Reading to Learn

A Content Teacher's Guide

Ross Bindon
STEPS Professional Development
Perth, Western Australia

Richard P. Santeusanio
STEPS Professional Development
Beverly, Massachusetts USA

STEPS Professional Development
Beverly, Massachusetts
Perth, Western Australia
Watchfield, United Kingdom

Reading to Learn: A Content Teacher's Guide
Ross Bindon and Richard P. Santeusanio

STEPS Professional Development
100 Cummings Center
Suite 421G
Beverly, MA 01915
Toll Free 866-505-3001
www.stepspd.org

STEPS Professional Development is a wholly owned subsidiary of Edith Cowan University, Perth, Western Australia. STEPS provides professional development and publishes resources for teachers in the areas of literacy (K-12), mathematics, and physical education. STEPS Professional Development has offices in Australia, the United States, and the United Kingdom and is represented in Canada by Pearson Professional Learning.

© STEPS Professional Development & Consulting 2006

All rights reserved. No part of this book may be reproduced in any form or by any electronic or mechanical means, including information storage and retrieval systems, without permission in writing from the publisher, except by a reviewer who may quote brief passages in a review.

ISBN 1-933775-50-5

Printed in the United States of America on acid-free paper.
06   RTL   10 9 8 7 6 5 4 3 2 1

TABLE OF CONTENTS

INSTRUCTIONAL ACTIVITIES INDEX	v
INTRODUCTION	vii
ACKNOWLEDGEMENTS	ix

1. **WHAT IS THE READING PROCESS?**   1
   Semantic Cues
   Syntactic Cues
   Graphophonic Cues
   The Context of the Reading Event
   The Reading Strategies
   Implications for Secondary Content Area Teachers

2. **HOW DO I TEACH THE READING PROCESS?**   7
   Before Reading
   During Reading
   After Reading
   Modelling the Reading Process
   Planning Modelling Sessions
   Conducting Sessions to Model the Reading Process

3. **WHAT ARE THE READING STRATEGIES?**   15
   Predicting
   Connecting
   Inferring
   Synthesising
   Visualising
   Self-Questioning
   Skimming
   Scanning
   Determining Importance
   Summarising/Paraphrasing
   Re-reading
   Reading On
   Adjusting Reading Rate
   Sounding Out
   Chunking

Using Analogy
Consulting a Reference
The Strategies and Technology

4. **HOW DO I CONNECT THE READING STRATEGIES TO MY CONTENT AREA?**   27

    BEFORE READING ACTIVITIES
        Activate Background Knowledge, Link to New Information, and Promote Active Reading
        Review and Clarify New Vocabulary
        Recognize and Clarify Purposes for Reading
        Predict Content, Text Structure, and Author Perspective
    DURING READING TEACHING ACTIVITIES
        Focus Attention on the Reading Task Activities
        Identify and Record Important Information
        Make Predictions during Reading
        Monitor Comprehension
        Making Inferences
    AFTER READING TEACHING ACTIVITIES
        Identify, Extract, and Recall Important Information
        Encourage Reading Reflection
        Summarizing Main Ideas and Details

5. **HOW DOES UNDERSTANDING OF TEXT STRUCTURE ENHANCE COMPREHENSION?**   87

    Where did the Idea for Teaching Text Structure Come From?
    Explaining Terms
    Locating Topic Sentences
    The Three Step Approach
    Summary Frames

6. **HOW DO I CONNECT TEXT STRUCTURE TO MY CONTENT AREA?**   97

    CAUSE/EFFECT PATTERN
        Cause/Effect Challenges
        Teaching Cause and Effect
        Cause Effect Pattern Guides
        Cause/Effect Focused Questions
        Cause/Effect Graphic Organizers
    PROBLEM/SOLUTION PATTERN
        Problem/Solution Pattern Guides
        Problem/Solution Focused Questions

Problem/Solution Graphic Organizers
SEQUENCE PATTERN
    Challenges
    Signal Words
    Sequence Pattern Guides
    Sequence Focused Questions
    Sequence Graphic Organizers
COMPARISON/CONTRAST PATTERN
    Signal Words
    Compare/Contrast Pattern Guides
    Compare/Contrast Focused Questions
    Compare/Contrast Graphic Organizers
Mathematics and Text Structure
Mathematics and Graphic Organizers

7. WHAT IS CRITICAL LITERACY?   161

Situational Context
Socio-Cultural Context
The Persuading Author; The Evaluating Reader
The Intensify/Downplay Schema Techniques
The Persuading Illustrator

8. HOW DO I CONNECT CRITICAL LITERACY TO MY CONTENT AREA?   175

Teaching and Learning Practices
Questions for Critically Analyzing Texts
Five Habits o f Mind
Pattern Guides
Graphic Organizers
SPECIFIC ACTIVITIES
    Critical Lens
    Fact/Opinion Continuum
    Four Corners
    Change the Point of View
    Possible Predictions
    Spot the Device
    Multiple Text Approach
    Great Debate

9. HOW DO I HELP MY STRUGGLING READERS?   191

What is the FIRST STEPS ® *Reading Map of Development?*
How Do I use the First Steps Reading Map?

WHAT IS AN APPROPRIATE TEACHING MODEL FOR MY STRUGGLING READERS?
- A Scaffold Approach
- Modelled Reading
- Joint Reading
- Guided Reading Sessions
- Independent Reading Sessions
- Research on Teaching Strategies

10. HOW DO I EVALUATE TEXTBOOKS? 203
- Science Textbooks
- Middle School Physical Science Textbooks
- History Books
- Literature Anthologies
- Mathematics Books
- Effects of the State Textbook Adoption System
- Weight of Textbooks
- Textbook Production
- Text Quest
- Alternatives to Textbooks
- Textbook Evaluation Form

APPENDIX

Bibliography B1

Adolescent Literacy: A Position Statement for the Commission on Adolescent Literacy of the International Reading Association

A Call to Action: What We Know About Adolescent Literacy and Ways to Support Teachers in Meeting Students' Needs. A Position/Action Statement from the National Council of Teachers of English Commission on Reading

The Fifteen Key Elements of Effective Adolescent Literacy Programs from *Reading Next – A Vision for Action and Research in Middle and High School Literacy: A Report to Carnegie Corporation of New York*

Overview of the FIRST STEPS® *Reading Map of Development*

READING TO LEARN
INSTRUCTIONAL ACTIVITIES INDEX

Activity	Page	Activity	Page
2R4C	59	Graphic Organizers	30, 109, 137, 150
66 Words	73		
A Scaffold Approach	194		
Alternative Headings	64	Great Debate	188
Anticipation Guides	45	Guided Reading	199
Before-and-After Charts	28	HEART Study System	158
Change the Point of View	185	Independent Reading	200
Cloze Procedure	62	Interviews	80
Critical Lens	181	Joint Reading	198
Crosswords	69	Linking Lines	86
Difficult Words Chart	60	Main Idea Pyramid	74
Directing Questions	38	Main Ideas	90
Five Habits of Mind	178	Missing Pieces	82
Focused Questions	105	Modeled Reading	196
Four Corners	184	Multiple Text Approach	187

Activity	Page	Activity	Page
Note Making	53	Strategy Demonstration Plan	11, 197
Pattern Guides	100	Summary Frames	94
Pinpointing Purposes	36	Synthesis Journals	66
Possible Predictions	186	Text Completion	83
Prediction Cloze	47	Text Reconstruction	55
Prereading Plan (Prep Plan)	33	Text-Connection Codes	51
Questions for Critically Analyzing Texts	177	The Reading Map	191
		The Text Quest	207
Read and Retell	71	The Three Step Approach	93
Reading Guides	49	Three Level Guides	76
Reciprocal Teaching	58	Transformations	65
Retrieval Chart	74	Verbed	85
Signal Words	99, 127, 143	Vocabulary Highlights	35
		Vocabulary Snowballs	34
Skim Sheets	41	Warm Ups	33
Split Pages	52	Who Said…?	81
Spot the Devices	187	Word Cline	70
SQ3R Study System	158		

INTRODUCTION

The primary goal of ***Reading to Learn: A Content Teacher's Guide*** is to help middle and high school subject matter teachers guide their students' reading of their textbooks. The idea is that better readers are better learners. The book is *not* intended to make reading specialists out of classroom teachers. That requires specialized training.

How do we achieve our goal? We offer you just enough theory to make sense out of the highly specific and practical ideas presented in the book. These ideas can be easily integrated with your teaching of content. Indeed, if you introduce reading strategies to your students and they practice them with your reading assignments, they will learn more. This book literally is your "guide" to helping your students increase their learning of content.

Many books on adolescent literacy cite numerous studies showing that adolescents cannot and will not read. You probably are familiar with these studies, so we will not dwell on them here. But we will focus on the fact that nearly all your students can read words and string them together. What they need help with is making sense out of what they read. If they cannot make sense out of what they read, they do not read.

To help your students with reading comprehension, we first concentrate on the reading process and discuss how to teach it. Then we review research supported strategies associated with the reading process and provide you with many activities that you can connect with your teaching of content.

Because understanding text organization is vital to comprehending text, we offer two chapters on this topic. We dedicate two subsequent chapters to critical literacy because it is so important for your students to question and evaluate everything they read and hear.

A separate chapter is devoted to struggling readers, so you will have some ideas on what to do with students who just cannot seem to comprehend what they read despite your best efforts. We end the book with a look at what critics have to say about textbooks and how you can deal with their legitimate criticisms.

Our appendices include two important statements on adolescent literacy, one from the International Reading Association and the other one from the National Council of Teachers of English. Finally, we reprint the Alliance for Excellent Education's "Fifteen Key Elements of Adolescent Literacy Programs." These elements provide teachers and administrators with research-supported suggestions on how to lead a middle or high school literacy initiative in their schools.

Subject matter teachers have many questions on what is involved in integrating supportive reading/learning activities with their teaching of content. We think our no-nonsense, direct approach to answering those questions can be found in the pages of this book. Our chapter titles take the form of "essential questions." These questions provide you with a "purpose for reading," an essential reading strategy that promotes comprehension. So read on!

Ross Bindon, Perth, Western Australia

Richard P. Santeusanio, Marblehead, Massachusetts

ACKNOWLEDGEMENTS

The authors and publisher wish to thank those who have generously granted permission to print the materials that appears in the Appendix.

Alliance for Excellent Education

Biancarosa, G. and Snow, E. E. (2004). *Reading Next – A Vision for Action and Research in Middle and High School Literacy: A Report to the Carnegie Corporation of New York.* Washington, DC: Alliance for Excellent Education.

International Reading Association

Moore, David W., Bean, Thomas W., Birdshaw, Deanna, and Rycik, James A. (1999). *Adolescent Literacy: A position paper for the Commission on Adolescent Literacy of the International Reading Association.* Reprinted with permission of the International Reading Association.

National Council of Teachers of English

A Call to Action: What we know about adolescent literacy and ways to support teachers in meeting student's' needs. A Position/Action Statement from NCTE's Commission on Reading, May 2004.

The authors wish to thank the **Department of Education and Training in Western Australia** for permission to reproduce the *First Steps Reading Map of Development* and for adaptations of materials from the texts *First Steps Reading Map of Development* and *First Steps Reading Resource Book,* 2nd ed. (2004).

CHAPTER 1   # WHAT IS THE READING PROCESS?

As a teacher of adolescents you know that the vast majority of your students can pronounce most of the words that appear in the readings you assign to them. But there is more to reading than pronouncing or "sounding out" words. In fact, there is a lot more to it.

It is not easy to describe how reading happens because it is a silent, motionless, personal act involving cognitive and social processes that are interactive. Most of these processes are not observable. For a skilled adult reader like you, reading is like riding a bike. You just do it and comprehending most text is automatic. You focus on the content of *what* you are reading, not *how* you are reading.

But what happens when reading in not like riding a bike, those times when you are challenged by complex text and/or topics unfamiliar to you? How do you make sense of what you are reading?

You read the title and introductory sentences and make a prediction about what the author will tell you. You connect this "new" text with whatever knowledge you already have on the topic. When you have trouble comprehending, you re-read sections and stop sometimes to figure out the meaning of unfamiliar words. As you read, you enhance your understanding by drawing on how the author has organized the text, and you summarize its main points.

When you try to make sense of challenging text, you approach it as a problem-solving process. You use visual information on the page and non-visual information in your head to make sense of a text. This visual displays the interaction of the two:

```
     ┌─────────────┐  ┌─────────────┐
     │   VISUAL    │  │ NON-VISUAL  │
     │  Headings,  │  │  Existing   │
     │   words,    │  │ information,│
     │  letters,   │  │ knowledge,  │
     │  captions,  │  │    and      │
     │ pictures,   │  │    prior    │
     │ and icons   │  │ experiences │
     │ on the page │  │ stored in   │
     │             │  │  the brain  │
     └─────────────┘  └─────────────┘
```

As a skilled reader, you comprehend text by drawing on a range of sources of information. These sources of information are often referred to as **semantic, syntactic,** and **graphophonic** cues. During the process of reading text, you draw on each of these cues simultaneously. The cueing systems are not sequential or hierarchical. They are equally important in contributing to your process of comprehending texts. Collectively, the three cues make up our prior knowledge or schema.

Semantic Cues

You draw on semantic cues to decide if what you are reading makes sense. These cues are associated with the overall meaning of a text, understanding both the words and the underlying messages. These cues include your cultural and world knowledge, concept or topic knowledge, and vocabulary knowledge. Semantic cues help you to make personal associations with a text.

Syntactic Cues

You draw on syntactic cues to decide if the text sounds right. These cues are associated with the structure of the language and include your knowledge of grammatical features, word order, and the organization of the text.

What is the Reading Process?

Graphophonic Cues

You draw on graphophonic cues to identify unknown words. These cues focus on the relationships between sound and symbols. They include your knowledge of letters and groups of letters and the sounds associated with them. Graphophonic cues also include your knowledge of print concepts and word structure.

The diagram below illustrates this multidimensional process of reading:

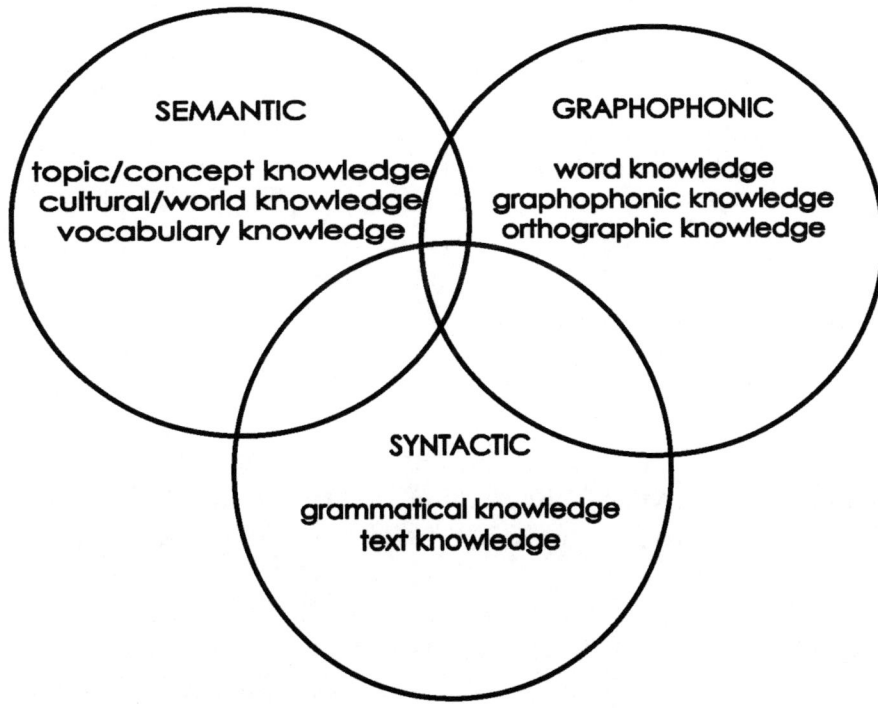

Figure 1. Linguistic Cueing System (Pearson, 1976)

Take a look at the following.

Heaven might be the apotheosis of medieval soul-space, but precisely because of its perfection, it is ultimately beyond human words. This is the realm of the ineffable.

> Margaret Wertheim, *The Pearly Gates of Cyberspace: A History of Space from Dante to the Internet*, W. W. Norton, 1999.

Consider how you need to access semantic, syntactic, and graphophonic knowledge to comprehend this piece of text. Among other things, you:

- Draw on your concept of "heaven." (semantic cue)

- Use the structure of the language to figure out the meaning of the unusual words like "apotheosis" and "ineffable" and note that the word "because" signals a cause/effect relationship. (syntactic cue)

- Use your knowledge of the sound/symbol relationships to pronounce the unusual words. (graphophonic cue)

The Context of the Reading Event

While the cues are important, your reading never occurs in a vacuum. Reading serves multiple purposes in your life. All reading happens within a social and cultural context and for a particular purpose. The purpose and context of a reading event helps you to decide what is important and what you need to understand to achieve your purpose. Purpose and context drives your selection of reading strategies and enables you to access appropriate cues, often without consciously being aware of the connections being made.

The Reading Strategies

As a skilled reader, you not only use the three cuing systems and take into account the context of your reading event; you also call upon a range of reading strategies to comprehend texts. These strategies include predicting, summarising, synthesizing and the like. (See Page 5.) Generally, you employ these strategies intuitively when you read familiar text. However, when the text is unfamiliar, you deliberately select and use those strategies that help you to comprehend unfamiliar text.

In summary, you comprehend text by interacting with the author. This comprehension occurs in a social and cultural context and is driven by your purpose for reading. The contextual elements contribute significantly to your motivation and interest to read. The authors contribute the message, and you actively integrate a range of strategies to draw interactively upon all knowledge available in the cues. As an effective reader you have automated most, if not all, the strategies. The Context for the Reading Event (Annandale, et. al.) illustrates the interplay of all that we have discussed in reviewing the process of reading:

What is the Reading Process?

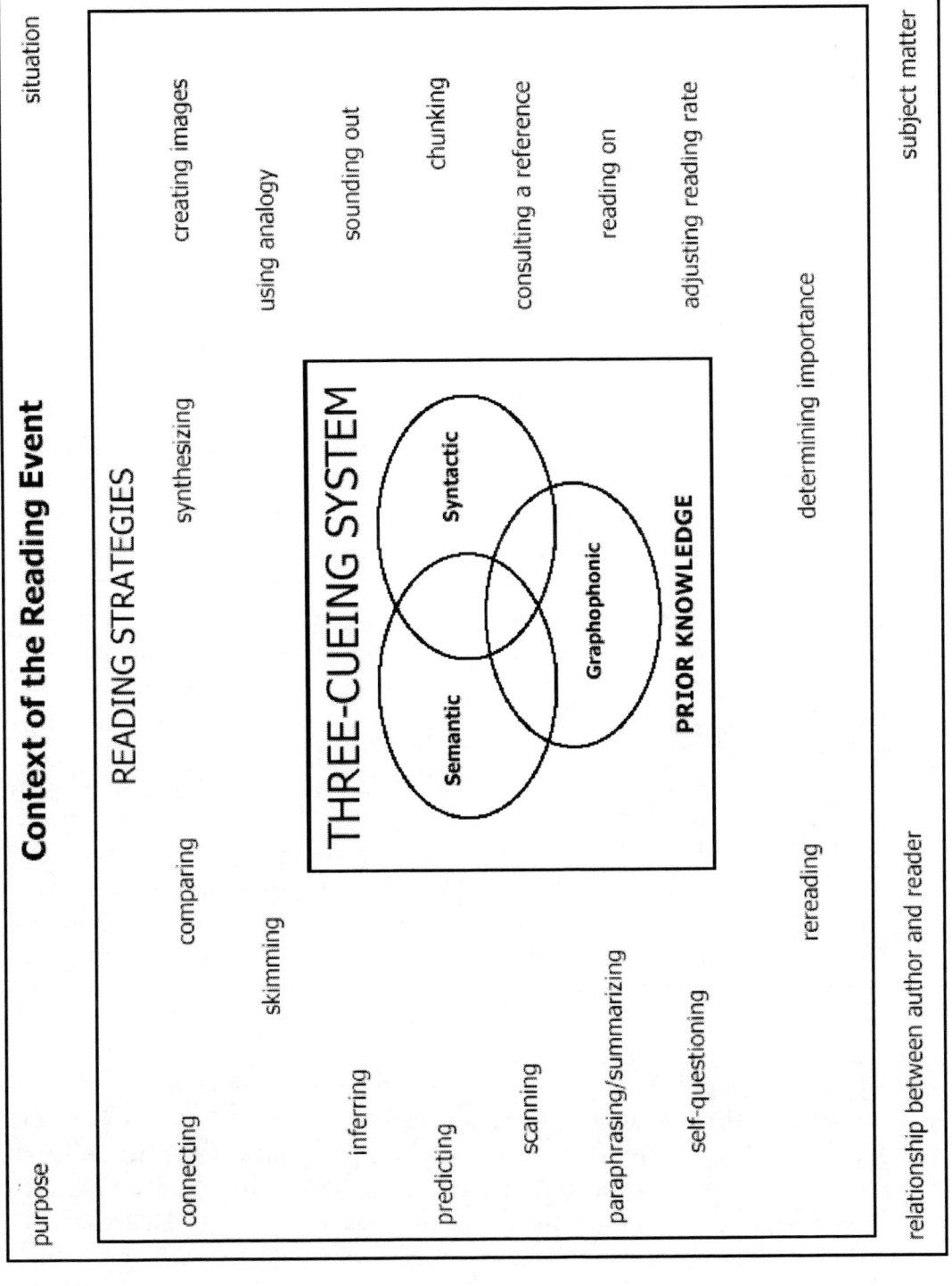

Implications for Secondary Content Area Teachers

We present this information to provide you with some background of what is involved in the process of reading and to provide a context for the remaining chapters in this book. For example, when we talk about the strategy of "determining importance," you will know where it fits as part of the reading process.

If you are a content area teacher, you are *not* expected to teach your students graphophonic skills like word structure and phonics. And with the exception of Language Arts teachers, you will not be teaching grammatical knowledge associated with the syntactic cues. However, your students will benefit when you help them with the text knowledge as it relates to your content area. You can address the other cue, semantic, by helping students activate their background knowledge related to readings you assign and providing background knowledge on that topic to your students. You can also help your students understand the difficult vocabulary associated with your subject. Finally, you also can assist your students with some of the reading strategies identified in the chart that are particularly important for secondary students such as predicting and comparing. The explicit teaching of reading strategies is vital to ensure that students are able to access successfully their cues to support the reading associated with your content area.

Several chapters in this book will show you how to teach the reading strategies. Although the thinking involved in carrying out the strategies is complex, we provide you with easy-to-implement activities designed to foster your students' development of these reading strategies so they can tackle the texts you use in your classroom. In short, these are strategies that will help your students *learn the content* of your courses.

These strategies help students carry out the process of reading. Before we look at these specific reading strategies, you need to know how to teach the three stages of the reading process – what competent readers do before, during, and after they read. And your students need to know how this process works in your particular content area(s). Therefore, in the next chapter we show you how, in general terms, to teach the stages of the reading process.

This framework is all you need to plan lessons on teaching the reading process as it applies to your content area(s). So let's move on to the next chapter and take a look at how to teach the reading process.

CHAPTER 2 **HOW DO I TEACH THE READING PROCESS?**

Now that you know what the reading process is, let's look at how you can you teach it to your students. Explaining and modeling are two "tried and true" approaches. The key is to break down the reading process into understandable and manageable steps for your students. While the emphasis on different aspects of the reading process may vary a bit in each of the different content areas, the process can be taught by explaining and modeling for students what proficient readers do *before*, *during*, and *after* they read texts. As pointed out by Trabasso and Bouchard (2002), if students are not taught the cognitive procedures or behaviors like those associated with the reading process, they will not learn, develop, or practice them spontaneously.

Let's now break down the behaviors and procedures involved in the reading process.

Before Reading
- Activate background knowledge
- Preview
- Set a purpose

During Reading
- Ask questions
- Predict
- Monitor understanding

- Make connections
- Fix up misunderstandings

After Reading
- Reread
- Remember
- Reflect

This format helps us to teach the reading process so that students can understand it. But it is very important to note that

- Proficient readers carry out many of the behaviors and procedures automatically, often without much thought.
- The behaviors are recursive, and a behavior listed in the "during" stage, say predict, will also take place for many in the "before" stage. Or the reread behavior, listed here in the "after" stage, often will take place in the "during" stage.
- The reading strategies listed in The Context for the Reading Event in Chapter 1 link to the behaviors listed in the reading process.
- There are a number of activities that you can carry out that will assist students in carrying out each of the behaviors successfully. These activities are discussed at length in the next two chapters.

Now let's review in a little more depth, the three stages of the reading process.

Before Reading

Before reading text closely we, as effective readers, first prepare ourselves for the task (Heilman, Blair, and Rupley, 2002; Paris, Lipson, and Wixson, 1994). We predict what the text might be about and how it might be structured, based on clues from the cover of the book, or the initial images on the website, or subheadings in a chapter. Typically, we quickly skim or preview the text. This activity tells us how the text is organized, gives us a sense of the major topics contained in the reading, and activates our background knowledge relative to the content. We connect this visual information with the non-visual information we have in our heads about the topic. These pre-reading behaviors combine to enable us to set a purpose for our reading.

During Reading

Our purpose established, we continue to connect the information in the text to our own experiences, to other texts we have read, and to what we know about the world. This connection makes the text more meaningful to us. Sometimes we visualize what is being described in the text. Where information is not explicit, we ask questions, infer, and draw conclusions about what the author means. We move quickly over some text and more slowly over other parts because we are determining the importance of information required to achieve our purpose. If our purpose is to find the date of an historical event, we will scan the text looking for related information. Where the meaning of the text is unclear, we reread, pose questions to ourselves, summarize, and paraphrase. When we get stuck on difficult words, we read on or reread, looking for clues. If the word is entirely unfamiliar, we may break it into smaller parts that make sense (chunking), relate it to another word we know (using analogy), or even sound it out. If it is essential to achieving our purpose for reading the text, we will check a glossary or dictionary, or ask someone if they know the meaning of the word.

After Reading

At this point we reflect on our reading and summarize important points to be remembered. We synthesize the key events, concepts, and aspects of the text, and we consider whether or not we have achieved our purpose. We reread parts of the text determined to be important, pose additional questions, and possibly write summary statements about what we've read.

Modeling the Reading Process

According to Annandale et. al. (2004), modeling is the most significant step of teaching any reading strategy. We also believe this is true for teaching the behaviors associated with the reading process. When you model the reading process, you are able to articulate all that is happening inside your head, making the reading process evident to your students. Thinking aloud is a vital part of modeling.

It will be necessary for you to plan your modeling lessons carefully. Rather than spontaneously thinking aloud, you should think through what aspect of the reading process you are modeling and the sections of the text that you will use to model, for example, making predictions. We suggest modeling only two or three of the reading process behaviors at a time.

Planning Modeling Sessions

Here, adapted from Annandale and her colleagues, are some questions you can ask yourself as you plan to model the reading process.

- How do I use this aspect of the reading process in my own reading?

- How does carrying out this aspect of the reading process help me to become a more efficient reader?

- What is important for my students to know about this aspect of the reading process?

- Which texts might be the most appropriate to model this aspect of the reading process?

- Where in the text will it be possible to demonstrate this aspect of the reading process?

- What language should I use to best describe my thinking and how I carry out this aspect of the reading process?

You may find the "Strategy Demonstration Plan" created by Annandale and her colleagues helpful as you conduct reading-process-modeling lessons.

STRATEGY DEMONSTRATION PLAN

Strategy to be introduced:
_____

When and why it is useful

Key points to model

-
-
-

Text selected

Pages to be used

Language to describe my thinking

Conducting Sessions to Model the Reading Process

Here, adapted from Annandale and her colleagues, are steps for you to consider as you model the reading process.

- *Introduce the reading process behavior and what it means.*
  "Today I am going to show you one of the things I do before I closely read a chapter in a text. I preview the chapter. Previewing means to skim quickly over the whole chapter."

- *Explain why the behavior is useful and how you use it.*
  "Previewing helps me a lot because before I start reading a chapter closely, I get an idea of what topics the author is going to cover and some of his key ideas. When I preview, I look at the name of the chapter and think about what I already know about what the chapter. Then I quickly look at all the major headings and subheadings. I also notice any graphs, tables, illustrations, and pictures. I make sure I read the captions of these visuals because they are often included in the text to illustrate a main point or important detail of the chapter, which may be included in the captions. And when I get to the end of the chapter, I read the summary. This is neat because by reading the summary first, I really get the author's important ideas before I read the chapter closely. It is like finding out what a T.V. program is going to be like by pressing the information button on my remote. I know what to expect. If there are questions at the end of the chapter, I look at those too. These questions also help me to figure out what the author thinks is important in the chapter."

- *Begin carrying out the reading process behavior, thinking aloud as you do it.*
  "Now I am going to demonstrate how I preview a chapter. Sometimes I am going to be reading right from the text. When I do that, my head will be down when I am reading material in the chapter. When I stop the reading to describe to you what I am thinking about, I will look up at you so you will know I am thinking out loud about what I just read."

- *Use precise, accurate language to describe your thinking while demonstrating the use of the reading process behavior.*
  "I see from reading this caption of this illustration on page 232

that different species of animals have very similar body structures. This is important to know about living things."

- ***After modeling, invite students to discuss their observations of the demonstration.***
  "So, tell me what you noticed as I modeled previewing for you."

- ***Summarize with the students the key points about the particular reading process behavior.***
  "Let's review now what we do when we preview a textbook chapter."

The thinking aloud that takes place during modeling is similar to what Ruth Schoenbach and her colleagues (1999) call "metacognitive conversations." Such conversations involve the act of "thinking about thinking" in which you and your students become consciously aware of your mental activity by describing and discussing it with each other. When these conversations take place, the invisible behaviors and cognitive dimensions of the process of reading are drawn out and made visible to all. Schoenbach and her colleagues note that "for adolescents, being shown what goes on behind the curtain of expert reading is especially powerful in helping them gain adult mastery."

Summary

In this chapter we reviewed the behaviors and procedures associated with the reading process. They were organized into what proficient readers do *before, during,* and *after* they read. Modeling, using a "think aloud" approach, was presented as a way to teach the reading process.

For most of your students, just introducing and modeling the reading process will not be enough to make them competent readers. They need to become familiar with and to learn how to use strategies associated with the reading process, especially the ones that will help them to comprehend what they read *during* the reading process. In the next chapter, we will review the strategies with you and then, in the following chapters, we offer specific teaching activities that will help your students to learn and practice the strategies.

CHAPTER 3

WHAT ARE THE STRATEGIES ASSOCIATED WITH THE READING PROCESS?

As we have pointed out, reading is a recursive process. Reading strategies are used many times rapidly, in unison with one another. Therefore, most reading strategies are evident *before*, *during*, and *after* reading, although not necessarily with the same emphasis.

The following descriptions of each strategy give some indication of when in the reading process they are generally employed. Different texts and different contexts require readers to use different reading strategies at different times. However, as you review each of these strategies it will become obvious to you when a reading strategy is emphasized the most. For example, "synthesizing" is used *during* and *after* reading while "scanning" is typically used *before* close reading. Here, then, for your review are the major reading strategies associated with the process of reading.

Predicting

Predicting helps readers to activate their prior knowledge about a topic, beginning the process of combining what they know with new material in the text. Predictions are not merely wild guesses, they are based on clues within the text such as pictures, illustrations, subtitles, and plot. Clues for predictions will also come from readers' prior knowledge about the author, text form, or content. Students should support why they make their predictions.

Readers can be encouraged to make personal predictions *before* and *during* reading. *During* reading, effective readers adjust and refine their earlier predictions as new information is gathered and new connections are made. They tend to rehearse what they have learned and move on with some expectations of what comes next (Graves & Graves, 2003; Slater & Hortsman, 2002).

Predictions are usually related to events, actions, or outcomes and will be either confirmed or rejected once the text has been read. Students can also use predicting to identify unknown words. Students can predict unknown words *before* or *after* decoding. These types of predictions usually are based on surrounding context clues, and on what would make the best sense within the text being read.

> **Significant research indicates that poor readers do not use their prior knowledge as effectively as good readers, particularly when comprehending expository text and activities that make explicit the connection between prior knowledge and the content of a text improves reading comprehension (Trabasso & Bouchard, 2002).**

Connecting

Efficient readers comprehend text through making strong connections between their prior knowledge and the new information presented in text. Activating students' prior knowledge *before* reading is important. However, students need to be able to continue to use this strategy *during* reading to make continual connections as they read.

Keene and Zimmerman (1997) categorise the type of connections made by efficient readers:

- **Text to Self Connections**

    Involves readers thinking about their life and connecting their own personal experiences to the information in the text.

- **Text to Text Connections**

    Involves readers thinking about other texts written by the same author or with common themes, style, organization, structure, characters or content.

- **Text to World Connections**

    Involves readers thinking about what they know about the world outside their personal experience, their family, or their community.

Effective readers limit their connections to those that enhance understanding of the text. Some students may make connections that have little relevance to text comprehension. Their conversations about the connections they make can help them focus on how connections may have assisted understanding.

> **Research suggests that weak readers are generally passive and do not attempt to connect ideas in the text to what they already know (Pressley and Wharton-McDonald, 1997). Successful readers, however, actively draw on their prior knowledge to connect to and within the text (van den Broek & Kremer, 2000).**

Inferring

Efficient readers take information from a text and add their own ideas to make inferences. During the process of inferring, readers make predictions, draw conclusions, and make judgments to create a unique interpretation of a text. Making inferences allows students to move beyond the literal text and to make assumptions about what is not precisely stated in the text. Inferences made by students may be unresolved by the end of text, neither confirmed nor rejected by the author.

Efficient readers also can infer the meaning of unknown words using context clues, pictures, or diagrams.

> **In their review of the research, Sinatra, Brown, and Reynolds (2002) found that students' ability to make causal inferences is important for building a coherent understanding of text.**

Synthesizing

When comprehending text, efficient readers use synthesising to bring together information within a text. Synthesising involves readers piecing information together, like putting together a jigsaw. As students read and use synthesising, they stop at selected places within a text and think about what has been read. This activity encourages them to keep track of what is happening in the text.

Students who are consciously aware of using this strategy are able to monitor continually their understanding of text. During the process of synthesising, students may be connecting, inferring, determining importance, posing questions, and creating images.

> **Brown and Day (1983) found that effective readers synthesize to enhance their comprehension of what they have read. Zwiers (2004) notes that learning how to synthesize benefits students because it leads them to new perspectives and insights.**

Visualizing

Efficient readers use all five senses to create images continually as they read text. The created images are based on their prior knowledge. Sensory images created by readers help them to draw conclusions, make predictions, interpret information, remember details, and assist with overall comprehension. Images may be visual, auditory, olfactory, kinaesthetic, or emotional.

Students may need extra encouragement to create images with greater detail or to create those that go beyond the literal information from the text. Support also can be provided to help students revise their images when new information is gained.

It is important that students also are given the opportunity to share their images and to talk about how creating images helps them better understand text. Images can be shared orally, as drawings, as jottings, or through drama.

> **In their comprehensive summary of research on imagery, Gambrell and Koskinen (2002) concluded that the teaching of imagery has a positive effect on students' ability to comprehend and remember what they read. Nokes and Dole (2004) believe visual imagery is an important strategy to teach struggling adolescent readers.**

Self-Questioning

Self-questioning is the strategy effective readers use to draw on existing knowledge, to investigate a text as it is read, to analyse the beliefs and motives behind the author's surface meaning, and to monitor comprehension. Whether posed in-head, sub-vocalised or noted in writing, self-questioning is critical to maintaining connections between existing and new knowledge. Self-formulated questions provide a framework for active reading by directing the reader's attention to key information.

Efficient readers continually form questions in their minds *before*, *during* and *after* reading to assist in comprehending text. Often these questions are formed spontaneously and naturally, with one question leading to the next. Questions may relate to the content, style, structure, important messages, events, actions, inferences, predictions, author's purpose, or may be an attempt to clarify meaning. Self-formulated questions provide a framework for active reading, engaging students in the text as they go in search of answers. It is important for students to be aware that answers to all questions may not always be in the text.

Helping students to become aware of questions they naturally ask is an important goal for teaching this strategy. Encouraging students to understand how the generation of questions helps to develop a deeper understanding of the text is also important.

> **Rosenshine, Meister, and Chapman (1996) note that many instructional studies demonstrate that students increase their reading performance after they receive instruction in self-questioning, and Cote and Goldman (1999) show that self-questioning is a strategy used by effective readers, but not by less effective readers. The National Reading Panel (2002) views question generation as a strategy that may be best used as part of a multiple strategy instruction program.**

Skimming

Skimming is glancing through material to gain a general impression or overview of the content. It involves passing over much of the detail to get the gist of a text. Skimming is the most common strategy used by a reader to assess quickly whether a text is going to meet his or her purpose. Effective skimming lets a reader know – in general terms – how difficult a text is, how long it is, how it is structured, and where the most useful information can be found.

Effective skimming strategies are critical for adolescents due to the volume of electronic text they read. Websites, CD ROMs, and multimedia texts are designed for, and subject to rapid reading practices where the reader gets the gist from sub-headings and key points, determine difficulty and usefulness, and assess the content flow.

Skimming is often used before reading to:

- Quickly assess whether a text is going to meet a purpose.
- Determine what is to be read.
- Determine what's important and what may not be relevant.
- Review text organization.
- Activate prior knowledge.

Students can be helped to use skimming by being encouraged to check any graphics, to check underlined, italicised, or highlighted text, or to read any titles and subheadings.

> **Block, Gambrell, and Pressley (2002) stress the prereading nature of skimming by referring to it as "tilling the text". They argue that students can be taught to "till the text" in the same way farmers till the earth before they plant. Research by Block (2001) indicates that students who are taught to skim increase their comprehension of a text significantly over those students who do not.**

Scanning

Scanning involves glancing through material to locate specific details such as names, dates, places, or some particular content. For instance, readers might scan a contents page or index to find the page number of a specific topic. They may scan a dictionary or telephone book in search of a particular word or name, or they may scan as they re-read a text to substantiate particular responses.

Like skimming, scanning is particularly important for comprehending selected parts of websites, CD ROMs, and multimedia texts. Readers may also scan a text looking for picture clues that may help them identify any unknown words.

Determining Importance

Efficient readers constantly ask themselves what is most important or what the main idea is of what they are reading. They benefit from understanding how to determine the important information, particularly in informational texts. Factors such as purpose for reading, knowledge of topic, prior experiences, beliefs, and understanding of text organization help readers to identify important information in a text.

Students can begin to identify important concepts or ideas from short pieces of texts. Key words, phrases and sentences can then be identified. It is beneficial to begin with informational texts and highlight organizational features that will help students to decipher important information from less important information. These features include: headings, subheadings, titles, illustrations, bolded text, icons, and font size. Students also need opportunities to determine important information in literary texts.

> **Widespread studies in the 1980s show that successful readers determine importance of ideas by excluding less important information (Baumann, 1986; Tierney and Cunningham, 1984; Winograd and Bridge, 1986). More recently, Brown (2002) notes that the considerable research on the positive effects of teaching students summarizing text shows how important it is for students to determine importance.**

Summarizing/Paraphrasing

Linked closely to the strategy of determining importance, summarising/paraphrasing is the process of identifying, recording, and writing the most important information from a text into your own words.

The ability to reduce a larger piece of text to its most important messages is done through summarising. The re-statement of the text in other words is referred to as paraphrasing.

Summarising/paraphrasing involves using key words and phrases to capture the general gist of a text.

> **Studies (Wittrock, 1990; King, 1992, O'Donnell and Dansereau, 1992) show that when students are taught to summarize, their comprehension improves and it helps them to monitor their understanding. After reviewing 18 studies on summarizing, Trabasso and Bouchard (2002) conclude that "Readers improve the quality of their summaries ...by identifying the main ideas ... generalizing and by removing redundancy" (p.182).**

Re-reading

Efficient readers understand the benefits of re-reading whole texts or parts of texts to clarify or enhance meaning. Reading or hearing a text more than once benefits all readers, allowing them to gain a deeper understanding of the text.

Re-reading can also be used as a word-identification strategy. Efficient readers sometimes re-read to work out the meaning of difficult words using context clues. The opportunity to re-read a text also helps to improve fluency.

> **The National Reading Panel (2000) reviewed the research literature relating to repeated reading and found that re-reading improves fluency, particularly for high school students experiencing reading difficulties.**

Reading On

When students cannot decode an unfamiliar word within a text, they can make use of the "Reading On" strategy. Skipping the unfamiliar word and reading on to the end of the sentence or the next two or three sentences often provides the reader with sufficient context clues to help determine the unknown word. Once the unknown word has been determined it is important for students to re-read that section of text.

"Reading On" also refers to continuing to read in an attempt to clarify meaning that may have been lost.

> **The research (Trabasso and Bouchard, 2002) on comprehension monitoring, knowing what to do when text does not makes sense, supports the use of the "Reading On" strategy.**

Adjusting Reading Rate

It is important that students give themselves permission to adjust their reading rate and recognize when this may be necessary. The purpose for reading will often dictate the most appropriate rate. Readers may **slow down** to understand new information, clarify meaning, create sensory images, or ask questions. Readers may also **speed up** when scanning for key words or skimming to get an overall impression of a text.

> **When readers lose meaning, they need to 'fix-up' their misunderstandings. One way they can do this is to adjust their reading rate, which usually means to slow down. Like the "Read On" strategy, adjusting reading rate is a strategy supported by comprehension monitoring research (Trabasso and Bouchard, 2002).**

Sounding Out

When adolescents meet new and unfamiliar words, they will use their knowledge of letter/sound relationships to identify them

> **Research has shown that an understanding of letter/sound relationships is positively related to reading ability (NRP, 2000), including students in the secondary school (Ryder and Graves, 1980).**

Chunking

As readers encounter greater numbers of multi-syllabic words, it is important to encourage students to break words into units larger than individual phonemes or single sounds (/b/). Readers might chunk words by pronouncing word parts such as onset and rime (spr-ing), letter combinations (ough), syllables, or parts of the word known as morphemes which carry meaning (ed, ing).

> **There is evidence to suggest that when students use common letter patterns or parts of words to decode, their word recognition is more efficient (Ehri, 1991).**

Using Analogy

When readers manipulate or think about words they know to identify unknown words, they are using analogy. They transfer what they know about familiar words to help them identify unfamiliar words. When using analogy, students will transfer their knowledge of common letter sequences, onset and rimes, base words, word parts that carry meaning, or whole words.

> **Several studies have concluded that reading instruction should include reading by analogy (Leslie and Calhoon, 1995; Greaney, Tunmer and Chapman, 1997).**

Consulting a Reference

The use of word-identification strategies such as "sounding out" or "chunking" may unlock both the pronunciation and meaning of words. However, if the word is not in a student's meaning vocabulary, the reader may not be able to understand the meaning of the word. Consulting a reference is an additional strategy that supports students to unlock word meaning. Being taught how to use a dictionary, thesaurus, reference chart, or glossary will help students locate the meanings, pronunciations, or derivations of unfamiliar words.

The Strategies and Technology

As we discussed strategies in this chapter, our examples came exclusively from traditional textbooks that permeate secondary classrooms. However, schools are increasingly integrating technology with their textbooks and adolescents spend many hours outside of school with technologies such as text-messaging, email, websites, and CD ROMs which are not as linear as traditional texts. For example, adolescents may have several text boxes open, comparing and relating information from each. They may be scrolling and scanning subheadings to find a particular detail. Or they may be retracing a line of thinking through hyperlinked sources or sites. These technological texts call for adolescents to call on reading strategies like skimming and scanning, predicting, determining importance, and rereading. Adolescents, then, must apply strategies flexibly.

The explosion in information that accompanies these technologies casts the spotlight on adolescent readers' ability to be aware of the context of a text, to be aware of the author's purpose, who the author is, and how the text and the reader are being positioned. For example, an email purporting to be from a government body may be bogus, and a website supplying supposedly objective information may be maintained by a commercial entity with a hidden agenda. An adolescent's capacity to self-question during reading is fundamental to the skill of reading critically. Middle and secondary school teachers can assist adolescent readers by making explicit the reading strategies that are being maximised when, for example, a reader follows a hyperlink to another website, or compares a range of print and non-print texts.

Now that you are familiar with the reading strategies associated with the reading process, let's look at some activities that you can use to integrate the teaching of these strategies with the teaching of your content.

CHAPTER 4

HOW DO I CONNECT THE READING STRATEGIES TO MY CONTENT AREA?

Now that you know what the reading strategies are, we offer you activities that will help your students to learn and use those strategies. As we note in Chapter 1, the process of reading takes place in three stages. Successful readers get ready and prepare for reading in the *before* stage. In the *during* stage, they read closely to comprehend. Finally, they ponder over and reflect on what they have read in the *after* stage.

While we have categorized the activities into the three stages, we want to say again that the reading strategies and activities presented in one particular stage can and should be practiced in other stages. This reflects the recursive nature of the reading process. Here is our "tool box" of teaching activities. Use the ones that you feel will work well in your content area and with your students. Naturally, we start with the *before* stage.

BEFORE READING TEACHING ACTIVITIES

The *before* stage of reading deserves a great deal of attention. There are several reasons for this. First, when the reading behaviors of effective and ineffective readers are compared, the difference is very dramatic in the *before*-reading stage. Ineffective readers will, for example, pick up a text and just start reading it. They fail to reflect on the purpose of their reading and using that purpose to drive the way they read.

Secondly, secondary teachers traditionally focus on the actual reading of a text and a series of comprehension questions that follow it. Too little is done to help students prepare for the complex task of reading. And finally, content area reading is challenging due to the inclusion of unfamiliar vocabulary and concepts and complex text structure and organization. It is these aspects of reading that many *before*-reading activities target. What happens *before* students read a text greatly affects their understanding of the material.

Effective readers activate their prior knowledge of the topic they are about to encounter in their reading assignment. When they do this, they bring to the text expectations about its purpose, medium (textbook, periodical, newspaper, email, and website), its form (essay, story, and procedure), its author, and its content. A schema, or mental map, based on previous experiences and knowledge, is activated to maximize comprehension.

ACTIVITIES TO ACTIVATE BACKGROUND KNOWLEDGE, TO LINK IT TO NEW INFORMATION, AND TO PROMOTE ACTIVE READING

BEFORE-AND-AFTER CHARTS

What are Before-and-After Charts?

Before-and-After Charts, derived from the work of Ogle (1986) provide an effective way of categorizing and recording all the information students (either individually or in small groups) know, want to know, and learn as a result of reading a text.

Why Before-and-After Charts Benefit Students

Research in the 80's (Anderson and Pearson, 1984; Beck, Omanson and McKeown, 1982) firmly demonstrates that students who are taught to make explicit connections between their prior knowledge and new information in a text improve their comprehension. The *before* sections of these charts make clear what is known prior to reading and what needs to be discovered through reading. The '*after*' sections provide a real purpose for reflecting on reading to find out what has been learned and what is yet to be learned.

How to Use Before-and-After Charts

Before-and-After Charts can be used with individuals, pairs, or with the whole class. However, be aware that when the whole class enters all they know about a topic in a chart (unless they know very little or the teacher summarizes constantly) the chart can become large and unwieldy.

Here are the steps to follow for this activity.

1. Group students in fours and have them brainstorm what they know about the topic associated with their reading assignment. They write key words or key clauses on index cards that can be seen by all group members. Word-association techniques help students to brainstorm. After an initial flurry of terms offered by students, teachers can circle those words that are most relevant to the reading. Associations with these key words will enhance the brainstorm.

2. Have the groups cluster and categorize the cards, arranging them to show relationships between them. Relationships can be shown by hierarchy, subheadings, lines, arrows, and other graphic- organizational techniques. What is produced can vary enormously depending on the nature of the topic and what students collectively know about it. Students may create a concept map or some sort of graphic organizer, like a Venn diagram or flowchart. The resulting overview can be represented on large chart paper, on a whiteboard, or temporarily on desk space.

3. From the overview, students list statements of what they know about the topic. Where a great deal of prior knowledge exists it is helpful for the teacher to highlight the areas of greatest relevance to the text. These statements are entered in the "*before*" column headed "*What we know about...*" as key words or clauses.

4. The question "*What we want to find out?*" is then posed and the responses are recorded in the appropriate column.

5. After reading, all new information learned is entered in the "*after*" column headed "*What we have learned.*"

6. Any unanswered questions are entered in the final "*after*" column headed "*What we still want to know*" and can provide the motivation for further reading.

Example   Before-and-After Chart

BEFORE READING		AFTER READING	
What we know about <u>plant behavior</u>	What we want to find out	What we learned	What we still want to know
A plant's roots always seem to grow downward.	Why do a plant's roots grow downwards?	A plant's roots respond to gravity and grow towards the Earth's center.	
Plants grow towards the sun.	Why do plants grow towards sunlight?	They are responding to light that they need for photosynthesis.	
Venus' flytraps can catch flies.	How does a Venus' flytrap plant work?	The leaf can return to its normal position in minutes.	How does the Venus' flytrap know that a fly has landed?

GRAPHIC ORGANIZERS

What are Graphic Organizers?

Graphic Organizers are visual representations of concepts designed to represent key ideas and their relationships. (In this book, semantic webs, concept maps, skeleton outlines, mind maps, diagrams, and structured overviews are collectively considered Graphic Organizers). Arrows and symbols are typically used to represent relationships. Information is organized around a word or phrase. Characteristics, attributes, and examples of the concept are included in the representation. Graphic Organizers can be used at all stages of the reading process. However, we feature them as a pre-reading activity because they are a powerful way to categorize prior knowledge. While each representation may have a claim to being unique in some way, they have in common the purpose of attempting to make visually explicit the structure of prior knowledge so the comprehension of new knowledge can be facilitated.

Why Graphic Organizers Benefit Students

A Trabasso and Bouchard (2002) summary of 11 research studies on graphic organizers led them to conclude that "Graphic organizers are appropriate for expository texts in content areas such as science and social studies." The Graphic Organizer makes explicit – in a useful visual representation – what is known *before* reading. The visual framework can then be added to, or amended, to accommodate new knowledge encountered in the text.

How to Use Graphic Organizers

Graphic Organizers can be used by individual students, pairs, or groups. However for initial instruction and when you want to assess the depth of knowledge of concepts across a class, whole class use is best.

1. In response to the question, "What do you know about...?" students offer responses that are recorded on individual slips of card.

2. As more responses are gathered, the students direct the teacher as to how the responses should be categorized.

3. The teacher groups and classifies related information using a card-cluster process.

4. Having consumed the available time or exhausted the responses, the students suggest a range of visual frameworks that would reflect relationships between the clustered information. Information can be sorted into concepts that are categorized in a logical, hierarchical way, with concepts leading to sub-concepts, or causes being linked to effects.

5. A number of techniques can be used to strengthen the meaning of a graphic organizer. Because the graphic organizer is being used to activate prior knowledge *before* reading, it can include question marks to indicate doubt about the accuracy of the information, dotted lines to show tenuous links, and color, size of print, and size of borders to imply relationships between concepts or elements.

Example   Graphic Organizers

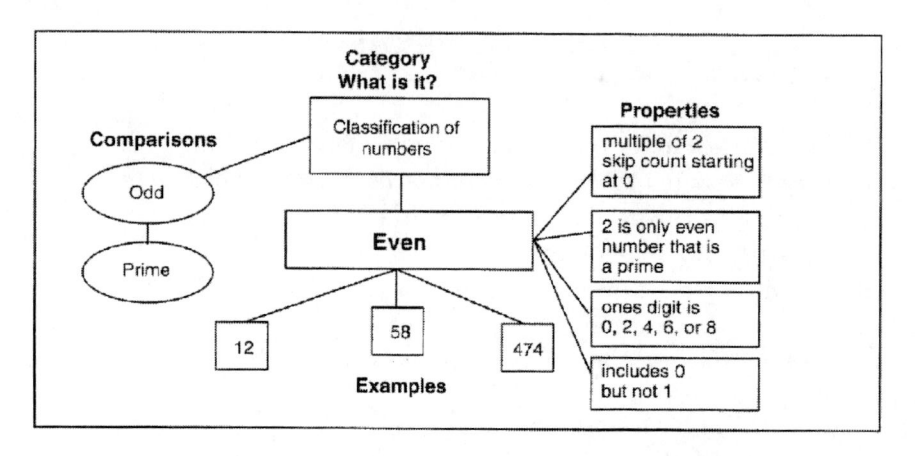

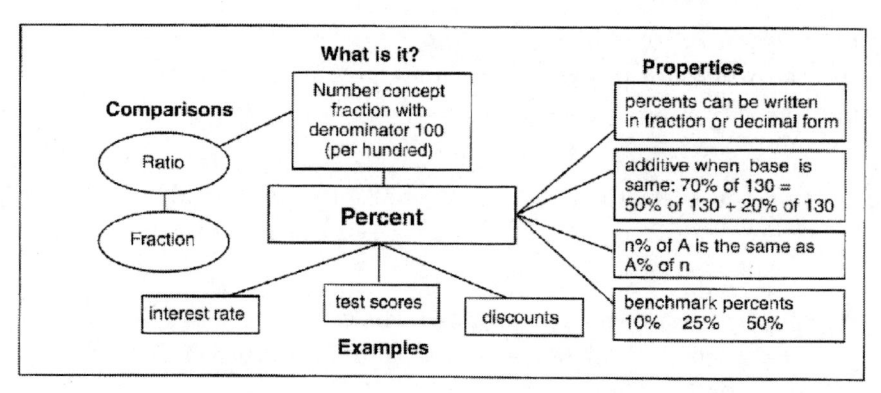

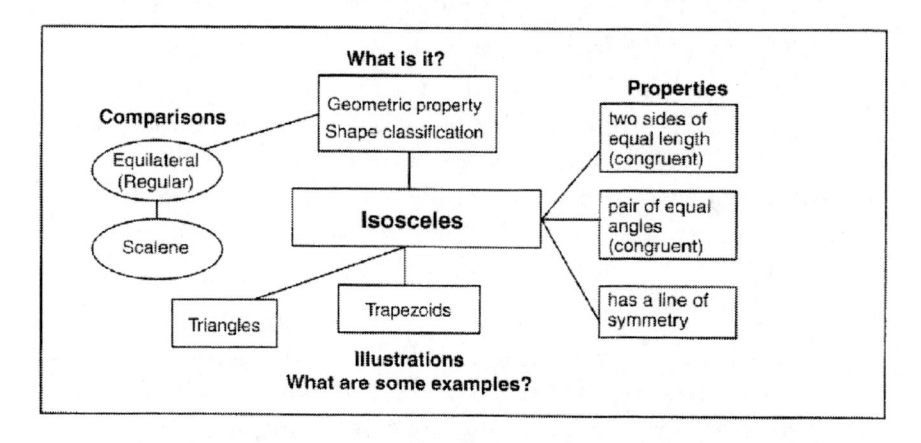

Even

- **Category / What is it?**: Classification of numbers
- **Comparisons**: Odd, Prime
- **Examples**: 12, 58, 474
- **Properties**:
  - multiple of 2 skip count starting at 0
  - 2 is only even number that is a prime
  - ones digit is 0, 2, 4, 6, or 8
  - includes 0 but not 1

Percent

- **What is it?**: Number concept fraction with denominator 100 (per hundred)
- **Comparisons**: Ratio, Fraction
- **Examples**: interest rate, test scores, discounts
- **Properties**:
  - percents can be written in fraction or decimal form
  - additive when base is same: 70% of 130 = 50% of 130 + 20% of 130
  - n% of A is the same as A% of n
  - benchmark percents 10%   25%   50%

Isosceles

- **What is it?**: Geometric property / Shape classification
- **Comparisons**: Equilateral (Regular), Scalene
- **Illustrations / What are some examples?**: Triangles, Trapezoids
- **Properties**:
  - two sides of equal length (congruent)
  - pair of equal angles (congruent)
  - has a line of symmetry

Barton, M.L. and Heidema, C. Teaching Reading in Mathematics. Aurora, CO: Mid-continent Research for Education and Learning, 2000. Reprinted with permission of McREL.

WARM UPS

What are Warm-ups?

Warm-ups are classroom experiences that prepare adolescent readers for a particularly new or challenging piece of text.

Warm-ups can include:

- pictures
- videos
- discussions
- visiting speakers
- excursions
- hands-on experiences
- computer experiences
- games

Why Warm-ups Benefit Students

Warm-ups help readers activate all they know about a topic before confronting new concepts and ideas in a text.

How to Use Warm-ups

1. Consider the key concepts within a piece of text, and reflect on what other media addresses the key concepts.

2. Ask students to collect pieces of text and other artifacts to share, discuss, and display, as an introduction to the text.

3. Taking into account time constraints, use the alternative media and/or artifacts to stimulate discussion and/or create a structured overview about the key understandings.

PREREADING PLAN (Prep Plan)

What is a Prep Plan?

Schema theory holds that readers' existing knowledge and experiences directly influence the content and form of new knowledge. Readers need assistance in activating their existing knowledge and experiences, and the Prep Plan is a three phase, teacher directed activity designed to do this task (Langer, 1981).

Why the Prep Plan Benefits Students

As noted in a later discussion of Text-Connection Codes, efficient readers activate their background knowledge of a topic *before* they read new material on that topic. Thus their comprehension of new information on the particular topic is enhanced. The important role of prior knowledge as it relates to comprehension is supported by Trabasso and Bouchard's (2002) review of 14 studies in which all but one support the notion that activation of prior knowledge improves comprehension.

How to Use the Prep Plan

1. The teacher introduces the class to a key word, phrase, or picture related to the text topic.

2. The teacher tells the students the topic (e.g. "cities").

3. The three phases of the Prep Plan are covered.

    - Phase one is *initial association with the concept*; the teacher says, "Tell me anything that comes to mind when you hear the word (e.g. cities"). Teacher writes students' responses on the board.

    - Phase two is *reflections on initial associations*; the teacher asks, "What made you think of ... (the responses given by the students"). This phase helps students to become aware of their network of associations, to listen, and to interact with other students. It helps students to weight, to reject, to accept, to revise, and to integrate their ideas.

    - Phase three is *reformulation of knowledge*; the teacher asks, "From our discussion and before you read the text, have you any new ideas about ... (e.g. cities?") Student responses are usually more refined than they are in phase one because they have had an opportunity to probe their memories and elaborate on their prior knowledge.

ACTIVITIES TO REVIEW AND CLARIFY NEW VOCABULARY

VOCABULARY SNOWBALLS

What are Vocabulary Snowballs?

Vocabulary Snowballs involve students working together to understand and/or refine their understanding of key vocabulary contained in the assigned text.

Why Vocabulary Snowballs Benefit Students

Middle and high school students are barraged with new concepts and words in all of their courses. Understanding the meanings of these words is essential to their ability to comprehend the text.

Marzano and his colleagues (2001) note that "powerful learning" takes place when teachers provide direct instruction on words that are critical to understanding new content. They cite the research of Stahl and Fairbanks (1986) which indicates that student achievement increases by 33 percentile points when vocabulary instruction focuses on specific words that are important to what students are being asked to learn. Vocabulary Snowballs pre-empt the difficulties adolescent readers may have with new, unfamiliar, or difficult vocabulary.

How to Use Vocabulary Snowballs

1. Identify a limited number of words that you feel are new, unfamiliar, or difficult vocabulary in the assigned text. Often textbook writers list them at the beginning of each chapter or section of a text.

2. Ask students to write each word on a card or slip of paper and attempt to write a simple definition on the back.

3. Once a definition or partial definition has been written for each word, ask students to work with a partner to amend or extend their definition.

4. When one definition or partial definition has been created from two definitions, combine the pairs to form groups of four. The process is repeated.

5. Ask a spokesperson for each group of four to share the group definitions word by word. Combine the key elements of the definitions without passing judgment on the accuracy of the class definition being formed.

6. After the text is read, consider the class definition. Predictions are made about its accuracy.

7. Verify the correct definition of the word by using the text glossary, a dictionary, or other reference.

8. Discuss why Vocabulary Snowballs are an aid to student comprehension.

VOCABULARY HIGHLIGHTS

What are Vocabulary Highlights?

Vocabulary Highlights serve the same purpose as Vocabulary Snowballs. However, they are teacher directed and involve no group work. When time does not permit a Vocabulary Snowball, Vocabulary Highlights can be used in its place.

Why Vocabulary Highlights Benefit Students

See "Why" section of Vocabulary Snowballs.

How to Use Vocabulary Highlights

Marzano and his colleagues (2001) suggest that students will learn the new terms and phrases best with multiple exposures, including non-linguistic representations such as graphic organizers. The suggested sequence is:

1. Present students with a brief explanation or description of the new term or phrase.//
2. Present students with a non-linguistic representation of the new term or phrase.
3. Ask students to generate their own explanations or descriptions of the new term or phrase.
4. Ask students to generate their own explanations or descriptions of the term or phrases.
5. Periodically ask students to review the accuracy of their explanations and representations (128-129).

ACTIVITIES TO RECOGNIZE AND CLARIFY PURPOSES FOR READING

PINPOINTING PURPOSES

What is Pinpointing Purposes?

Pinpointing Purposes is a brief exercise in which students self-question to clarify their reading purpose.

Why Pinpointing Purposes Benefit Students

When students pinpoint their reading purpose they monitor their comprehension more successfully with respect to the extent to which their purpose is being met. Being aware of purpose equips readers to skim, to scan and to determine importance more flexibly and efficiently. Regular involvement with Pinpointing Purposes will prepare adolescents to respond more effectively to test questions and examination tasks.

How to Use Pinpointing Purposes

1. Provide students with their reading assignment.

2. Provide students with sample self-questions that help them to clarify what their purposes for reading will be. Here are some sample questions.

   - What do I have to find out?
   - What do I have to do with this text?
   - What do I need from this text?

3. Direct students to pair, and merge their purpose statements by discussing and refining the statement.

4. Direct students to join another pair to form a group of 4 in order to discuss and refine the purpose statement again.

5. Contribute the group purpose statements for a class discussion, highlighting the cues that helped each group refine the purpose.

Example   Pinpointing Purposes

Student 1: Purpose	Student 2: Purpose
I think my purpose for reading this section about Profits and Losses (p 43 Heinemann Mathematics 2) is: *to find out what a profit is and what a loss is.*	I think my purpose for reading this section about Profits and Losses (p 43 Heinemann Mathematics 2) is: *to find out what the bolded words mean and to find out how you work out the percentage profit on something.*

Joint Purpose

I think our purpose for reading this section about Profits and Losses (p 43 Heinemann Mathematics 2) is: *to find out what the bolded words like profit, loss, break-even, and percentage profit mean and to find out how you work out the percentage profit on something.*

DIRECTING QUESTIONS

What are Directing Questions?

Directing Questions are detailed questions with background information that can prepare and motivate an adolescent to read a text for specific purposes.

Why Directing Questions Benefit Students

Where teachers can substitute "read pages 95 to 98 by tomorrow' with some Directing Questions, there is a greater probability that students will become engaged and focused in their reading because they will be reading for specific purposes. Providing background information prepares readers for the task, and supplying directing, open-ended questions enables students to target key information.

How to Use Directing Questions

1. Decide on your assigned reading and consider the main ideas your students need to develop as a result of reading the text.

2. Create questions that compel readers to examine the main ideas and also to draw conclusions and to form opinions. Directing Questions should heighten curiosity and challenge general knowledge.

Example   Directing Questions

Many industrialized nations in the world have recycling programs. Which country in the world do you think would be most advanced in their recycling? Why? For homework, read pages 142 and 143: Recycling – the Costs and Benefits. Find out which country in the world is most advanced in their recycling and why this is so.

READING PLANS

What are Reading Plans?

Reading Plans are brief statements or diagrams that make explicit how the reader intends to achieve his or her reading purpose.

Why Reading Plans Benefit Students

Effective readers plan how they are going to read texts. Encouraging adolescents to document briefly how they intend to

How Do I Connect the Reading Strategies to My Content Area?

tackle texts increases the likelihood that they will undertake their reading in a prepared and systematic way.

How to Use Reading Plans

1. Ask students to look at the text to be read and the task.

2. Instruct students to complete the sentence stem "I am reading this to…."

3. Have students refer to the Reading Plan guide sheet (or poster) and list a number of steps that they will follow to accomplish their reading task.

4. After the reading task is completed, direct students to return to the plan and place a check next to the parts of the plan that worked, a cross next to those parts that didn't, and a wavy line next to those parts of the plan that were moderately useful.

READING PLAN GUIDE			
Skim to get an overall picture	*Re-read* to check my answer	*Predict* to think about what might be in the text	*Scan* to find specific information
Discuss the content with a partner to compare your understanding	*Summarize* the information to condense what it was all about	*Compare* this text with other texts to make connections in meaning	*Self-question* to direct reading of the next part or re-reading
Write the main idea to clarify the gist	*Read silently* to understand	*Skip over* to avoid distraction	*Read aloud* to sense author's style
Scan the index to find out if specific information is in the text	*Draw a diagram* to show how the different parts of the text are related	*Write key words* to remember what has been read	*Scan the contents* to find out if broad information is in the text
Ask myself what is needed to complete the task or solve the problem	*Write the task* in other terms like algebraic expressions to help solve the problem	*Re-read* to get a clearer idea of the message or to check	*Write the task* in my own words to clarify what needs to be done
Visualize to picture what is happening	*Unlock the meaning* of difficult vocabulary	*Tag the information* so I can return to it	*Pause and reflect* to ensure my reading is making sense

Example   Reading Plan

You and three friends are having a dim sum lunch at a Chinese restaurant that charges $2 per plate. You order lots of plates of wontons, egg rolls, and dumplings. The waiter gives you a bill for $25.20, which includes tax of $1.20. Solve the equation for how many plates your group ordered.

My Reading Plan	My calculations
Re-read to get a clearer idea of the message	
Write the task in my own words	*The cost of each plate multiplied by the number of plates will come to the bill without the tax.*
Write the task in other terms, e.g. algebra	*2 plates = 25.20 – 1.20* *or* *2p = 25.20 – 1.20* *2p = 24.00* *p = 12* *The group ordered 12 plates.*
Re-read to check my answer	

ACTIVITIES TO MAKE PREDICTIONS ABOUT CONTENT, TEXT STRUCTURE, AND AUTHOR PERSPECTIVE

SKIM SHEETS

What are Skim Sheets?

Skimming is quickly glancing through material in order to gain a general impression or overview of a chapter or section of text. It involves passing over much of the detail and focusing on "signposts" to get the gist of what a chapter or section is about. The structure of Skim Sheets, derived from the work of Raphael (1982, 1986) directs students on how to skim by quickly focusing on the "signposts" including:

- Headings
- Introductory statements
- Subheadings
- Captions
- Dot points
- Icons
- Bolded or italicized text
- Boxed or shaded text
- Illustrations, photos, and diagrams
- Tables
- Signal words or phrases (such as *finally, for example, in contrast to*)
- Summary statements

Why Skim Sheets Benefit Students

Research conducted by Block (2001) indicates that students who are taught to skim increase their comprehension of a text. Electronic texts such as websites require readers to skim effectively in order to predict content and to process large amounts of information efficiently.

How to Use Skim Sheets

1. Use a specific chapter or section of a text that has signposts. Where texts lack signposts, students can be taught to use topic sentences where they are regularly located by the author (e.g. beginning of the paragraph).

2. List the headings and sub-headings from the text in the left hand column of the Skim Sheet.

3. Give students a limited amount of time to skim the section of the text, with the intention of predicting what sort of

information might be included under each heading and subheading.

4. Ask students to form pairs to discuss and record their predictions on the Skim Sheet.

5. Have students read the section of the text to assess the accuracy of the predictions.

6. Tell students to complete the rest of the Skim Sheet.

7. Discuss why using Skim Sheets aids student comprehension of text.

SAMPLE OF COMPLETED SKIM SHEET

HEADING / SUB-HEADING	IN ONE SENTENCE, WHAT DO YOU THINK THIS SECTION IS ABOUT?	PREDICTION WAS ACCURATE	PREDICTION WAS PARTLY ACCURATE	PREDICTION WAS INACCURATE. THE SECTION WAS ABOUT…
Animal Behavior	*Why animals behave the way they do.*		X	*It included how animals learn to behave.*
Migration	*What migration is.*	X		
Hibernation	*What hibernation is.*	X		

Skim Sheet

Heading / Sub-heading	In one sentence, what do you think this section is about?	Prediction was accurate	Prediction was partly accurate	Prediction was inaccurate. The section was about…

ANTICIPATION GUIDES

What are Anticipation Guides?

Anticipation Guides (Readence, Bean, and Baldwin, 1995) are a series of statements developed by the teacher to focus students' attention on the most important concepts in a text. Some of the statements are common misconceptions about a topic or challenge a reader's existing knowledge about a topic. Prior to reading, students use their existing knowledge to categorize each statement as true or false, or to agree or disagree with a statement.

Why Anticipation Guides Benefit Students

Anticipation Guides encourage readers to consider what understandings and attitudes they bring to a text. This activity helps them to predict the information in the text and to determine the importance of what is read. Anticipation Guides have the added benefits of motivating students to read, and revealing misconceptions or preconceived notions that might interfere with their learning.

How to Use Anticipation Guides

1. Consider the most important explicit and implicit ideas in the text for the students.

2. Write the ideas as short, simple, declarative statements, highlighting contentious issues or common misconceptions.

3. Ensure that the statements are related in some way to the students' world.

4. Arrange the statements in an order that is logical, enhances anticipation, and builds to the main ideas.

5. Provide time for students to read the statements alone and respond to them (true/false; agree/disagree) based on existing knowledge.

6. After reading the text, provide opportunities for students to reflect on the accuracy and/or consistency of the judgments made before reading.

7. Encourage students to discuss how their existing knowledge and beliefs have been challenged or confirmed by the important ideas of the text.

Examples   Anticipation Guide

Anticipation Guide **Statistics**
Directions: In the column labeled "Me," place a check next to any statement with which you agree. After reading the text, compare your opinions on those statements with information contained in the text. **Me**   **Text** ___   ___   1. There are several kinds of averages for a set of data. ___   ___   2. The mode is the middle number in a set of data. ___   ___   3. Range tells how far apart numbers in a data set can be. ___   ___   4. Outliers are always ignored. ___   ___   5. Averages are always given as percents.

Anticipation Guide **Multiples and Divisors**
Directions: In the column labeled "Me," place a check next to any statement with which you agree. After reading the text, compare your opinions on those statements with information contained in the text. **Me**   **Text** ___   ___   1. Multiples relate to multiplying and divisors relate to dividing. ___   ___   2. 0 is a multiple of any number. ___   ___   3. 0 is a divisor of any number. ___   ___   4. Multiples of 2 are called even numbers. ___   ___   5. Multiples of 1 are odd numbers. ___   ___   6. Every number is a multiple of itself. ___   ___   7. Every number is a divisor of itself.

Barton, M.L. and Heidema, C. Teaching Reading in Mathematics. Aurora, CO: Mid-continent Research for Education and Learning, 2000. Reprinted with permission of McREL.

PREDICTION CLOZE

What is Prediction Cloze?

Prediction Cloze is a template that students can use to predict

- what a text might be about.
- whether a text is fiction or non-fiction.
- what its purpose might be.
- how it might be structured.
- what vocabulary it might include.
- what writing style might be used.
- what layout features it might include.

Why Prediction Cloze Benefits Students

Prediction Cloze encourages adolescents to activate everything they know about a topic and a text form. By activating their background knowledge, students' predictions are made explicit. Therefore students anticipate what sort of text they're about to confront.

How to Use Prediction Cloze

1. Select texts that have some introductory element to them like books (cover), websites (home page), newspapers (sections/headings), and magazines (sections/headings). The text needs to have some clues such as headings, subheadings, illustrations, and format that will provide a basis for predictions to be made.

2. Have students look at the surface features of a text (book cover, website homepage, chapter heading).

3. Have students complete the Prediction Cloze template, based on what they know about the text.

4. After reading the text, students look again at their Prediction Cloze and reflect on how accurate the predictions were.

Example   Prediction Cloze Template

I predict that this text will be about _____. I expect that it will be a narrative/informational text and the purpose will be to entertain/recount/socialize/inquire/inform/persuade/explain/instruct. This text will probably have mostly pictures/photographs/diagrams. I predict that it will have a text structure that is sequence/problem-solution/cause-effect/comparison-contrast. I expect that the following important words will be in the text:

Word List:

- _____
- _____
- _____
- _____
- _____

DURING READING TEACHING ACTIVITIES

To the onlooker the *during*-reading stage appears passive. Typically, the reader is silent, eyes fixated on the page. This appearance deceives. There is nothing passive about effective reading. There is real substance to the interaction between the reader and the text.

In the *during*-reading stage, competent readers are aware of their reading strategies and use them to monitor and adjust their reading. They use a cyclic, recursive process of predicting, sampling, confirming, or rejecting at the word, sentence, and text level. Competent readers are also constantly questioning the view of the world presented by the author. They consistently ask themselves questions related to *awareness*:

- What is my purpose in reading this?
- What information might be next?

They ask questions that help them to *monitor* their understanding:

- Is the text making sense to me?
- Is this information something I need to remember?

- How does this information connect to what I read earlier in the text?
- How does this information connect to what I know?
- Where do I have to infer the author's meaning?
- How am I being positioned by the author?

They ask questions to help them *fix up* misunderstandings:

- What does that word mean?
- How can I work out what that word means?
- How can I figure out the author's main idea?

ACTIVITIES TO FOCUS ATTENTION ON THE READING TASK

READING GUIDES

What are Reading Guides?

Reading Guides provide students with a set of written directions, questions, and activities intended to guide students through the independent reading of text. Reading guides can be thought of as a marriage between the direction a teacher would like to give verbally during a reading task, and the enjoyment of a reading puzzle.

Why Reading Guides Benefit Students

When students are asked to read independently, many still require support in monitoring their reading. Reading Guides assist comprehension by

- highlighting significant ideas and the relationships between them.
- indicating sections that are peripheral or irrelevant and can be skimmed.
- stimulating thinking about key ideas.
- reinforcing the importance of regular monitoring of comprehension (summarizing, questioning, and locating troublesome vocabulary).

How to Use Reading Guides

To design a reading guide:

1. Determine the overall purpose for reading.

2. Select the sections of the text that are most important to achieving the purpose.

3. Plot a path through the text by directing students to sections of text. Guide students' reading by posing questions, suggesting they make predictions, and prompting them to summarize what they read.

Example Reading Guide
based on *The First Lunar Landing* by Rodney Martin, Magic Bean, In-fact series.

Reading Directions	**Task**	
Read the introduction to the book on page 3.	Look at the Contents page opposite. The next page, page 4, is about the Apollo Spacecraft and the Saturn V Rocket. Quickly draw what you think the rocket might look like in this space. How tall do you think it might have been? Put an X in your drawing where you think the astronauts might sit.	
Read page 4 and look carefully at the diagram.	How tall was the rocket? Were you right about where the astronauts sat? You can see the astronauts on the opposite page. Page 6 is about their training for the journey. What sort of training do you think they would need to do?	
Read page 7.	Check the training needs you predicted that were listed on page 6. The next two pages are about the journey. How long do you think it might have taken them to get to the moon and back? What would they do during a day in space?	
Skim pages 10, 11, and 12. Read page 13.	Check the parts of your prediction that were correct. Close the book and write down the main ideas that you can recall from your reading today.	

TEXT-CONNECTION CODES

What are Text-Connection Codes?

Text-Connection Codes are ways of ensuring that the reader is actively connecting elements in the text with their own personal experiences, other texts, and what they know about the world that is outside their personal experiences.

Why Text Connection Codes Benefit Students

Psychologists and reading specialists have long emphasized the importance of readers' background knowledge and how it affects their ability to comprehend new material. Efficient readers typically activate their prior knowledge before and as they read (National Reading Panel, 2000). Text-Connection Codes are a good way to help students to activate their prior knowledge during their reading of text.

How to Use Text-Connection Codes

1. Explain to students the three different types of text connections they can make as summarized by Keen and Zimmerman (1997):

    - **Text-to-Self Connection**

        This involves readers thinking about their life and connecting their own personal experiences to the information in the text.

    - **Text-to-Text Connection**

        This involves readers thinking about other text written by the same author or with common themes, style, organization, structure, characters, or content.

    - **Text-to-World Connections**

        This involves readers thinking about what they know about the world outside their personal experience, their family, or their community.

2. Provide students with sticky notes so they can record their connections in the different sections of the text you have assigned to them.

3. Explain to students that as they read and come to something within the text that triggers a connection, have them place a sticky note there. They should use the code S for connection to self, T for connection to another text, and W for connection to general world knowledge. Each code should be

accompanied by a key word or phrase that triggered the connection.

4. Ask students to reflect on their text connections after reading. You may want them to summarize their connections by using the form contained in the Course Booklet.

5. In pairs or small groups ask students to share and explain their most useful text connections.

6. Discuss why using Text-Connection Codes aids comprehension of texts. It is important that readers learn to refine and limit their connections to those that help them understand the text better. At first, students may make connections that have little relevance to helping comprehension. Conversations about connections being made can help students focus on how connections may have assisted understanding.

SPLIT PAGES

What are Split Pages?

Split pages are formats that provide students space on notebook pages to generate and answer their own questions.

Why Split Pages Benefit Students

Santeusanio (1990) cited 13 studies that support the practice of having students generate their own questions from text in order to improve learning. A goal of middle and high school teachers is to help their students to become independent learners, and a characteristic of such learners is the ability to generate and answer their own questions. The theoretical support for this practice is found in Wittrock's (1974) "generative" model for learning which states that when learners generate their own learning aids, knowledge is enhanced.

How to Use Split Pages

1. Have students rule notebook pages with a 2 ½-inch margin on the left, leaving about a 6 inch area on the right.

2. Explain to students that the left side of the page is where they create their questions and the right hand side is where they record their answers.

3. Remind students to create questions that represent the author's main ideas and reflect the author's organization of

those main ideas such as cause/effect relationships or the comparison and contrast of information.

4. Also remind students, particularly if this technique is used with literature, to create questions and answers that reflect the author's inferred ideas.

5. Tell students to use their own words, not the author's, when recording answers to questions.

6. Encourage students to use their "Split Pages" as learning aids. Cover the 6 inch column. Using the questions as cues, they try to recall the answers to their questions as fully as possible. (This is usually done in the *after*-reading stage).

ACTIVITIES TO IDENTIFY AND RECORD IMPORTANT INFORMATION

NOTE MAKING

What is Note Making?

Note making is the recording of key words in a text, usually nouns or verbs, as a means of identifying and extracting important information from texts.

Why Note Making Benefits Students

Note making allows readers to recall extended and dense text, to organize and summarize information, and to record it for later use (Faber, Morris & Liberman, 2000). It enhances a reader's ability to recall significant concepts and the relationships between them in a text.

How to Use Note Making

1. Present students with a descriptive text about three paragraphs long. The paragraphs should have distinct main ideas marked by either subheadings or topic sentences. For example, an extended text on the water table could have one paragraph titled *Groundwater*, one titled *Aquifer* and a third titled *Pollution*.

2. Ask students to select a nominated number of key words to answer the question, *what is groundwater?* The number of

key words should be adjusted to reflect the density of ideas in the text.

3. Share which paragraph was chosen as the source of the key words. Explain the importance of using subheadings and/or topic sentences to ignore some information in pursuit of more important information.

4. Discuss the key words selected.

5. Put the key words in a sentence or two which summarizes the paragraph.

6. Ask students to choose one question from a list designed to be answered within a selected text. Examples: What is groundwater? What is an aquifer? What is the water table?

7. Provide students with the text about the water table and model how, using an example question as a starting point, a reader could use the contents page, index, chapter headings, subheadings, and topic sentences to find the information required in the text.

8. Ask students to follow the demonstration, to locate the information, and to select the key words necessary to answer the question.

9. Ask students to use the key words to write a sentence or two that answers the question. A table like the one below may be useful in guiding the process

Example   Note Making

Topic: the water table	
Question: What is the water table?	
Key words	**Sentence answers**
Groundwater cracks rocks layer aquifer upper surface	*When groundwater collects in cracks between rocks and makes a layer, called an aquifer, the upper surface is called the water table.*

Generating a Question

Here are some ways to help students generate questions:

- Provide students with a text that is motivating and interesting.

- Ask students to skim the contents page and pose a question that provides a purpose for reading. That is, "what would you like to know about this topic that this text could answer?"

- Students find the information they need by using the contents page, index, chapter headings, subheadings and topic sentences.

- Ask students to locate the information and select the key words necessary to answer the question.

- Ask students to use the key words to write a sentence or two that answers the question.

- Provide an opportunity for students to share their findings.

TEXT RECONSTRUCTION

What is Text Reconstruction?

Text Reconstruction is the process of reassembling whole text that has been fragmented.

Why Text Reconstruction Benefits Students

When students reconstruct text they become aware of the structure and cohesive devices of a text type. This type of activity aids comprehension. Text Reconstruction activities are most useful with text types with a distinct sequence of paragraphs. However, when the sequence of paragraphs is not prescriptive, excellent discussion can arise as students generate reasons to justify why their order of elements is more effective than alternatives. For example, students may argue that a report reads better with details about location first and description of appearance later. Of course, there will not always be one solution, but the discussion will focus on links in meaning which are crucial.

Texts that are arranged in time-order sequence and have dates or time 'signposts' such as *firstly*, *secondly*, *following*, and *after*, are generally the easiest texts to reconstruct. Those organized in a cause-effect or compare-contrast pattern are usually more difficult, although again, this depends on how the author has used signal words and phrases.

How to Use Text Reconstruction

1. Select a text with 4 or more paragraphs that has some words or phrases that are 'signposts' to the sequence of the text.

2. Photocopy the text and cut it between the paragraphs.

3. Provide students with the challenge of reconstructing the text.

4. Encourage students to use the main idea of each piece of text (often a paragraph), linking words and phrases to establish the sequence of events.

5. Direct students to compare their reconstructions and to justify their sequences by referring to the content. Having the correct sequence is less important than being aware of how the concepts in the information relate to each other.

How Do I Connect the Reading Strategies to My Content Area?

Example   Text Reconstruction

Arrange the following paragraphs about the discovery of radioactivity in the order that you think makes most sense. Be prepared to explain why.

In 1895, Wilhelm Roentgen observed that cathode rays in a tube from which all air had been evacuated caused certain substances to fluoresce or glow. To study this phenomenon, he darkened his lab and wrapped his cathode-ray tube in black cardboard. When he looked away from the tube across the room, he noticed that some chemically treated paper glowed when the electricity in the tube was turned on. He reasoned that when cathode rays hit the anode, other unknown rays were emitted that could penetrate solid substances like cardboard, glass, and even walls of a room. Because the nature of these rays was unknown, Roentgen called them x-rays.

Beginning in 1898, Pierre Curie, who once worked with Becquerel, and his wife Marie set out to further investigate substances which she termed "radioactive." After four years' effort, in 1902, they reduced a ton of pitchblende into a fraction of an ounce of substance 400 times more radioactive than uranium. They called the newly discovered, powerfully radioactive element polonium. Later that year they also isolated radium from the pitchblende. The radium, too, was more powerful than uranium.

Few Scientific discoveries occur suddenly and unexpectedly; rather, they come about through the dedicated efforts of several people over long periods of time. The discovery of radioactivity resulted from many years of persistent investigation.

The Discovery of Radioactivity

Antoine Becquerel took the next step in the discovery of radioactivity when in 1896 he began to study materials that fluoresced in sunlight. He covered a photographic plate with black paper, placed a bit of fluorescent uranium substance on top, and put it in sunlight. Ordinary light couldn't pass through the black paper, but x-rays could. And they affected the film. Next, he noticed that even when the uranium substance wasn't exposed to sunlight, the film still fogged. From this he realized that whatever fogged the film was spontaneously emitted from the uranium substance. He had discovered something more powerful than x-rays –radioactivity.

Adapted from E.M. Fitzpatrick (1982) *Study Skills Program Level III*. Used by permission of Scarecrow Press, The Rowman & Littlefield Publishing Group.

Other Activities Two previously discussed activities, *Text-Connection Codes* and *Graphic Organizers* can also be used to help students to identify important information.

AN ACTIVITY TO MAKE PREDICTIONS DURING READING

RECIPROCAL TEACHING (Also used for questioning, clarifying and summarizing)

What is Reciprocal Teaching?

Reciprocal teaching is an activity to enhance students' reading comprehension. The teacher and students take turns leading a dialogue about different sections of text. During this dialogue, participants make predictions, raise questions, summarize, and clarify their understanding of difficult text. The teacher and students take turns assuming the role of teacher in leading the dialogue.

Why Reciprocal Teaching Benefits Students

Because the focus of Reciprocal Teaching is on comprehension, its use helps students to understand what they are reading. It also provides students with opportunities to monitor their learning. Reviews of research (Rosenshine and Meister, 1994; Slater, 2004) indicate that Reciprocal Teaching is an effective way to improve students' reading comprehension.

How to Use Reciprocal Teaching

1. Be sure students understand what the reading strategies are that are emphasized in Reciprocal Teaching. You may want to make charts that include information that is presented below.

   - **Summarizing**

     When you summarize you are finding the most important information in the text. We sometimes refer to this as the "main idea." You can summarize single paragraphs, a series of paragraphs, or a whole section of your text. Use your own words when summarizing.

   - **Questioning**

     Create questions on what you are reading by using the "5 Ws": who, what, where, when, and why. Why questions are good ones because they help you to learn the material more deeply. The other "W" questions generally focus on details of the text. Using "How Questions" is also a good way to formulate questions.

- **Clarifying**

    A lot is going on as you read, so you need to be sure of what you do and do not understand as you read. When what you read does not make sense to you, then slow down, re-read, figure out the meaning of unfamiliar words, or ask for help. Do whatever is necessary to clarify when you do not understand what you are reading.

- **Predicting**

    When you anticipate what the writer is going to say next, you are predicting. After you make your prediction, read on to see if you were correct. Always think ahead as you read.

2. Model the process by emphasizing the four strategies listed above.

3. Give students the opportunity to become the teacher.

4. Have students work in fours and provide each with a card that signifies the student as the summarizer, questioner, clarifier, or predictor. Each student takes a turn analyzing the text in the way indicated by the card. Cards are switched as the group moves to the next section of text. This process continues until each person in the group has had an opportunity to carry out each of the four roles.

5. Have students work in pairs, taking turns "teaching" each other by carrying out all four roles.

6. Discuss why Reciprocal Teaching aids student comprehension of text.

ACTIVITIES TO MONITOR COMPREHENSION

2R4C

What is 2R4C?

2R4C is a repeated pattern of systematic steps that adolescent readers can use when they do not understand a word.

Why does 2R4C Benefit Students

If students do not have a plan to unlock the meaning of unfamiliar vocabulary, they will not understand the readings you assign to them. Effective readers have a well-rehearsed plan of action for occasions when they cannot identify a word.

How to Use 2R4C

In the course of reading any text students should be encouraged to use the following process when they are confronted with a word that they can't identify:

Re-read the sentence that includes the difficult word.

Read on past the difficult word.

Consider the context (the subject, surrounding pictures).

Chunk the word into meaningful parts such as syllables, prefix, suffix, and base word.

Compare the word with others you know.

Check a reference like a glossary, a friend, or a dictionary.

DIFFICULT WORDS CHART

What are Difficult Words Charts?

Difficult Words Charts, an adaptation of Interesting Words Charts (Morris and Stewart-Dore, 1984) is a method for clarifying new or unknown vocabulary.

Why Difficult Words Charts Benefit Students

Difficult Words Charts helps students use 2R4C to work out word meanings and benefit students for the same reasons we noted above in the 2R4C section.

How to Use Difficult Word Charts

Difficult Words Charts can be used *before, during* or *after* reading. As a *during*-reading activity, the chart encourages students to practice using the context – the words and graphics around a difficult word – to identify a difficult word.

1. Pair students and provide a Difficult Words Chart.
2. Encourage students to use the 2R4C process to develop some idea of what the difficult words mean.

How Do I Connect the Reading Strategies to My Content Area?

3. Enter the word in the word column; the page, paragraph or line number is recorded in the next column, and context clues are listed in the appropriate column.
4. Have students share their findings at appropriate breaks in the reading or following the reading. Clarify any misunderstandings.

Example Difficult Words Chart
based on *Natural Disasters* by Janeen Brian
(Magic Bean, In-fact series)

Word	Page / ¶ / Line	Context Clues	Our Explanation	Definition
molten	P. 4, ¶ 2, L. 3	hot lava, magma	melted rock	
topple	P. 7, ¶ 1, L. 5		knock over	
tsunamis	P. 7, ¶ 3, L. 1	giant waves caused by earthquakes	giant waves	
evaporate	P. 14, ¶ 6, L. 5	water turns into water vapor	water turns into a gas	

Other Activities Two previously discussed activities, *Text-Connection Codes* and *Split Pages* can be used to teach comprehension monitoring.

An Activity to Aid Making Inferences

CLOZE PROCEDURE

What is the Cloze Procedure?

The Cloze Procedure is the omission of single words or groups of words from text for the purpose of testing or teaching comprehension, particularly making inferences.

Why the Cloze Procedure Benefits Students

Cloze can be manipulated to provide practice in the use of syntactic, semantic, and graphophonic cues. This practice leads to making inferences.

How to Use the Cloze Procedure

There are several varieties of cloze. Each can be configured to achieve a different purpose. For example, a cloze p_____ that leaves initial letters encourages the use of initial l_____ as a cue to word identification. What is most important in the use of cloze when teaching the comprehension of non-fiction text is that the cloze procedure is used to teach reading skills rather than to test knowledge. Compare the following cloze passages.

	Cloze Test	Cloze Exercise
Example	Pyramid of Cheops A few facts on the Pyramid of Cheops: 1. It is made out of _____ blocks. 2. These blocks are made of _____.	Pyramid of _____ A few facts on the Pyramid of _____: 1. It is made out of 2 300 000 _____. 2. These blocks are _____ of limestone.
Features	Relies on the recall of previously encountered information.	Provides context clues to help pupils decide on the deleted words.
Purpose	• Test of pupil knowledge • Test of reading ability	• Exercise to teach the use of context clues

Deleting words directly from a piece of text read recently tends to encourage recall of literal details, in a way similar to a memory test. One very effective way of focusing cloze exercises on comprehension is to write a summary of a piece of non-fiction text to be read by pupils. Delete selected words which carry meaning and ask pupils to complete the passage.

The way in which the cloze passage is completed also affects its worth as a reading-comprehension strategy. When students have an opportunity to substantiate their choice of word - and any reasonable choice is accepted - cloze becomes an exercise in reading and thinking. Students should be encouraged to generate their own answers, but then encouraged to discuss them and revise them on the basis of what sounds right. It is useful to stage cloze exercises so the discussion takes place after a section of text. This staging prevents weaker readers from being misled by inappropriate selections early in the text. So the lesson would incorporate teacher modeling, individual attempts at the words missing in a paragraph, discussion with a peer or group, revision of answers, and reading of the next paragraph to continue the cycle. Teacher input to discussion at a group, or later at a whole class level, should focus on how the reader was able to choose an appropriate word for the space. Discussion centers on the context clues that were used to decide upon a logical word. Where the text is enlarged, arrows and color might be used to highlight their role in completing that part of the cloze.

Other Activities

Three previously discussed activities, Reciprocal Teaching, Text-Connection Codes and Graphic Organizers, can be used to teach making inferences.

AFTER READING TEACHING ACTIVITIES

The *after*-reading stage has traditionally been dominated by teacher-assigned comprehension tests that consist of a series of questions or a written task. While there is a place for students to demonstrate their comprehension after reading, it needs to be balanced with opportunities for students to, among other things:

- reflect on the text, including opportunities to clarify meaning.

- evaluate and respond to the text by expressing an opinion in a discussion.

- organize, synthesize, and analyze new information gained from the text.
- extend new knowledge by planning to read more texts of a similar author or genre.

In the *after*-reading stage, effective readers ask themselves questions such as:

- Did I achieve my purpose in reading this?
- Did I understand what I read?
- How does this text now make me feel?
- What do I do with this text now?
- What information is critical?
- How can I recall this text if necessary? What summary of text structure will enable me to remember key parts of the text?

ACTIVITIES TO IDENTIFY, TO EXTRACT, AND TO RECALL IMPORTANT INFORMATION

ALTERNATIVE HEADINGS

What is Alternative Headings?

Alternative Headings is an activity whereby students read to find main ideas of sections of text and then suggest alternative headings for them. It helps them to crystallize main ideas and to understand that there may be differences between what the author thinks is important and what they think is important.

Why Alternative Headings Benefit Students

Vacca and Vacca (2004) note that what a reader identifies as the main idea may not be what the author intended as the main idea. They make the distinction between *textually* important ideas, or what the author considers important, and *contextually* important ideas, or what the reader thinks is important. By using Alternative Headings, this distinction can be made explicit to students who need to differentiate what is textually important from what is contextually important in the texts that they read.

How to Use Alternative Headings

1. Provide students with a text that has various sub-headings.

2. Have students read those sections to determine main ideas and then brainstorm key words that would be suitable to produce an alternative to the heading.

3. Have students create an alternative heading.

4. Organize students into pairs to combine their ideas and reach consensus. Discussion need not be lengthy, but should be based upon literal and inferential information in the text that supports a particular heading being chosen.

5. Once pairs have agreed on the heading, organize pairs to form a group of four. Encourage this group to again reach consensus. Students may find themselves debating the relative meanings of a number of synonyms in an effort to choose the most appropriate heading.

6. Discuss the alternative headings produced by each group.

7. Discuss why using Alternative Headings aids student comprehension. Engage in a discussion on the extent to which there is a difference between what the author thinks is important (her heading) versus what students think are important (their headings). Do the differences in headings really reflect a difference in what each party thinks is important?

TRANSFORMATIONS

What are Transformations?

Transformations involve students changing text information into a different genre, form, mode, medium or format. Examples of transformations suitable for adolescents include:

- A fairy tale re-written as a news article.
- A novel re-created as a board game.
- A math problem re-created as a diagram.
- A short story represented as a comic strip.
- A poem or historical event represented as a performance.

Transformations can vary greatly in their degree of difficulty. Factors that contribute to this include the text content, the text form, and the compatibility between the original and new text form. Although a fairy tale may be familiar to a student, the text structure and organization of a newspaper article may not. Similarly, a student may have played many board games but rarely considered how one might be constructed. Students attempting Transformations require significant support in the understanding and manipulation of the two text forms. You can best support students with extensive modeling, sharing, and guiding.

Explicit modeling and support are necessary to teach transformation. Note-making skills must be sufficiently developed to draw facts from fictional texts and to represent them in the text structure and style of a non-fiction text. An awareness of the characteristics of both text types is therefore necessary. It is also necessary to consider the purpose and audience for the transformed text.

Why Transformations Benefit Students

Transformations require students to select relevant detail and to reshape the main ideas of the text in a different form. As a result, students gain a deeper understanding of the text while developing their note-making skills.

How to Use Transformations

Here is a suggested procedure for teaching Transformations:
1. Select the text you want students to transform.
2. Provide students with choices regarding what shape the transformation will take.
3. Model, as necessary, how to make the transformations.
4. Have students make notes on the original text.
5. Have students make the transformation.

SYNTHESIS JOURNALS

What are Synthesis Journals?

A Synthesis Journal (McAlexander & Burrell, 1996) provides a framework for students to use when synthesizing information about a topic from a variety of sources written by authors who often represent a range of perspectives.

Why Synthesis Journals Benefit Students

Zwiers (2004) believes that learning how to synthesize benefits students because by being involved in research they are led to new perspectives and insights that are formed from the unique combination of information they take into their brains, their unique backgrounds, and their thinking process. Completing Synthesis Journals helps them to gain these new perspectives and insights. Zwiers feels synthesizing is one of the most creative skills of thinking.

How to Use Synthesis Journals

Because synthesizing is a complex process, it should be modeled several times by the teacher before asking students to independently create their own journals. Here are directions for students to follow for using the journals:

1. Select a topic or assign a topic to them.

2. Gather information from a variety of sources such as books, videos, speakers, the teacher, newspapers, periodicals, and websites.

3. Record key information from each source onto the Synthesis Journal framework located in the Course Book.

SYNTHESIS JOURNAL

Source 1 Key Info	Source 2 Key Info	Source 3 Key Info	Source 4 Key Info

CROSSWORDS

What are Crosswords?

Crosswords are made up of a series of intersecting words of which some of the letters are common, and the words are indicated by clues. Any text with difficult vocabulary or new concepts to be learned is ideal for the construction of Crosswords. While there are software packages available for the creation of crosswords, students benefit from working together to manually complete the process as it helps consolidate vocabulary and word understandings. It is important to model the creation of clues. Clues could include:

- Simple definitions, e.g. *the process whereby organisms containing chlorophyll use the energy in sunlight to produce sugar and oxygen from carbon dioxide and water.*

- Cloze sentences, e.g. *Plankton produce 80 per cent of the ------ on our planet.*

- Stating a relationship, e.g. ADD

- Offering a synonym or antonym, e.g. ADD

Why Crosswords Benefit Students

Creating and completing Crosswords requires adolescent readers to focus on defining features of words as well as investigating both the structure and meaning of key words.

How to Use Crosswords

1. Arrange students in pairs.
2. Provide each pair with two crossword grids, e.g. *15 squares by 15 squares.*
3. Have students select thematic words, subject specific words, or words from discrete sections of a text and arrange them on one of the grids ensuring some of the letters intersect.
4. On the same grid, direct students to number the first letter of each word.
5. Direct students to transfer these numbers onto the blank grid. Have students shade grid boxes that will not contain a letter when the crossword is complete.
6. Direct students to create clues for each of their selected words.
7. Have students swap crosswords with another pair to complete.

WORD CLINE

What is a Word Cline?

A Word Cline is an activity that involves students arranging words that are similar in meaning to show a graduating intensity, according to a given criterion. Any text with new concepts or difficult vocabulary that can be categorized suits a Word Cline. For example, a health education text might deal with a range of foods that include Vitamin A. Word Clines can include a vertical axis. For example, the Word Cline dealing with forms of energy would have one axis relating to sustainability, and one relating to cost.

Why Word Cline Benefits Students

Word Cline helps build students' understanding of concepts including their connotations.

How to Use Word Cline

1. After students have read a common text, select a key word e.g., *coal*. It is important for students to be able to find other words in the same category (e.g. *forms of energy*) or generate at least four synonyms for a chosen key word (*poor*).

2. Have students generate synonyms (or words that are closely related) for the key word, e.g., *working class, destitute, needy, impoverished*.

3. Invite students to arrange the words in rising intensity against a criterion, e.g. *forms of energy – more sustainable to less sustainable; poverty – more desperate to less desperate.*

4. Arrange students into small groups to discuss the words and reach a consensus about the order of the words.

5. Have students reflect on the factors that influenced their choice of placement. Students need to be aware that readers' perceptions of the meanings of words will vary according to their prior knowledge.

6. Discuss how the use of the different words from the Word Cline would influence the text.

AN ACTIVITY TO ENCOURAGE READING REFLECTION

READ AND RETELL

What is Read and Retell?

Read and Retell (Browne and Cambourne, 1987) is a simple activity that is flexible in its use and provides an opportunity for students to recite and reflect on what they have learned in a variety of ways. Retelling requires students to read or listen to a text, organize key information they understand from the text, and then share and compare their retellings with others. While secondary students typically "retell" or recite their learning in a written form, students can retell orally, through drawings and diagrams, and even through drama. Any text is suitable for Read and Retell.

Why Read and Retell Benefits Students

Retelling provides an excellent context for students to analyze texts and identify ideas that are explicit and implicit within a text. Santeusanio (1990) identifies a number of studies that demonstrate the positive effects on students when they recite what they have learned from text.

How to Use Read and Retell

1. Have students activate background knowledge about the topic and make predictions about the content of the text.//
2. Direct students to read the text.
3. Allow students to re-read as necessary.
4. Provide time for students to prepare their retell and to include only key information.
5. Have students create their retell in one of the following forms:

    - **Written to Written Retells** – students read a text and retell it in writing.
    - **Written to Oral Retells** – students read a text and retell it orally.
    - **Written to Drawing/Design Retells** – students read a text and retell it through a drawing or a graphic design.
    - **Written to Drama Retells** – students read a text and retell through drama.

- **Diagram to Oral or Written Retells** – students read a diagram and retell orally or in writing.
- **Drama to Written Retells** – students view a dramatic presentation and retell in writing.

6. Have students share their retells with a partner, small group, or the whole class.
7. Provide time for students do discuss and compare their retells.
8. Discuss why Read and Retell is an aid to student comprehension.

ACTIVITIES FOR SUMMARIZING MAIN IDEAS AND DETAILS

FACTS AND FALSEHOODS

What is Facts and Falsehoods?

Facts and Falsehoods consists of a series of statements created by the students that include accurate and inaccurate information from assigned text. The challenge is for another student to determine which statements are facts and which are false. The activity changes in orientation depending on how the reading is done. For example, students can read texts about individual areas of interest in a subject and create Facts and Falsehoods for their peers. This is a good test of their classmates' general knowledge. With more time, peers can investigate these statements using information such as the Internet and reference material. Alternatively, all students can read the same text and create Facts and Falsehoods for each other. This is more a test of comprehension for all students.

Why Facts and Falsehoods Benefit Students

Facts and Falsehoods require students to categorize items and clarify concepts, both of which are essential to effective comprehension. In addition, students need to respond to text at both the literal and interpretive levels of comprehension.

How to Use Facts and Falsehoods

1. Ask the students to read about a particular topic and list facts. If the task is to be completed orally, 3 or 4 statements are sufficient. If the list is to be read, up to 10 items would be possible. Generally, the greater the number, the greater

the difficulty of the task for the person who must distinguish between accurate facts and inaccurate ones.

2. Have students write some facts and some falsehoods to be included in the list.

3. Provide opportunities for students to present their lists to another student, challenging them in particular to find the falsehoods and the reason they are falsehoods.

66 WORDS

What is 66 Words?

66 Words is a framework that can be used to record the key events or themes of a text. Students are challenged to read a text and create a summary recording this in sixty-six words or less. By providing students with a grid with sixty-six rectangles, the focus is on the concise crystallization of the text not the exact number of words.

Why 66 Words Benefits Students

Understanding *main ideas* is the ability to identify the author's topic and to summarize what the author says about the topic. *Details* are the specifics that support or add meaning to the summary main idea statement. Typically, writers express or imply a main idea statement in each of their paragraphs. Good readers can summarize not only the main idea of the individual paragraphs, but summarize a number of paragraphs that make up a section.

To summarize *main ideas*, readers must decide what is important, what is trivial, and what is repetitive. Therefore the reader must generalize, delete, or ignore some information and reword some ideas.

How to Use 66 Words

1. Have students individually write their 66 Word summary in sentence form.

2. Organize students into small groups. Each small group merges individual ideas to create a single summary in sixty-six words or less. If consensus is difficult, each group member may have a turn at making the final decision about at least one sentence.

3. Have groups share their 66 Word summary. Discuss what was included, what was left out, and why.

MAIN IDEA PYRAMID

What is a Main Idea Pyramid?

The Main Idea Pyramid is a graphic organizer that helps students to determine important information within a paragraph or entire text. Texts that have paragraphs with clear topic sentences and simple listing structures are ideal texts when beginning to use Main Idea Pyramids.

Why Main Idea Pyramid Benefits Students

The completion of a pyramid helps students to understand main ideas and how details are related to them.

How to Use Main Idea Pyramid

1. After reading a text or sections of a text, have students brainstorm important facts. Encourage students to refer back to the text if necessary.
2. Have students record facts on cards or notes so they can be moved.
3. When the brainstorming process is complete, direct students to cluster the cards or notes into common sub-topics. Transfer clustered information to the base of the pyramid.
4. Direct students to re-read the combination of words/phrases in each cluster and record a main idea statement for each. These statements form the second level of the pyramid.
5. Direct students to then use all the information at the second level to create a main idea of the text. This forms the top level of the pyramid.

RETRIEVAL CHART

What is a Retrieval Chart?

A Retrieval Chart is a format for recording information about a number of categories or topics in a way that allows comparisons to be made.

Why Retrieval Charts Benefit Students

Creating a Retrieval Chart involves students in scanning text to extract important information in order to make generalizations. It helps them to comprehend text written in the comparison/contrast pattern. Retrieval Charts can be completed using key words or pictorial representations, or can include references to page, paragraph, and line numbers.

How to Use Retrieval Charts

1. Construct the headings for the Retrieval Chart based on the type of information being sought.
2. Introduce the Retrieval Chart headings to the students.
3. Allow students time to read the text/s.
4. Provide time for students to re-read the text/s, scanning to identify relevant information.
5. Allocate time for students to record the information they have identified onto the Retrieval Chart.
6. Discuss with students similarities and differences within categories.

Example   Retrieval Chart

Analysis of Insulators			
MATERIAL	COST	ADVANTAGES	DISADVANTAGES
wool			
paper			
polystyrene foam			
rubber			

Other Activities

Three other previously discussed activities, Alternative Headings, Transformations, and Graphic Organizers can be used to help students to summarize main ideas.

AN ACTIVITY TO RECOGNIZE DIFFERENT LEVELS OF COMPREHENSION

THREE LEVEL GUIDES

What are Three Level Guides?

Three Level Guides consist of a series of statements based on information found in text. The statements reflect different levels of comprehension.

Level One statements require readers to locate relevant information directly from the text. The wording of the statements may not always be exactly the same as in the text, but the meaning is similar. This requires literal level comprehension. Literal level comprehension has been referred to as *reading on the lines*, *right there*, and *the author said it* comprehension.

Level Two statements require readers to reflect on literal information and to see relationships between statements. They require students to think and search for answers. This is interpretive level comprehension. Inferential level comprehension has been described as *reading between the lines*, *think and search*, and the *author meant it* comprehension.

Level Three statements require readers to apply and evaluate information by relating it to their own background knowledge. This is applied level comprehension. Applied and evaluative comprehension is often called *reading beyond the lines*, *on my own*, or *the author would agree with it* comprehension.

Why Three Level Guides Benefit Students

A Three Level Guide ensures that students reflect on the material they have read, first at the literal, then the interpretive, and finally the applied and evaluative level. This means that students are guided to use facts to form meaningful concepts as they:

- identify the most important literal details and concepts (level 1).

- interpret relationships between these literal statements (level 2).

- apply and evaluate this information so that deeper understandings or new ideas evolve (level 3).

How to Use Three Level Guides

The Three Level Guide requires consistent modeling and shared use at a class and group level before students are able to use it independently.

1. Determine the content objectives of the reading. The statements at all three levels must be aimed at these objectives. This is what gives direction and purpose to the guide.

2. Write the applied/evaluative level statements first (level 3). These should be based on the content objectives and the main idea(s), major concepts, and generalizations beyond the text.

3. Write literal level statements next (level 1). These should include information on which the applied/evaluative level statements are based.

4. Finally, write interpretive level statements (level 2). These should help pupils draw inferences from the information in the text.

5. Include a number of incorrect statements at each level.

Examples   Three Level Guide
based on *Viewpoints on Waste* by Rodney Martin (Magic Bean, In-fact series).

Level 1: Right There

Check the statements that say what the author actually said.

_____ 1   The expense of waste disposal is a problem.

_____ 2   People throw away approximately 30 kg of household waste every year.

_____ 3   One way to reduce waste is to refuse to buy goods that have unnecessary packaging.

_____ 4   Lots of kitchen and garden waste can be recycled.

Level 2: Think and Search

Check the statements that you think the author meant:

_____ 1   We buy and use too many disposable things.

_____ 2   We need to find special ways for dealing with toxic waste.

_____ 3   Industries are being creative in finding uses for recycled materials.

_____ 4   Recycling is a government and industry responsibility.

Level 3: On My Own

Check the statements that you think the author would agree with.

_____ 1   The disposal of waste is affecting our environment more than ever before.

_____ 2   Every piece of waste ultimately has an impact on humans and other living things.

_____ 3   Ways in which we can prevent waste disposal problems are limited.

_____ 4   People can lessen the waste problem by changing their habits.

Like the Reading Guide, the Three Level Guide takes time to produce. However, it must be remembered that it only needs to be done once, and by sharing the workload teachers can benefit from the work of others.

Example Three Level Guide for Mathematics

A three-level guide to a math problem

Read the problem and then answer each set of questions, following the directions given for the set questions.

> Problem: Sam's Sporting Goods has a markup rate of 40% on Pro tennis rackets. Sam, the store owner, bought 12 Pro tennis rackets for $75 each. Calculate the selling price of a Pro tennis racket at Sam's Sporting Goods.

Part I

Directions: Read the statements. Check Column A if the statement is true according to the problem. Check Column B if the information will help you solve the problem.

A (true?)	B (help?)	
_____	_____	Sam's markup rate is 40%.
_____	_____	Sam bought 12 Pro tennis rackets.
_____	_____	Pro tennis rackets are a good buy.
_____	_____	Sam paid $75 for a Pro tennis racket.
_____	_____	The selling price of a Pro tennis racket is more than $75.

Part II

Directions: Read the statements. Check the ones that contain math ideas useful for this problem. Look at Part I, Column B to check your answer.

_____ Markup equals cost times rate.
_____ Selling price is greater than cost.
_____ Selling price equals cost plus markup.
_____ Markup divided by cost equals markup rate.
_____ A percent of a number is less than the number when the percent is less than 100%.

Part III

Directions: Check the calculations that will help or work in this problem. Look at Parts I and II to check your answers.

_____ 0.4 x $75   _____ 12 x $75
_____ $75 x 40   _____ 40% of $75
_____ 1.4 x $75   _____ $75 + ($\frac{2}{5}$ x $75)

Barton, M.L. and Heidema, C. Teaching Reading in Mathematics. Aurora, CO: Mid-continent Research for Education and Learning, 2000. Reprinted with permission of McREL.

AN ACTIVITY TO SUBSTANTIATE INFORMATION

INTERVIEWS

What are Interviews?

Interviews involve students in role-playing a question-and-answer situation. One student takes on the role of a character/person while the other student asks the questions. Texts that involve human participants or characters are especially suited to interviews. Where participants are not explicit in a text (e.g. the description of a newly discovered land by an explorer) it is still possible for students to create an interview, but the interview material will be inferred.

Students role-playing the character/person are required to respond orally to questions asked by their partner. Responses made will require students to make inferences, draw conclusions and make connections, presenting their own interpretation of the text.

Students conducting the interviews need to create questions that will elicit personal interpretations of the information in the text. It is important to model the types of questions that will help students to focus on finding out about the characters/person's actions, feelings, and behaviors.

Why Interviews Benefit Students

Participating in Interviews supports readers to make inferences about a characters/person's actions and behaviors.

How to Use Interviews

1. Organize students into pairs. Have students select a character/person from a previously read text.
2. Have students negotiate who will be the character/person and who will be the interviewer.
3. Have the pairs work together to develop questions.
4. Provide time for students to conduct their interviews.
5. Invite students to share some interviews with the class.
6. invite the students to discuss which parts of the text influenced the questions and answers.

Other Activities Two previously discussed activities, *Facts and Falsehoods* and *Synthesis Journal,* can be used to help students to substantiate information.

ACTIVITIES TO DRAW CONCLUSIONS AND MAKE GENERALIZATIONS

WHO SAID…?

What is Who Said…?

Who Said…? is an activity that encourages students to infer characters/people's actions and behaviour using implicit information from texts with numerous human participants, such as historical recounts, narratives, and some newspaper articles.

Why Who Said…? Benefits Students

This activity encourages students to use two important comprehension skills, making inferences and drawing conclusions.

How to Use Who Said…?

Provide students with the following directions:

1. Read a text that has several characters/people.

2. Select a character, and write on a slip of paper something that the character/person might typically say. This should not be a direct quote from the text.

3. Draw out a slip of paper from a container.

4. Read the statements aloud, declaring who in the story would say something like that. Substantiate your choice with reference to the story.

MISSING PIECES

What is Missing Pieces?

Missing Pieces is an activity that requires students to draw on explicit and implicit information from a text as they guess the name of an element from a text. During the activity, a small number of students are allocated an element and are required to ask a series of questions to determine their identity. Restricting the questions to yes/no responses encourages students to listen critically, to remember information supplied, and to build on questions already asked.

Why Missing Pieces Benefits Students

Missing Pieces helps students reflect on and clarify the attributes of concepts in a text. Texts that include numerous elements of one category or deal with a concept that can be generalized to numerous elements of one category are suited to Missing Pieces. For example, a text about the various political systems in the world has numerous elements that belong to the category of political systems. On the other hand, a text about the attributes of plants may not make reference to mosses and seaweed, but may define what attributes plants have, and therefore enable students to generalize.

How to Use Missing Pieces?

1. After reading a text or texts, make headbands each featuring the name of a different element.

2. Make a list of the possible elements as an aid for students to create effective questions.

3. Select students to wear a headband (sight unseen).

4. Have these students take turns to ask the class questions to try and determine their identity. A 'Yes' response from the class allows the students to ask another question. A 'No' response passes the questioning to the next student.

5. Conclude the questioning when one student successfully identifies his/her element.

TEXT COMPLETION

What is Text Completion?

Text Completion is a variation of Text Reconstruction. Students are given a text that has a distinct section (paragraph or stage) missing. The students must decide which paragraph is missing and complete it. Texts that have a clear structure and organizational pattern, or are familiar to students, are most appropriate for Text Completion activities. In each instance, the text used must be immediately recognizable as lacking an element because many elements at a whole text level or paragraph level are optional.

At the paragraph level, using the lead from a newspaper report, or an historical recount, teachers can explain that a necessary element from the who, when, where, and why details has been omitted. To focus on the reading strategy of visualizing, delete a diagram from an informational text and ask students to approximate what sort the diagram may have looked like.

Why Text Completion Benefits Students

Text Completion encourages students to consider all the essential components of a text and how they work together to achieve a purpose.

How to Use Text Completion

1. Delete a key paragraph or component from a text and ask students to read the text and suggest what is missing.
2. Ask students to work in pairs or groups to write the missing component.

Example   Text Completion

Algae, fungi, and lichen were once considered as the most primitive plants on Earth. Not only did they not produce flowers or seeds, but they also did not have roots, stems, or leaves. On the basis of current information, many biologists no longer consider them as plants.

Some of the characteristics of algae, fungi, and lichens are outlined below.

Algae

Characteristics:
- all live in water
- often unicellular

- no true roots, stems, leaves or flowers
- no special tissue for transporting food or water
- divided into groups depending on their color
- make their own food using photosynthesis

Examples: diatoms, euglena, 'Neptune's necklace', sea lettuce.

Fungi

Characteristics:

- .
- .
- .
- .
- .
- .

Examples:

Lichens

Characteristics:

- found on bare rocks, bark of trees, or in cold polar regions and on mountain tops
- no true roots, stems, leaves or flowers
- made up of two different organisms: an alga and a fungus
- algal cells live among tiny fungal tiny threads
- algal cells photosynthesize and supply the fungus with food
- fungus provides protection and anchorage for the algal cells
- grow very slowly and are extremely long-lived
- often responsible for breaking down rocks, allowing other organisms to grow.

VERBED

What is Verbed?

This activity involves students selecting a verb that encapsulates the situation or outcome for each character/person/participant in a content-area text. This activity works best with newspaper/magazine articles, short informational texts and literary texts, with strong characterization or clear participants. Literary texts may require a chapter-by-chapter analysis to account for the character's changing situation.

Why Verbed Benefits Students

Verbed helps students to draw conclusions by analysing explicit and implicit information in text.

How to Use Verbed

1. Create small groups and have students read a selected text.
2. Have students list characters/people/ participants from the text.
3. Have students work individually to generate a past tense verb for each character/person listed.
4. Invite students to share and justify their selected words in the small group. Have the students discuss the words and choose the most effective. Discussion could revolve around:
    - justifying the choice of verb by referring to the text
    - the vocabulary used by the author
    - the perspective chosen – through whose eyes are the verbs selected

Have groups share their text and selected verbs providing justification.

AN ACTIVITY TO MAKE CONNECTIONS AND RESPOND TO TEXT

LINKING LINES

What is Linking Lines?

Linking Lines helps readers make connections between different texts.

After re-reading a text, students make lines between text titles explaining how the texts are linked.

Why Linking Lines Benefit Students

When students make connections to other texts they have read that refer to the same topic, they enhance their comprehension and strengthen their knowledge of the topic.

How to Use Linking Lines

1. At the conclusion of reading a text, organize students into small groups.
2. Have students discuss and make connections between the text they have read and other texts, including television documentaries, computer games, and conversations.
3. Direct students to draw lines between the text titles and record any connections they have made.
4. Invite students to share the connections.

A Word of Caution

We believe the activities we have shared with you are very valuable. Indeed, research (Davis, Kushman & Spraker, 2004) supports the practice of explicitly teaching comprehension strategies. But, as you can see, there are many ways to go about teaching comprehension strategies.

You should not use all of them. Pick a few from each of the reading stages that resonate with you and are likely to meet the needs of your students. Use them several times so that students become comfortable with them and can see the benefits of engaging in the activities. Follow the recommendations we offer on how to teach the strategies and, of course, bring your own ideas and creativity to teaching them. And *always* connect them to the texts you are using in your classroom.

CHAPTER 5
HOW DOES STUDENT UNDERSTANDING OF TEXT STRUCTURE ENHANCE COMPEHENSION?

In Chapter 3 we discussed the strategies associated with the reading process, including the strategy of Re-reading. This strategy, we suggest, is one of the actions readers should take when they don't understand what they have read. But sometimes, just going back to re-read doesn't do the trick. What if the reader still doesn't "get it"?

When this happens, we tell our students to read each paragraph very slowly (the Adjusting Reading Rate strategy) to figure out what the author's main idea is (the Determining Importance strategy). "Look," we say "at how the author's thoughts are organized. At the paragraph level, the author typically summarizes main ideas in a single sentence while the other sentences are details to support, clarify, or explain her main idea."

What we are telling students, without using the technical term, is to look at the author's *text structure*. Did the author start with the main idea in the first sentence and follow up with details? Did the paragraph begin with the details and then lead to the main idea in the last sentence? Are the details included at the beginning and end of the paragraph, with the main idea placed in the middle of the paragraph? This is looking at *text structure* at the paragraph level. (Notice in this paragraph we placed our main idea in the *last* sentence).

We also tell students to take a look at the way authors organize ideas in larger sections of text containing several paragraphs. Does the author present ideas in *sequence?* Is the focus on *cause/effect* relationships? Is the text about a *problem* that will lead to a discussion of *solutions?* Are two or more ideas or events being *compared* and *contrasted?* When students analyze *text structure* in larger pieces of writing such as chapters or sections of chapters, they may have to use both the "Re-read" strategy as well as the "Read On" strategy to figure out the text's structure or organizational pattern.

Students' knowledge and use of text structure or organizational patterns definitely helps them to comprehend text. Let's look at the research that supports this statement.

What Research Supports Text Structure as an Aid to Comprehension?

Throughout the 70's, (Bartlett, 1978; Meyer, 1975), the 80's (Armbruster and Anderson, 1984; Meyer, Brandt, and Bluth, 1980; Slater, Graves, and Piche, 1985; Taylor, 1980; Taylor and Beach, 1984), and the 90's (Block, 1993; Chambliss, 1995; Scuggs and Mastropieri, 1990) research demonstrates that when students can perceive a writer's plan and writing pattern, they understand and retain more of what they read. After analyzing 14 studies on the relationship between text organization and comprehension, Dickson, Simmons, and Kameenui (1995) conclude that students' awareness and use of text structure are highly related to their ability to comprehend text.

Now, into the 21st century, analysis of research (Goldman & Rakestraw, 2000) supports the conclusions drawn by Dickson and her colleagues. And college textbooks, such as Vacca and Vacca's (2004), as well as authors of professional articles (Ciardiello, 2002; Rhoder, 2002) continue to recommend teaching text structure to students.

Where did the Idea for Teaching Text Structure Come From?

The idea of helping students comprehend text through an analysis of text structure is based, in part, on ideas drawn from the theory of Gestalt (German for "form" or "pattern") psychology. Gestalt psychology is concerned with perception, its patterns, its organization, and its holistic character.

Gestalt psychology places priority on creating greater meaning by looking at the parts that comprise and connect to each other and to the whole rather than looking at the parts separately or in isolation (Hergenhahn, B. R. and M.H. Olson, 2004). The cliché that the whole is more than the sum of its parts is derived from this organizing principle of Gestalt psychology. The concern of Gestalt psychologists is with relationships and interactions. Humans, as they take in information, look for relationships in order to create meaning or understanding.

There are a number of applications of Gestalt psychology to writing and reading. For example, when writers express or shape their ideas, they tend to organize them in certain ways, depending on the nature of their message. They don't simply dash off a mass of isolated details or a jungle of ideas; rather, they break ideas down and organize them so that their readers can perceive how the ideas interact and how they are related. It is the responsibility of all writers to perform this task.

On the other hand, the responsibility of readers is to interact with the writers in such a way as to concentrate on the essential ideas contained in the writer's message. This idea of focusing on essential ideas is similar to the psychological phenomenon of *figure ground*. The figure in the perceptual field is clearly outlined, well shaped, and prominent, whereas the stimulus of the ground constitutes the fringe or background. For each paragraph they write, authors usually focus on a main idea (the figure) which they support with details (the ground).

How do I Teach Text Structure at the Paragraph Level (Main Idea)?

When explaining main ideas, you might start by comparing writers of texts to artists and song writers. Artists use similar colors and shapes in their various paintings, but the placement of them in the paintings gives each work its unique distinction, configuration, and idea. Andrew Lloyd Webber used similar notes when he wrote "The Music of the Night" and "Don't Cry for me Argentina," but the timing and sequence of the notes gave each composition its distinct sound and unique message. Likewise, writers use similar words, phrases, and grammatical structures, but they are organized in a variety of ways in order to express a variety of ideas. And most writers try to focus on main ideas (the figure) that are supported by details (the ground).

Explaining Terms

Be sure students know what the following terms mean: *topic, main idea* and *details*.

The **topic** is the subject matter of the passage, the one or two things the passage is about. It is usually a noun or phrase. When readers ask themselves, "What is this all about?" they are looking for the topic.

The **main idea** is a declarative statement about the topic. This statement reflects the most important idea about the topic. It usually is stated in a sentence from the passage or it may be implied. When readers ask themselves, "What, in general, does the writer say about this topic?" their answer should reveal the author's main idea.

Details are bits of information that support, clarify, or explain the main idea. Their function is to tell when, where, how, or why. They also may serve as examples of the main idea. When readers ask, "When (how, where, why) did this happen?" they are asking questions that require detailed responses. These questions should help them to find information that supports their main idea statements.

Locating Topic Sentences

At the beginning of this chapter we suggest that students find *topic sentences* in paragraphs that contain the main idea. Here are some examples from different subject-matter text that illustrate the different placement of main ideas in a paragraph.

MAIN IDEA STATED IN FIRST SENTENCE

Math

Ratios help us keep things in proportion. If a lemonade recipe calls for 4 cups of water, 1 cup of lemon juice, and 1 cup of sugar, than twice as much lemonade would mean using twice as much of *each* ingredient: 8 cups of water, 2 cups of lemon juice, and 2 cups of sugar. You get the idea – everything in proportion means the lemonade tastes the same no matter how much you make. (Kaplan & Petroni-McMullen, 1998, pg. 423)

Social Studies

The thoughts, speech, and action a person performs during a lifetime are called karma. Buddhists teach that both an individual's wholesome karma (or good deeds) and the unwholesome karma (or bad deeds) travel into the next life. This karma causes rebirth. However, a person's personality does not make this journey. Buddhists do not believe in a soul or in any kind of creator God. What continues lifetime after lifetime is the karma that has been set in motion by all one's thoughts, words, and deeds – like the ripples caused by a stone thrown into a pond. (Armento, et. al, 1999, p.238)

Science

Intertidal zones are shoreline areas that are covered by water at high tide and not covered by water at low tide. In this zone live many shelled animals that have adaptations for clinging to surfaces or burrowing in sand to avoid being carried out to sea. Periwinkles, snails, and other species often live near the tops of rocks, where they are exposed to sunlight, salt spray, and wind for much of the time, only to be covered by salt water during high tide. (ScienceSaurus, 2002, pg. 149)

Language Arts

Characters are the people, animals, and imaginary creatures in stories. Generally, the action of a story centers on one main character. Usually, there are some minor characters that interact with the main character and with one another. Characters are revealed by their traits, or qualities. These include their physical characteristics; their speech, thoughts, feelings, and actions; the writer's directed statements about them; and the thoughts, speech, and actions of other characters. (*The Language of Literature*, 2001, pg. 23)

MAIN IDEA STATED IN LAST SENTENCE

Math

If you were to pick a number that best describes all the data in a set, what number would you pick? People most often choose a number somewhere in the middle of the data ordered from least to greatest, or a number with a lot of data clustered around it. *This number is known as an average, or a measure of central tendency.* (Kaplan & Petoni-McMullan, 1998, pg. 273)

Science

Soon after a disease is successfully stopped, the level of the antibody that fought against it drops. For example, a person who has recovered from chicken-pox will have only a small amount of chickenpox antibody left in his or her bloodstream. But a few of the white blood cells that made the chickenpox antibody remain in the blood stream to fight the chickenpox virus if it returns. These white blood cells "remember" how to make the antibody of chicken pox. If the virus that causes chickenpox enters the body again, these cells will make a lot of new antibodies in a very short time. They will eliminate the virus before it can do any damage and before you become ill. That is why a person usually gets diseases like measles, mumps, whooping cough, scarlet fever, and chickenpox only once. *This resistance to a disease is called acquired immunity.* (Morrison, Earl S., 1997)

Social Studies

The cuneiform system was used in the Middle East for about 2,000 years. Later, around 900 B.C., the Phoenicians devised a simpler way to keep records. The Phoenicians lived on the east coast of the Mediterranean Sea. They were seafaring merchants who traded throughout the area. Cuneiform, with its many symbols, was just too complicated to use in their growing trade. They invented a new writing system with only 22 symbols. If you think this system sounds familiar, you're right. *The Phoenicians invented the alphabet.* (Armento, et. al., 1999, pg. 161)

Language Arts

The pillared hall of Hades opened before the hero's song. The ranks of long-dead heroes who sit at Hades' board looked up and turned their eyes away from the pitiless form of Hades and his pale, unhappy queen. Grim and unmoving sat the dark king for the dead on his ebony throne, yet the tears shone on his rigid cheeks in the light of his ghastly torches. *Even his hard heart, which knew all misery and cared nothing for it, was touched by the love and longing of the music.* (Coolidge, 1977)

Although these last four examples illustrate topic sentences placed at the end of a paragraph, our own perusal of textbooks as well as one study (Aikman, 1997) tells us that writers most often place their topic sentences at the beginning of paragraphs. On occasion, they will place them in the *middle* of the paragraph as in the following example.

In the 50's and 60's, women had made up between 5 and 8 percent of the students in medical, law, and business schools. By the mid-80's, they were at 40 percent and heading upward. *Educated women could now make choices.* They could work as veterinarians or as housewives. They could be Supreme Court justices, brain surgeons or like that pioneer Lucille Ball, television producers. (Hakim, 2003, p.143)

The best advice to give adolescents when they find themselves "looking back" to determine the main idea is to focus on the first sentence in the paragraph and then see if the remaining sentences help to clarify it and/or provide details to support the topic or main-idea sentence. If the main idea is not stated in the first sentence, then it probably is in the last sentence.

While locating main-idea sentences often works for students, sometimes writers do not state clear topic or main-idea sentences. In addition, looking for one topic sentence can become a mechanical process that discourages readers from mentally interacting with writers.

THE THREE STEP APPROACH

An alternative to the topic sentence approach is The Three Steps Approach.

1. *Find the topic.* This is usually a word or phrase that is repeated several times.

2. *Find the main idea.* Students ask themselves, "What, in general, is the author telling me about the topic?

3. *Check it out.* Questions like the following help students to determine how the authors support their main ideas: "Does the author tell me more about the main idea? Am I told when, where, how, or why? Does the writer give examples?"

Try using this approach you with the following passage.

> Websites differ from books and other publications in another important way: quality of information. Books, while subject to error, are carefully edited, and publishers try to uphold high standards of accuracy and expertise. Anyone can have a website. Once you click your way into a website, whether it's a reputable one or a random site you've never heard of before, you need to know how to evaluate what you find there. Reading a website demands that you use the

reading process and your critical eye. (Burke, Kemp, and Swartz, 2002).

1. *Find the topic.* What word is repeated?

2. *Find the main idea.* What, in general, is the author telling you about the topic?

3. *Check it out.* Does the author tell you more about the main idea? Are you told when, where, how, or why? Did the writer give examples?"

- The repeated word is "website(s)."

- In general, the author says that websites need to be read carefully.

- The author answers the "why" question by telling us that anyone can create a website and they are not edited by professionals.

SUMMARY FRAMES

Summary Frames are very similar to the **Three Step Approach**, except students are given a "frame" and there is one additional question: What details *do not* support your general or main idea statement? Here is what a summary frame looks like.

Summary Frame	
1. What is the **topic** of this section?	
2. What, in general, does the author say about the topic?	
3. What **details** *do not* support your general or main idea statement?	
4. What **details** do support your main idea statement?	

Let's look at a summary frame based on the Phoenicians paragraph we looked at earlier in this chapter.

> The cuneiform system was used in the Middle East for about 2,000 years. Later, around 900 B.C., the Phoenicians devised a simpler way to keep records. The Phoenicians lived on the east coast of the Mediterranean Sea. They were seafaring merchants who traded throughout the area. Cuneiform, with its many symbols, was just too complicated to use in their growing trade. They invented a new writing system with only 22 symbols. If you think this system sounds familiar, you're right. *The Phoenicians invented the alphabet.* (Armento, et. al., 1999, pg. 161)

1. What is the **topic** of this section?	The Phoenicians
2. What, in general, does the author say about the topic?	The Phoenicians invented the alphabet.
3. What **details** *do not* support your general or main idea statement?	Cuneiform system used in Middle East for 2,000 years. The Phoenicians lived on east coast of Mediterranean Sea. They were seafaring merchants.
4. What **details** *do* support your main idea statement?	Cuneiforms were too complicated to use in trade. The new writing system had 22 symbols.

Using the **Three Step Approach** and **Summary Frames** takes time. But after using them a few times with teacher guidance, students find main ideas come to them more quickly, and they do not have to rely so much on the self-questioning associated with these activities to determine important ideas in text.

SUMMARY

In this chapter we reintroduced the strategy of "Re-reading" as an action readers can use when they are having difficulty comprehending text. When they re-read, they can try to determine the author's main idea and how the author's ideas are organized. When readers understand the organizational pattern of a text, their comprehension improves. We supported this point by citing a great deal of research. Discussion of some of the theoretical background supporting the teaching of text structure followed. Finally, we showed you how you can teach text structure/main idea at the paragraph level.

In the next chapter, we will look at how main ideas and details are related to each other in larger sections of text when writers choose to discuss *cause/effect* relationships, present material in *sequence, compare and contrast* ideas, and focus on *problems and solutions*. Models for teaching these organizational patterns in different content areas will be presented.

CHAPTER 6

HOW DO I CONNECT TEXT STRUCTURE TO HELP MY STUDENTS LEARN CONTENT?

In the last chapter we introduced you to the role text structure plays in improving student understanding of text. The focus of that chapter is on ideas contained in paragraphs. The focus of this chapter is on how main ideas in single paragraphs are related in longer pieces of text.

Sometimes textbook authors will simply present information with a focus on related topics. Their focus is on *who, what, where, when, why,* and *how* much like articles that appear in newspapers and information contained in websites. When paragraphs are connected in this way, the text structure is called *informational*. With this type of text structure, readers need to follow the text by focusing carefully on each paragraph's main idea and connecting the main ideas included in each section of text.

Often, rather than presenting information in this straight forward way, authors will provide an analysis of their topics by discussing *causes and effects* related to them, *comparing and contrasting* them, showing how events are *sequenced* and looking at *problems and solutions*. These ways of writing text are sometimes referred to as the writers' *organizational patterns,* another term for text structure.

It is important to note that in a single piece of writing or a textbook chapter, authors almost always switch from one organizational pattern to another. It is not unusual to see single chapters written in two or more of the organizational patterns.

In this chapter we will look more closely at the organizational patterns. We will focus on how you can alert your students to the way text chapters are organized and then, with this knowledge in hand, use it to read and learn from texts.

THE CAUSE/EFFECT PATTERN

When writers explain *why* certain events take place and what the results of them are, they are writing in the cause/effect pattern. In one of the first professional texts devoted entirely to the topic of reading comprehension, Pearson and Johnson (1978) point out why some students are challenged by material written in this pattern.

Cause/Effect Challenges

One challenge is referred to as *reversible causal relations*. This is when writers place the effect(s) before the cause(s). Readers expect writers to state causes first and the effects second. But notice how just the opposite happens in this sentence: "The fact that English is spoken widely in so many parts of the world results from the history, development, and expansion of the British empire after the sixteenth century." Check out your textbooks. How often do the authors reverse causal relations?

Another challenge is referred to as *multiple events*. Readers expect a single cause to be followed by a single event. But authors often present multiple causes with a single effect, multiple causes with multiple effects, and a single cause with multiple effects. Notice, for example, in the passage below that the single cause (stress) has multiple effects.

All of us experience stress. Sometimes the effects are negative; we feel bad, get headaches, and our stomachs are upset. Sometimes the effects are positive. For example some athletes find that stress helps them meet the challenges of a match or game.

Check out your textbooks. How often do the authors present multiple cause/effect relationships?

Despite these challenges, there is a great deal you can do to help your students to follow texts expressed in the cause/effect pattern.

How Do I Connect Text Structure to Help My Students Learn Content?

Teaching Cause and Effect

Signal Words

You can share with your students certain *signal* words that alert them to the fact that authors are discussing cause/effect relationships. Here is a list of them.

Cause and Effect Signal Words

- because
- if
- consequently
- led to
- as a result
- since
- so
- therefore
- hence
- due to

If you think your students are unfamiliar with the cause/effect pattern, you can give them relatively simple passages and have them circle the signal words. This activity will help them when this pattern occurs in their more complex textbooks. Here is an example.

Joshua became angry (because) he struck out. (Because) Joshua was very upset, he slammed his hand against the water cooler. (As a result) he bruised his hand and put a dent into the water cooler.

99

PATTERN GUIDES

First introduced to elementary school teachers nearly 70 years ago by Donald Durrell (1956) and then presented to secondary content area teachers in the early 70's by Harold Herber (1970), the use of pattern guides or reading/study guides to help support students' reading continues to be recommended today (Vacca & Vacca, 2004).

Pattern guides alert students to a text's organizational pattern enabling them to have greater understanding of the content. Furthermore, pattern guides emphasize both the process and the products of reading.

Here are some guidelines for creating pattern guides:

1. Determine the section of text you wish to guide your students' reading and the prominent organizational pattern used by the author.
2. Determine the important ideas in the text.
3. Construct a pattern guide that simulates what students need to do to comprehend the text. In this case, the focus will be on cause/effect relationships.
4. Have students preview the guide *before* they read and then have them refer to it *during* and *after* they read.

Following are some samples of reading/study guides based on text from a variety of content areas.

How Do I Connect Text Structure to
Help My Students Learn Content?

PATTERN GUIDE   CAUSE/EFFECT   Social Studies

Listed below are some situations that are related to ideas you will find in this chapter. Study the situation and complete the guide by providing what you think may have caused the situation or what you think would be an effect of the situation.

1. (a) *Causes.* The city of Pittsburgh depends on the production of coal and steel. As of yesterday, all mines have dried up.

   (b) *Effects.*

2. (a) *Causes.* Crayton is a small town. Recently a large corporation discovered rich deposits of raw materials (various metals and petroleums) within and around the town. The town is situated near the Mississippi River, and one can reach it by taking a train. The next largest city is five hundred miles away.

   (b) *Effects.*

3. (a) *Causes.* Electricity is no longer transmitted by wires. Everyone now gets their energy directly from the sun.

   (b) *Effects.*

4. (a) *Causes.* A law has been passed. Zinc and lead are poisons. They must be taken out of all products.

   (b) *Effects.*

PATTERN GUIDE CAUSE/EFFECT   Auto Mechanics

Directions: In your reading assignment on transmissions, find the causes that led to the effects listed. Write each cause in the space provided.

1. Cause:_____

   Effect: Grinding occurs when gears are shifted.

2. Cause:_____

   Effect: Car speed increases but engine speed remains constant while torque is decreasing.

3. Cause:_____

   Effect: Car makers changed over to synchronizing mechanisms.

4. Cause:_____

   Effect: Helical gears are superior to spur gears.

5. Cause:_____

   Effect: Some cars cannot operate correctly with three-speed transmissions and require extra speeds.

6. Cause:_____

   Effect: Most manuals have an idler gear.

7. Cause:_____

   Effect: All cars require some type of transmission.

How Do I Connect Text Structure to Help My Students Learn Content?

PATTERN GUIDE   CAUSE/EFFECT   Science

This guide is designed to assist you in understanding the cause/effect relationships in the chapter on "Infectious Diseases."

Use this guide as you read to help you understand these relationships. Four disease causing agents are listed with one example of their effects. Add to each list other effects of each disease causing agent.

Disease Causing Agent	Effects of Agent
Bacteria	tuberculosis
	_____
	_____
	_____
Viruses	common cold
	_____
	_____
	_____
Protozoans	malaria
	_____
	_____
	_____
Fungi	athlete's foot
	_____
	_____
	_____

PATTERN GUIDE   CAUSE/EFFECT   English

Not at Home by Jean Anderson

This short story contains many cause/effect relationship. As you read the story, use this guide to help you identify these relationships.

Determine if statement A **caused** statement B.

1. a. Alison was late for school.

    b. She had to leave her bike next to the "skeleton."

Did A cause B? _____   If no, why?

2. a. Alison forgot to remove her front lamp from the bike.

    b. Trayner removed and saved the lamp for Alison.

Did A cause B? _____   If no, why?

3. a. The fog was heavy.

    b. Alison could not see the on-coming truck.

Did A cause B? _____   If no, why?

4. a. Alison was frightened by the people in her house.

    b. She ran out of the house.

Did A cause B? _____   If no, why?

5. a. Alison sought out Mrs. Cullen for help.

    b. Mrs. Cullen comforted Alison.

Did A cause B? _____ If no, why?

Focused Questions

In chapter 3, we identified "self-questioning" as a valuable reading strategy for students. However, we should not forget the important role the teacher plays in asking questions. Indeed, formulating and asking good questions has been the stock and trade of teachers for years. Trabasso and Bouchard (2002) suggest why answering questions advances students' reading comprehension. This practice, supported by 17 studies they reviewed, facilitates reasoning, increases memory, and encourages meaningful rereading of text.

When we use the term "focused questions," we mean the questions are intentionally focused on the pattern of organization used by the author. According to Davis, Kushman and Spraker (2004), the types of questions and the way teachers ask them have a direct impact on the quality of understanding students acquire. In this case, the questions are focused on improving students' ability to understand and recall cause/effect relationships.

Here are some guidelines for formulating focused questions:

1. Emphasize what is important, not what is unusual.

2. Create questions that help students to follow the author's organizational pattern.

3. Include "higher level" questions because they produce understanding more deeply than "lower level," or literal questions.

4. Provide students with questions *before* reading because this will increase their understanding of the text.

5. When asking questions orally, give students enough "wait time." Students need the time to formulate their answers, especially when you ask "higher level" questions.

Following are some samples of cause/effect questions based on text from a variety of content areas.

FOCUSED QUESTIONS 　　　CAUSE/EFFECT　　　English

The Secret Garden

Chapter 1 in *The Secret Garden* contains several cause/effect relationships. As you read the chapter, these questions will help you to focus on and understand the causes and effects of a number of events in the chapter.

1. What *caused* Mary's face to be yellow?

2. Mary's mother had not wanted a little girl. What *effect* did this have on Mary?

3. What *caused* Mary's English governess to leave after only three months?

4. What *caused* the servants to wail in their huts?

5. Mary drank a glass of wine. What were the *effects* on Mary?

6. What *caused* Mary to be lonely?

7. What were the *effects* of the breakout of cholera?

FOCUSED QUESTIONS   CAUSE/EFFECT   Social Studies

Supply and Demand in a Market Economy

This section of your text discusses causes and effects related to the economization of supply and demand. These questions will help you focus on and understand the cause/effect relationships.

1. A business person produces something at a cost that is higher than the price people are willing to pay. What *effect* does that have on the business person?

2. What *causes* business suppliers to produce more of their products?

3. What *effects* do price increases have on the public?

4. What *causes* the public to demand more of a product?

5. What *causes* a surplus?

6. What *causes* a shortage?

7. What are the *effects* of a decrease in supply?

FOCUSED QUESTIONS CAUSE/EFFECT Science

Plants Respond to Stimuli

This section of your text discusses what *causes* plants to respond in certain ways. Stimuli, such as light and touch are *causes* and the responses to the stimuli are the *effects*. These questions will help you to focus on these cause/effect relationships.

1. What *causes* a plant to grow toward light?

2. What are the *effects* of touch on the mimosa plant?

3. What *effects* are evident when the hairs of a Venus' Flytrap are touched?

4. What *causes* the Wood Sorrel to fold its leaves?

5. What are the *effects* on a mimosa when placed in a dark closet?

6. What *causes* a crocus flower to close or open?

7. What are the *effects* on an earthworm when the temperature changes?

8. What are the *effects* of sound and light on fish?

Graphic Organizers

Graphic Organizers are visual representations of concepts and ideas that enable learners to visualize, represent and retrieve information from text. They are especially effective in helping students to understand text structure because the graphic organizers clearly show the relationship of ideas through the use of diagrams.

Research (Block, 1991, 1993) indicates that teacher training in the use of graphic organizers helps students learn. Trabasso and Bouchard (2002) reviewed 11 studies on the use of graphic organizers with elementary and middle school students. They conclude that when students use graphic organizers to organize authors' ideas, students' comprehension and achievement improves, especially in social studies and science.

Here are some guidelines for teaching graphic organizers:

1. Share a completed graphic organizer with students, emphasizing the relationship between ideas as expressed through one of the organizational patterns: (*informational, cause-effect, problem-solution, sequence, compare/contrast*).

2. Create a graphic organizer that is partially completed. Have students complete the graphic organizer.

3. Present a graphic organizer with no information in it. Have students complete the graphic organizer.

4. Have students create their own graphic organizers in a way that makes sense to them.

Following are some examples of how graphic organizers can be created for cause/effect relationships. The first three are templates containing no information and the remaining ones are examples of completed graphic organizers from a variety of content areas.

GRAPHIC ORGANIZER   CAUSE/EFFECT

Multiple Causes, Single Effect

Causes

1. _____
2. _____
3. _____
4. _____

Effect

GRAPHIC ORGANIZER CAUSE/EFFECT

Multiple Causes, Multiple Effects

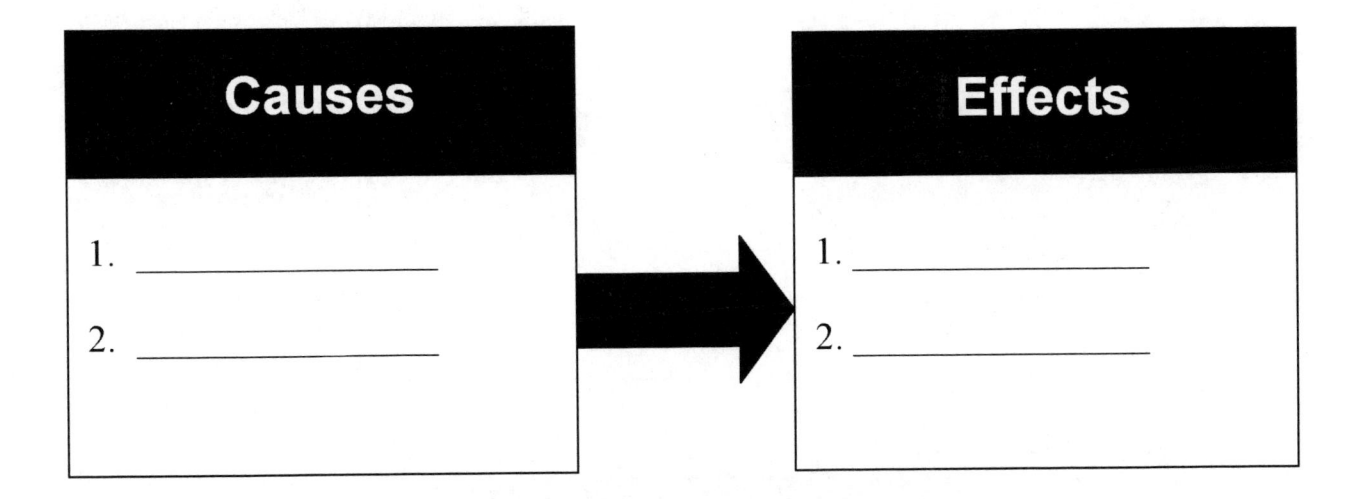

Causes		Effects
1. _____ 2. _____	→	1. _____ 2. _____

GRAPHIC ORGANIZER   CAUSE/EFFECT

Single Cause, Multiple Effects

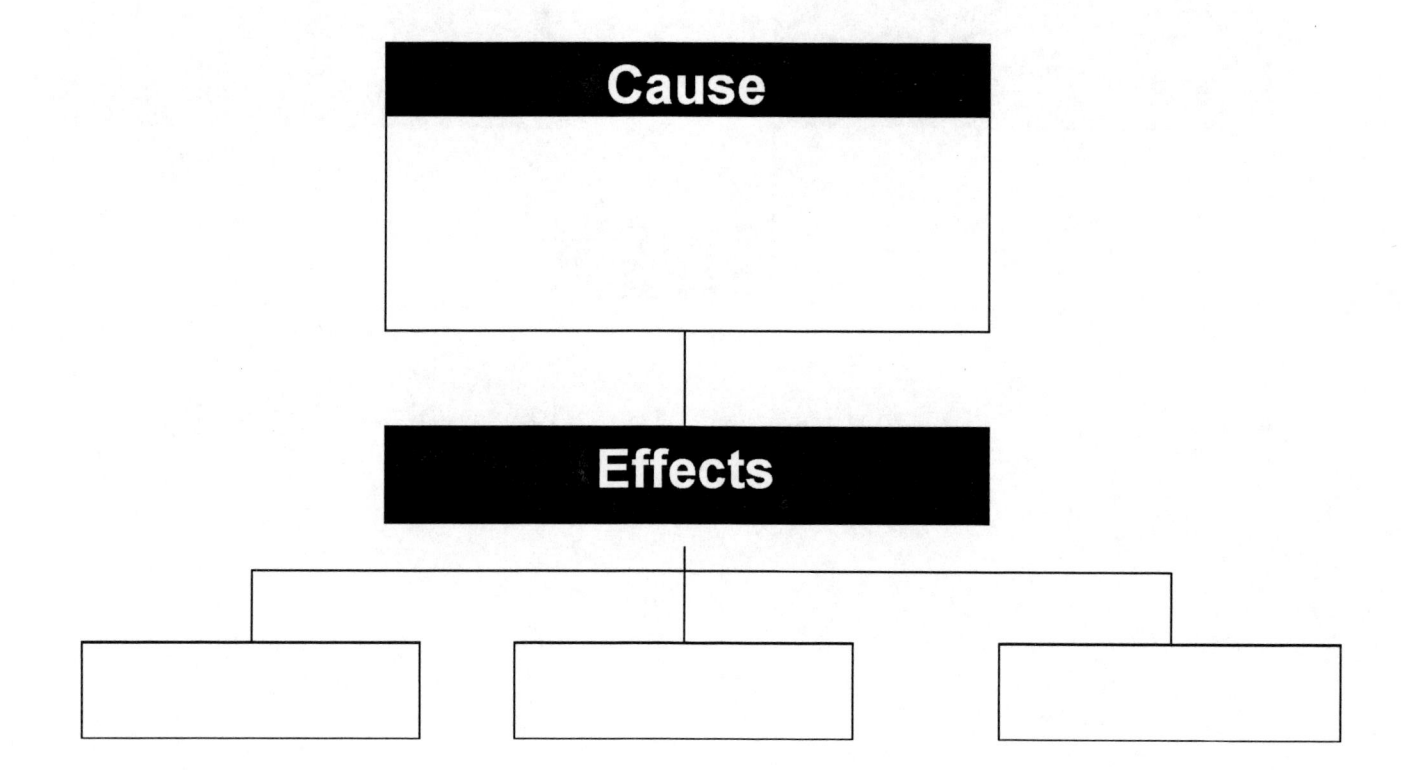

Cause

Effects

How Do I Connect Text Structure to Help My Students Learn Content?

Graphic Organizer Cause/Effect Science

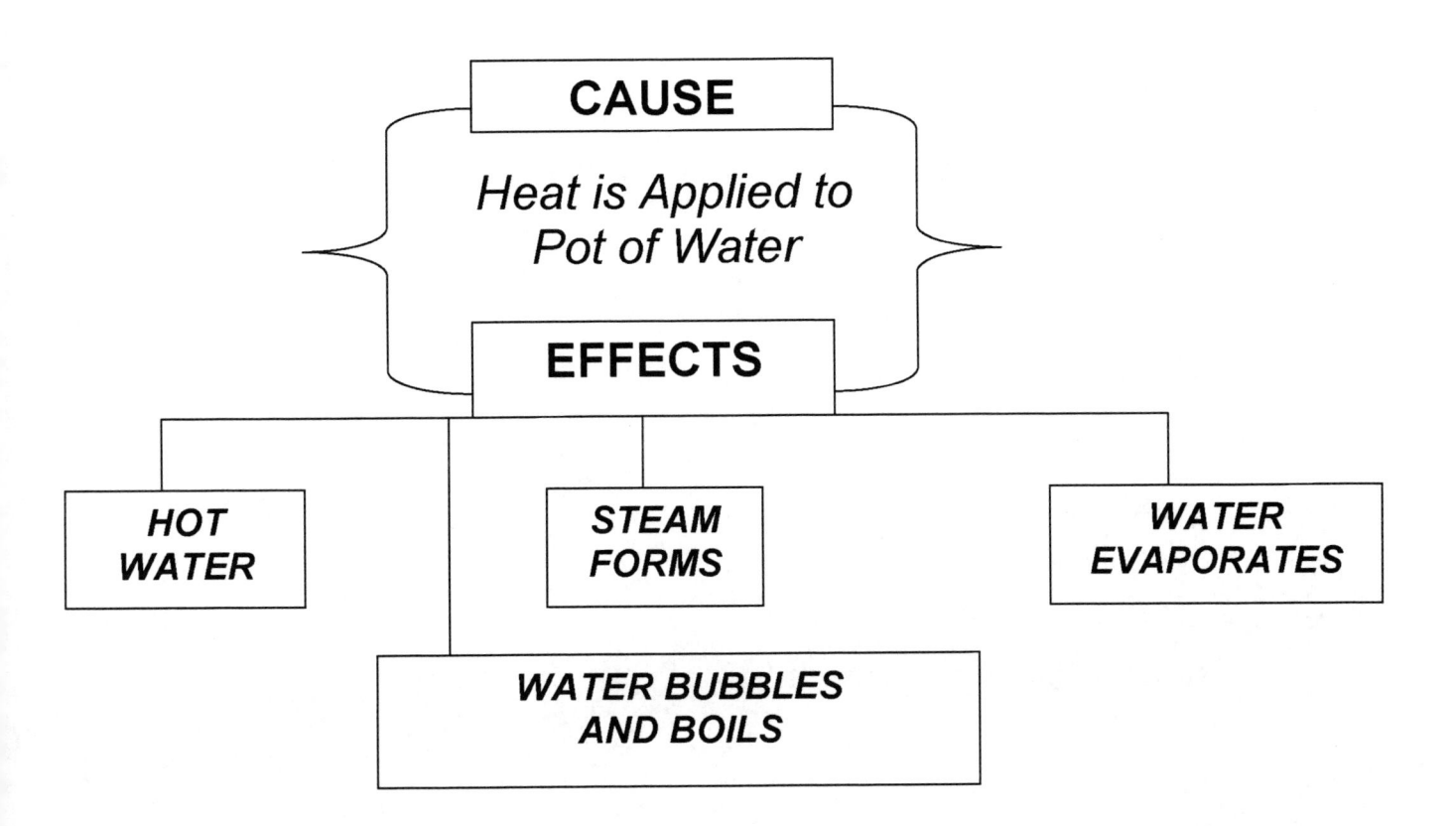

CAUSE

Heat is Applied to Pot of Water

EFFECTS

- HOT WATER
- STEAM FORMS
- WATER EVAPORATES
- WATER BUBBLES AND BOILS

Graphic Organizer　　Cause/Effect　　　Social Studies

Why Does the U.S. Still Have a Two Party System?

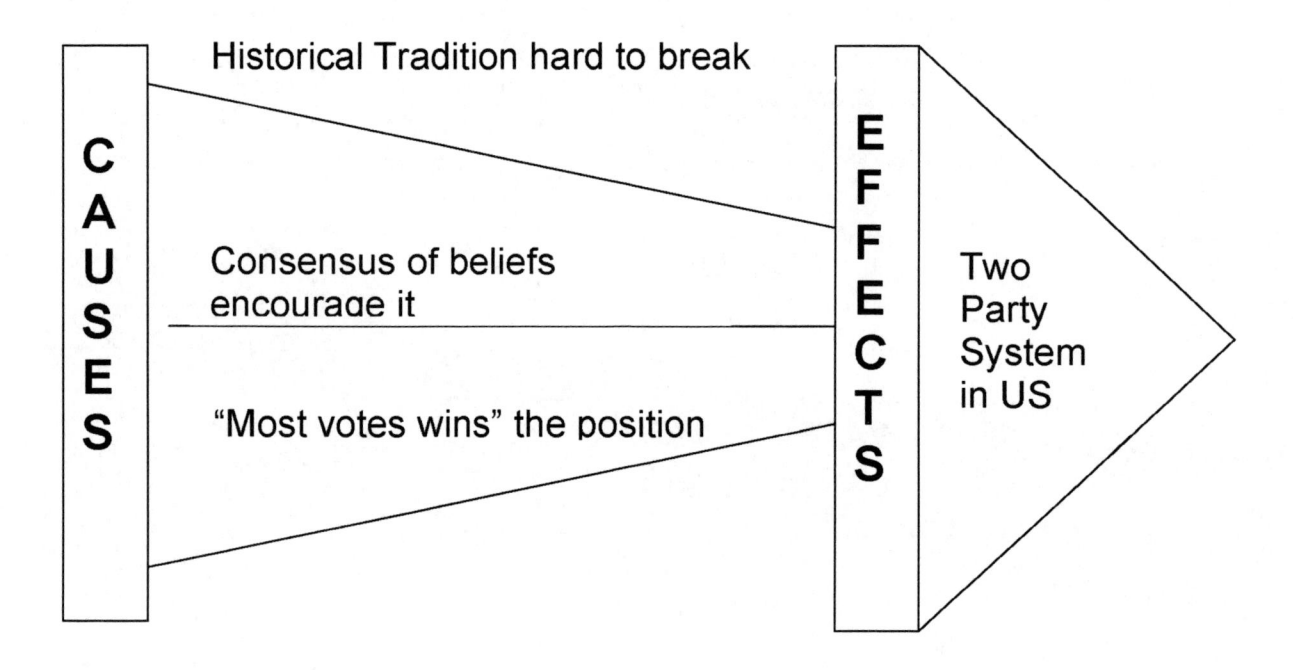

CAUSES:
- Historical Tradition hard to break
- Consensus of beliefs encourage it
- "Most votes wins" the position

EFFECTS: Two Party System in US

GRAPHIC ORGANIZER CAUSE/EFFECT ENGLISH

Based on *Lob's Girl* by Joan Aiken

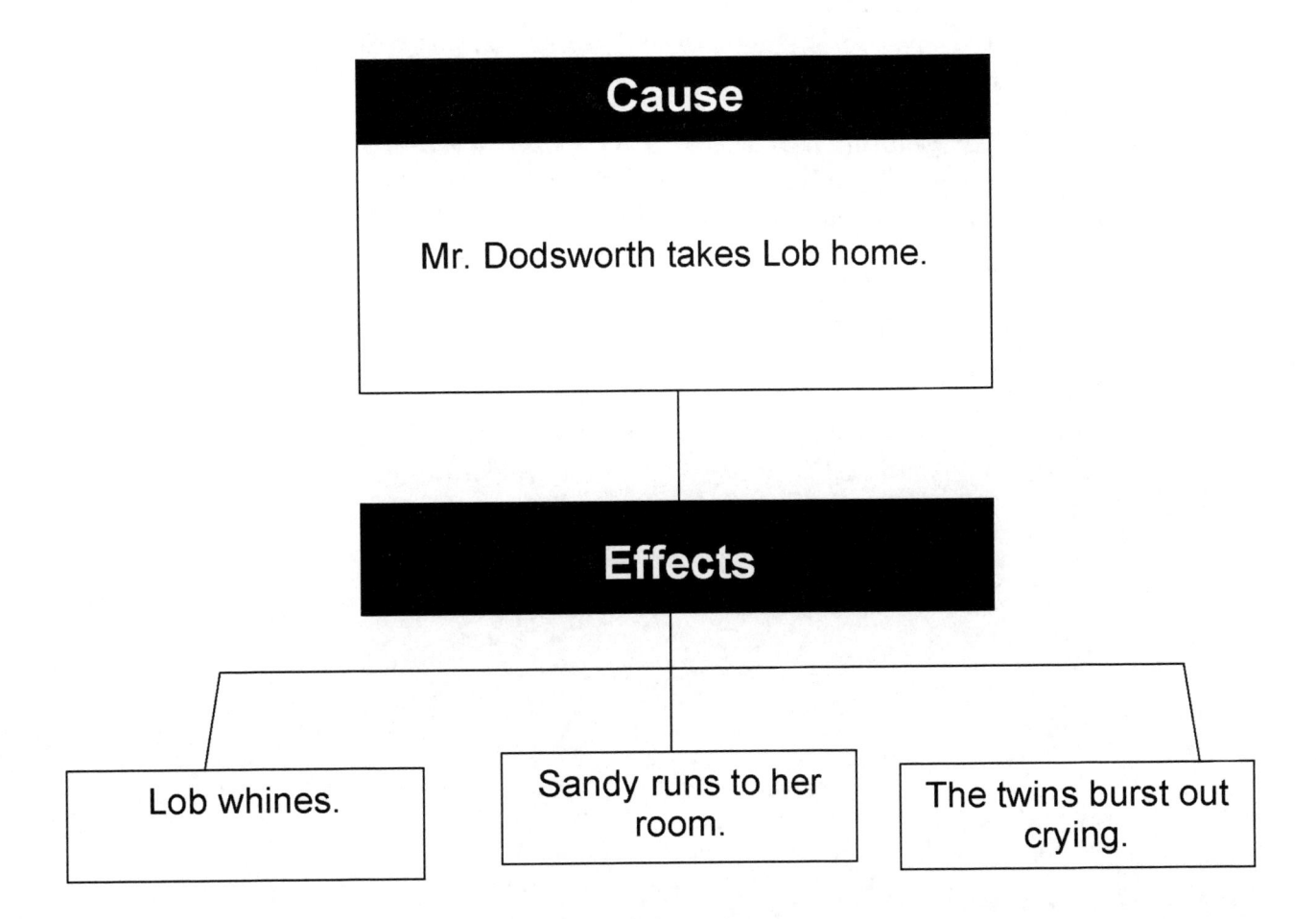

Cause

Mr. Dodsworth takes Lob home.

Effects

- Lob whines.
- Sandy runs to her room.
- The twins burst out crying.

The Problem/Solution Pattern

Often authors discuss cause/effect relationships as they connect to a *problem* which leads to some suggested *solution*. For example, a chapter in a high school business text deals with the *problem* of poor morale among employees of a business. The *effects* of the problem are low profits for the company. The *causes* of the problem are overly controlling supervisors whose goals are in opposition to employee goals. The *solution* is for management to discover ways of involving workers in planning, organizing, and controlling their own work.

The problem/solution pattern is relatively easy for readers to identify because the problem is often stated in the title of a chapter or article. Once readers realize that the content deals with some type of a problem, their *purposes for reading* are to discover the causes, effects, and solutions to the problem. The solutions most often are found at the end of the article or chapter, while the causes and effects are most often found in the middle.

Following are examples of teaching the problem/solution pattern through the use of pattern guides, focused questions, and graphic organizers.

How Do I Connect Text Structure to
Help My Students Learn Content?

PATTERN GUIDE   PROBLEM/SOLUTION   English

To the student: The short story you will read is "The Scribe" by Kristin Hunter. An overriding problem of society is addressed in this story as well as problems that the narrator has. Use the guide below to understand the **problems** as well as some **effects, causes,** and **solutions**.

I. Check the statement that best represents the societal **problem** addressed in this story.

    a. ____ Shortage of housing

    b. ____ Unemployment

    c. ____ Illiteracy

II. Check the statement that represents the **cause** of the problem.

    a. ____ Lack of education

    b. ____ Lack of available land to build houses

    c. ____ Bad economic times

III. Check the statement that represents the **effect** of the problem.

    a. ____ People have to pay to have their bills and letters read to them and to fill out forms.

    b. ____ People must live on the streets and shelters.

    c. ____ People must go on welfare.

IV. When the narrator tries to help the people with their problem, what happens?

    a. ____ The police threaten to put her in jail.

    b. ____ She is harassed by Old man Silver and Old man Dollar.

    c. ____ The police tell her she needs a license to set up a business.

V. How does the narrator ultimately try to help the people? What do you think are some long-term **solutions** to the societal problem addressed in this story? Write your answer below.

Reading to Learn: A Content Teacher's Guide

PATTERN GUIDE   PROBLEM/SOLUTION   Social Studies

To the student: Chapter 3 describes many problems involved in the settling of Virginia. There were a number of attempts to solve them. Below is a list of some of the problems discussed in the chapter. Next to each **problem**, list one or more ways attempts were made to **solve** each problem.

Problem   **Solution(s)**

A. The settlers had little they could sell   A._____
for profit.   _____

B. There were insufficient funds to start   B._____
a colony.   _____

C. The Virginia Company of London was   C._____
poorly managed.   _____

D. Some settlers refused to work hard.   D._____
                                                                   _____

E. Conflict existed between Powhatan   E._____
and the settlers.   _____

How Do I Connect Text Structure to
Help My Students Learn Content?

PATTERN GUIDE   PROBLEM/SOLUTION   Science

To the student: The reading that has been assigned to you presents the **problem** of global warming. When writers discuss problems, you can expect them to discuss **solutions** to the problem and sometimes the **causes** and **effects** related to the **problem.** This reading/study guide is designed to help you to follow the reading to identify the important ideas contained in it.

I. The **problem** discussed in this article is global warming and the **greenhouse effect.** In the space below, explain what the greenhouse effect is.

_____

_____

II. Below is listed one of the effects of global warming. Add other effects discussed in the reading.

Air Pollution_____

_____

III. Below is listed one of the causes of global warming. Add other causes discussed in the reading.

Burning coal and oil_____

_____

IV. Below is listed one of the solutions to global warming. Add other solutions discussed in the reading.

Plant trees_____

FOCUSED QUESTIONS PROBLEM/SOLUTION Social Studies

To the student: The reading that has been assigned to you discusses the growth of new cities in the early-to-mid 1800's. A number of **problems** were created as a result of this growth. The authors discuss these **problems** as well as attempts to **solve** them. They have used the **problem/solution** writing pattern in this reading to discuss these issues. The following questions are designed to help you to focus on and remember the important ideas related to these various **problems** and **solutions.**

1. Lack of drinking water is presented as a **problem** for growing cities. What **solutions** are discussed?

2. The **problem** of sewage and garbage is presented. What **effect** did this have on people?

3. Farmers fed corn to hogs. What **problem** did this solve?

4. Newspapers were too expensive for most people to buy. How was this **problem solved?**

5. Robert Fulton launched a successful steam-powered board. What **problem** did this solve?

6. Skilled workers had the **problem** of competing with half-skilled and unskilled workers. How did the skilled workers **solve** their problem?

FOCUSED QUESTIONS   PROBLEM/SOLUTION   Science

To the student: The reading that has been assigned to you discusses the **problem** of deforestation. The questions that follow are designed to help you understand deforestation, its **causes** and **effects** as well as **solutions** to the **problem.**

1. The **problem** discussed in this reading is deforestation. What is this process?

2. What will be some of the **effects** of this problem if the current rate of deforestation continues?

3. What are some of the **causes** of deforestation?

4. What does the reading state about the rate of deforestation?

5. What are some ways of **solving** the problems related to deforestation? Are some solutions more viable than others? Why?

Reading to Learn: A Content Teacher's Guide

FOCUSED QUESTIONS   PROBLEM/SOLUTION   English

To the student: The short story you will read is *Ta-Na-E-Ka* by Mary Whitebird. You have already learned about how the parts of a plot apply to works of fiction and drama as well as some nonfiction and poetry.

Another way of analyzing such works is recognizing the **problem** in the piece (the **rising action** when the main **conflict** takes place), the **effects** of the problem, (usually how the problem effects the **characters),** the cause of the problem (who or what was responsible for the **conflict** or problem**),** and the **solution** to the problem. The following questions will help you focus on these aspects of the short story.

1. What **problem** does Mary and her cousin, Roger Deer Leg, have as their birthdays draw near?

2. What is the major **cause** of the problem?

3. What are the **effects** of this problem on Mary and other members of her family?

4. What are some of the ways Mary attempts to **solve** the more unpleasant aspects of her problem?

5. How do members of Mary's family react when she tells them how she **solved** her problems related to Ta-Na-E-Ka?

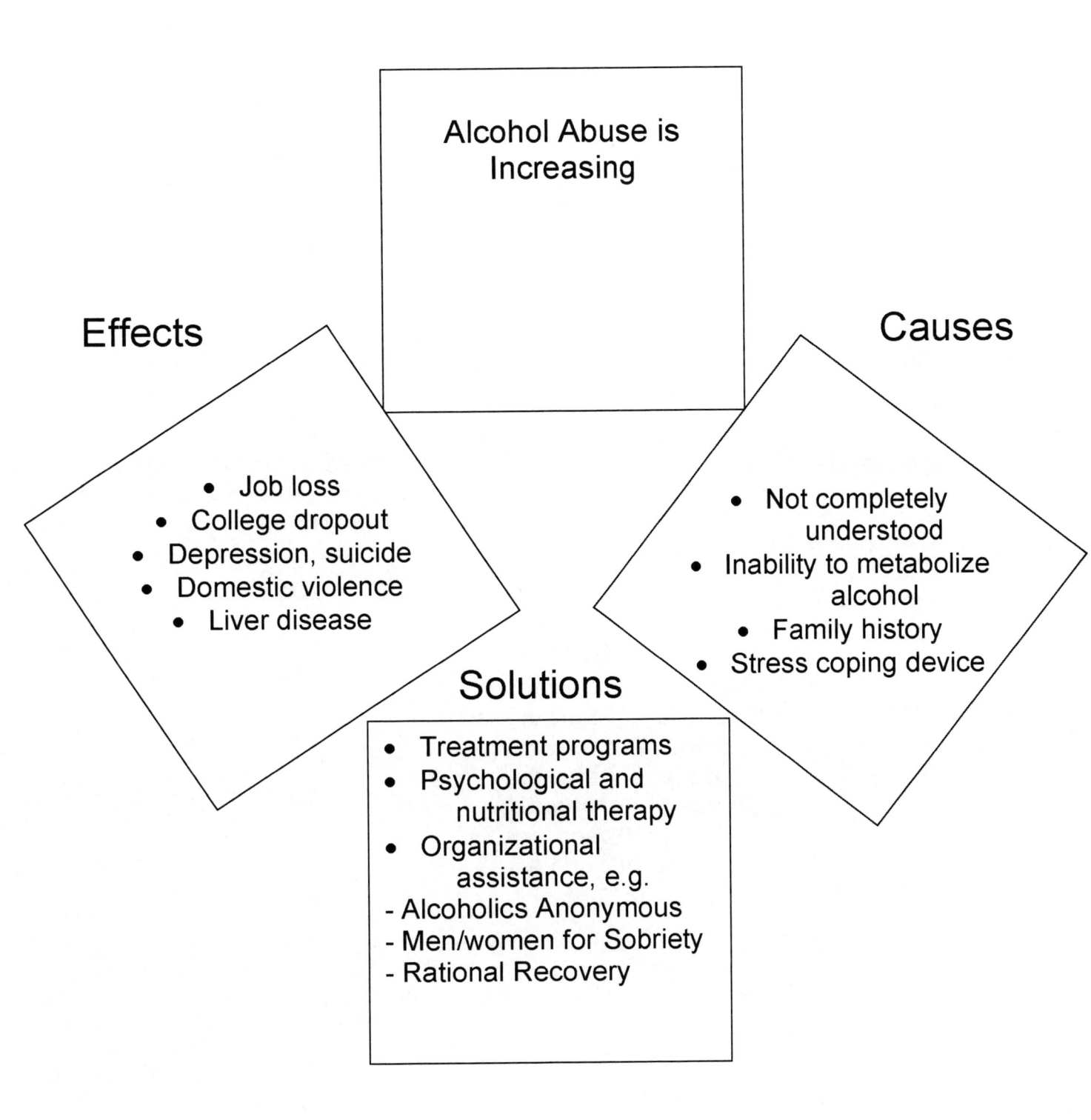

How Do I Connect Text Structure to
Help My Students Learn Content?

GRAPHIC ORGANIZER PROBLEM/SOLUTION Science

Problem

Alcohol Abuse is Increasing

Effects

- Job loss
- College dropout
- Depression, suicide
- Domestic violence
- Liver disease

Causes

- Not completely understood
- Inability to metabolize alcohol
- Family history
- Stress coping device

Solutions

- Treatment programs
- Psychological and nutritional therapy
- Organizational assistance, e.g.
  - Alcoholics Anonymous
  - Men/women for Sobriety
  - Rational Recovery

GRAPHIC ORGANIZER PROBLEM/SOLUTION Social Studies

Problem

The Soviets beat the U.S. in exploring outer space with their launching of Sputnik.

Effects

Americans are shocked; politicians seek action.

Cause

Soviets more determined than the U.S. Their research on rockets and missiles is more advanced than the U.S.

Solution

The National Defense Education Act provides money for science education, and the National Aeronautics and Space Administration (NASA) is formed.

How Do I Connect Text Structure to
Help My Students Learn Content?

GRAPHIC ORGANIZER PROBLEM/SOLUTION English

Based on *The Scholarship Jacket*

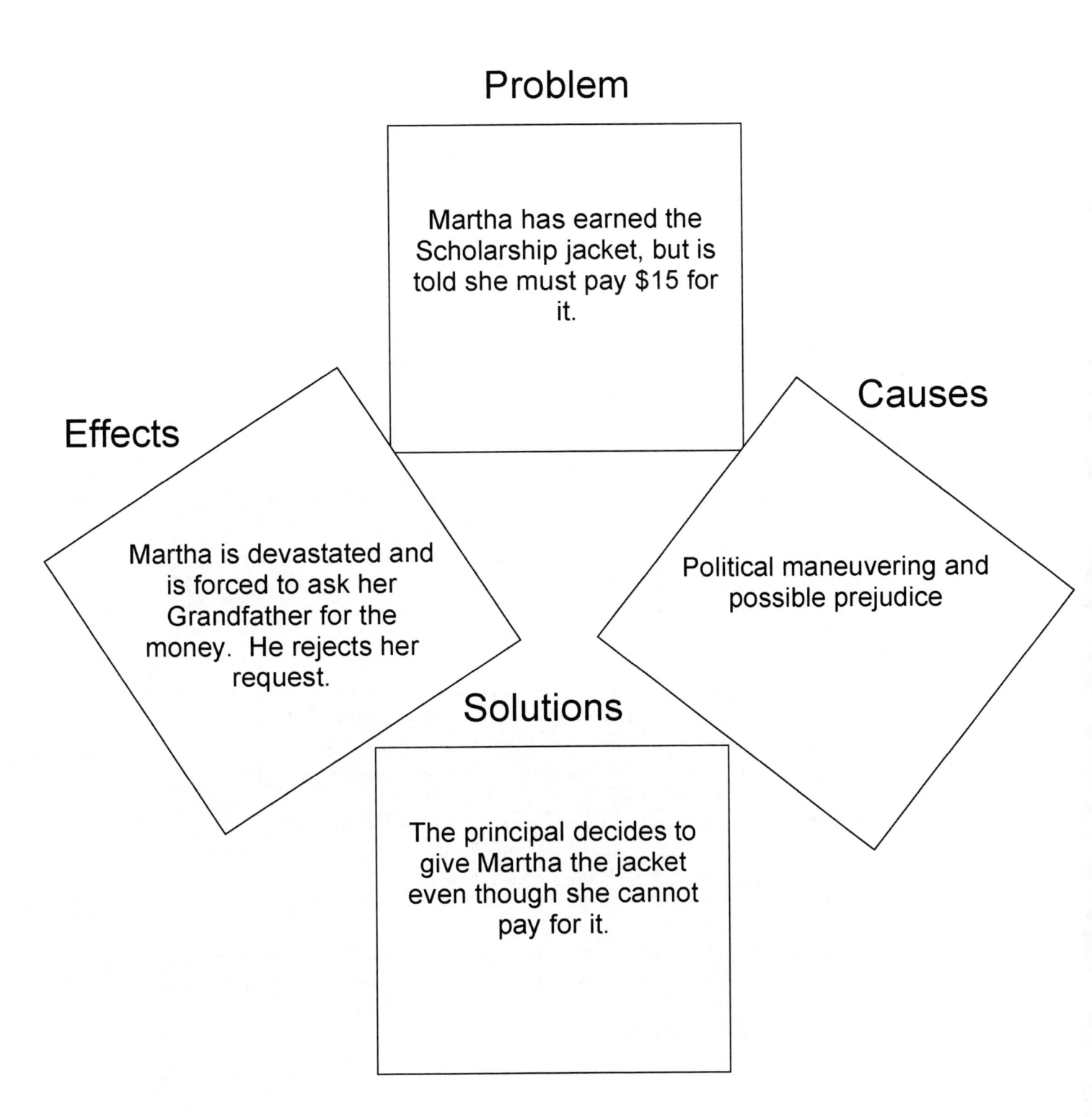

Problem

Martha has earned the Scholarship jacket, but is told she must pay $15 for it.

Effects

Martha is devastated and is forced to ask her Grandfather for the money. He rejects her request.

Causes

Political maneuvering and possible prejudice

Solutions

The principal decides to give Martha the jacket even though she cannot pay for it.

THE SEQUENCE PATTERN

When the order of events is important to convey to readers, authors write using the *sequence* pattern. Sometimes the events are stated in a clear-cut fashion from beginning to end and sometimes they can be presented in reverse. Or the flashback technique can be used, especially in literature.

The sequence can also be *spatial*. This occurs when writers emphasize a sequence of area to area or region to region. For example, a history author might discuss the route followed by frontiersmen, or a science author might discuss the parts of the body through which food travels as it is digested.

Challenges

Pearson and Johnson (1978) note a number of challenges readers face when they try to figure out the sequence of events in their reading. One is *reversibility of events*. This is when the sequence of events is not predictable as in this example: "The Jones family watched the tennis match after they went shopping." Because the actions of the Jones family are arbitrary, recalling the sequence can be troublesome for some students.

Another challenge is when the *stated* order of events is different from the *actual* order of events as in this example: "Before logs are transported to paper or lumber mills, they must be sorted by intended use and graded for quality." Readers can mistakenly conclude that logs are first transported to paper or lumber mills and then sorted.

A final challenge has to do with the *multiplicity of events*. This is when many events are discussed sequentially. For example, science authors discuss mitosis and the four phases that occur during mitosis: prophase, metaphase, anaphase, and telephase. Then each phase has its own sequence of events, so we have sequence within a sequence.

Check out your textbooks. To what extent will your students be confronted by these challenges?

Signal Words

One way you can help your students overcome the challenges associated with the sequence pattern is to share *signal* words that alert them to the order of events. Here is a list of them. You may want to make a chart for the class on these and other signal words.

How Do I Connect Text Structure to
Help My Students Learn Content?

> **SEQUENCE SIGNAL WORDS**
>
> - first, second
> - next
> - after that
> - before
> - finally
> - later
> - then
> - on (date)
> - not long after
> - to begin with

You can give students practice in identifying sequence signal words by having them circle them from some passages. Note the example below.

(First) Joan completed the petition for naturalization. (After that), she sent it to the federal court in Boston. (Then) she had to wait for a month. (During) this time, the Immigration and Naturalization Service completed a security check on her. (Finally,) she attended a hearing and was granted citizenship.

Following are some examples of teaching sequence with pattern guides, focused questions, and graphic organizers.

PATTERN GUIDE SEQUENCE Science

This guide is designed to help you to understand the **sequential events** as discussed in your textbook section on "Food Chains." Below are some events discussed in this chapter. Write each statement in the correct section of the sequence steps on the chart.

- A. Bacteria and fungi act as decomposers.
- B. The pondweed acts as the producer.
- C. The perch acts as the tertiary consumer.
- D. The minnow represents this stage of the food chain.
- E. The snail is the primary producer.

Stage 1	Stage 2	Stage 3	Stage 4	Stage 5

How Do I Connect Text Structure to Help My Students Learn Content?

PATTERN GUIDE SEQUENCE English

The Ceremony by Nigel McKeand

Directions: Read the information below on the parts of the plot. Then write the plot parts from "The Ceremony" on the dotted lines on the diagram. Use the lines of dialogue to make your decisions. Each sentence of the dialogue fits under a part of the plot in the diagram, but the sentences are not in correct order. Write the sentence numbers on the diagram's solid short lines. Be sure to put them under the correct part of the plot. The sentences will not necessarily be in chronological order.

Sequential Parts of the Plot

The *exposition* usually comes at the beginning of the play, although bits of exposition will occur throughout the play. A good script writer often gives us a bit of exposition just before we need to know it to appreciate an important moment in the play. The exposition usually deals with what has happened in the past; it explains all that is necessary to understand what follows (setting, mood, main character, point of view, background).

The *complication* is the next part of the teleplay or script. It presents the problem or conflict implied in the beginning situation. In George M. Cohan's terminology, you "get your man up a tree."

The *turning point* or crisis is the third part of the story, the part that takes a *decisive* turn. In George M. Cohan's scheme, this is the point at which "you throw rocks at the man in the tree." The turning point in tragedy was identified long ago by the Greek philosopher Aristotle: "Reversal of Situation is a change by which the action veers round to its opposite, subject always to our rule of probability or necessity.... Recognition...is a change from ignorance to knowledge, producing love or hate between persons destined by the poet for good or bad fortune. The best form of recognition is coincident with a reversal of the situation. This recognition, combined with Reversal, will produce either pity or fear in a tragedy."

129

The *climax*, the point of highest emotional intensity, is the point of highest suspense. Sometimes this moment coincides with the turning point. In other stories it replaces the resolution, as in stories that have an exciting ending, particularly twist endings.

The final section is the *resolution* or *denouement*, the part where the author unravels the complication and thus provides the answer to the main questions. This part is where George M. Cohan "gets the man down from the tree." This resolution in fairy tales (and other stories) is the and-they-lived-happily-ever-after part.

Lines from *The Ceremony*

1. *David*: (holding out the gift, a prayer shawl) I bought this for you a long time ago.

2. *Jim-Bob*: His daddy won't let him have his birthday.

3. *News Announcer*: In Adolf Hitler's Germany, the persecution of the Jews goes on. Jews are forbidden to marry non-Jews. No Jew may teach or hold public office. Meanwhile, books by foreign authors are disappearing from Germany. One night recently, in Berlin, more than 20,000 books were burned.

4. *Grandpa*: If you deny your heritage, you'd be false to yourself. It would fester inside you like a disease.

5. *Paul*: Today I am thankful for many things – my father and mother for bringing me through these troubled times to manhood . . . and my friends here for giving us back our faith in people.

6. *Paul*: You see. . . I am a Jew.

7. *Ike*: They just arrived in the United States. Doc Harrison's lending them his summer cottage here.

8. *Paul*: John-Boy helped me find the rabbi. I talked to him about my Bar Mitzvah. He says it is the birthright of every Jew to have a Bar Mitzvah. He says I can have it even if my father is not present.

9. *Grandpa*: You know, Professor, all my life, I've lived in the shadow of this mountain. My father – and his father

before him – were born here. Generations of Waltons rest up there in the family graveyard. This is my heritage. Compared to yours it's small, but it's mine. If my ancestors had ever denied who they were, my grandchildren wouldn't be the people they are today. I think those same feelings are in your heart . . . just as they've been in the hearts of your people for five thousand years.

10. *Eva*: We loved Germany. It was our native land. Suddenly, everything changed. My husband, for no reason, was forced out of his job. In school, Paul was taunted. On the streets, our neighbors turned away and would not speak to us. Then one night every window of our house was smashed. Our door was smeared with paint and filthy words.

11. *Paul*: You mean I can't have my Bar Mitzvah?

12. *David*: Not even that. We cannot take any more risks.

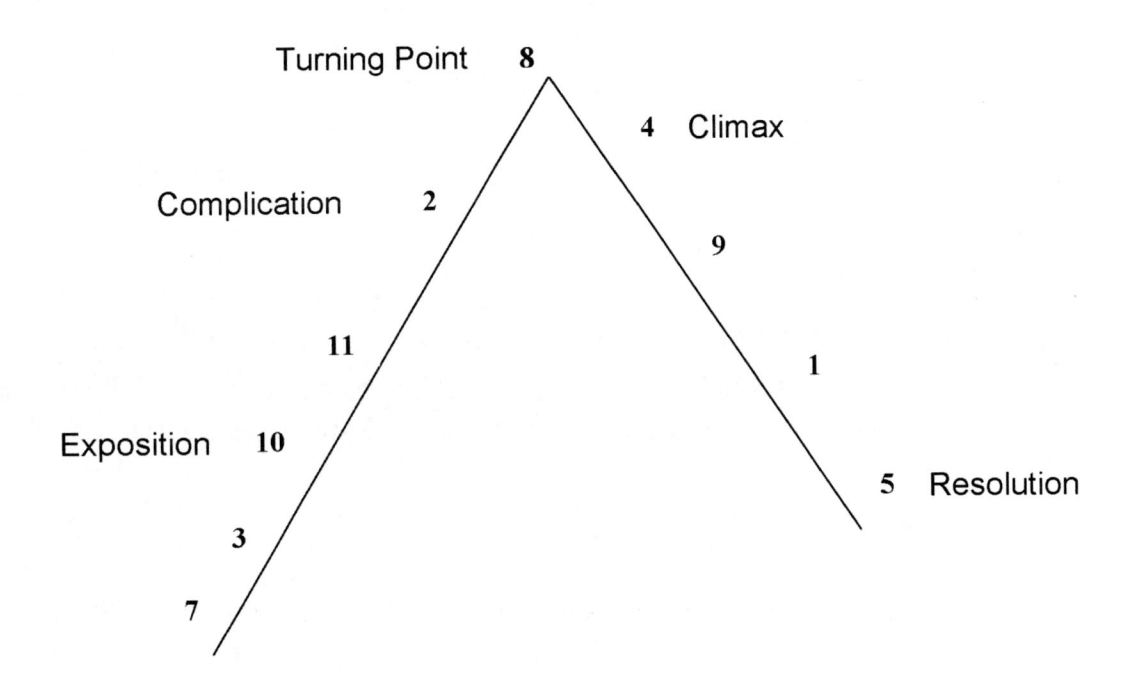

```
                    Turning Point    8
                                    / \
                                   /   \    4   Climax
                                  /     \
              Complication   2   /       \
                                /         \   9
                               /           \
                          11  /             \
                             /               \    1
              Exposition  10/                 \
                           /                   \
                        3 /                     \   5   Resolution
                         /
                      7 /
```

PATTERN GUIDE   SEQUENCE   Business

Directions: This pattern guide will help you to see how the writer organized his thoughts. In this case the sequential pattern begins with an Introduction in which the writer presents a background to the six-column work sheet and the sequence of steps that are needed to prepare a six-column sheet. In each step of the sequence (steps 1-9) you are required to read each question and place your answers in the space provided. Complete the guide as you read the chapter.

Background: Answer T for true and F for false in the following statements.

___   1.   The owners of businesses want to know how well the business is doing.

___   2.   A paper with several amount columns, used for analysis, is known as a work sheet.

___   3.   The length of time for which an analysis of business operations is made is a fiscal period.

___   4.   All the ledger account balances are sorted and summarized in the balance sheet section.

___   5.   The finished work sheet is used in preparing the financial reports for the fiscal period.

STEPS

Step 1. What are the three lines of the heading?

(a) _____

(b) _____

(c) _____

Step 2. What are the column headings, reading from left to right, on a standard six-column work sheet?

(a) _____

(b) _____

(c) _____

(d) _____

(e) _____

Step 3. Write Step 3 here:

_____

Step 4. What is extended from the balance sheet items into the balance sheet section?

(a) _____

(b) _____

FOCUSED QUESTIONS   SEQUENCE   English

In the "Author Study" section of Unit 3 in your textbook, Gary Soto is featured. These questions will help you to keep the major events of his life in the proper order or **sequence.**

1. When and where was Soto born?

2. When did his grandparents arrive in the United States?

3. How old was Soto when his father died?

4. What kind of work did Soto do as a teenager?

5. What did Soto do **after** graduating from high school?

6. What did Soto discover about himself **during** his sophomore year in college?

7. What are Soto's interests as an adult?

How Do I Connect Text Structure to
Help My Students Learn Content?

FOCUSED QUESTIONS   SEQUENCE   Science

The section of your science textbook that discusses volcanic eruptions uses Mount Pinatubo as an example. The **sequence** or order of events associated with that eruption is emphasized. The following questions will help you to identify the events and the order in which they occurred.

1. What conditions existed **before** the eruption that helped scientists to predict that the eruption would occur?

2. When did Mount Pinatubo **first** begin to erupt?

3. What could observers see **as** the eruption took place?

4. **Minutes after,** how did the sky look?

5. **How long** did the volcanic activity last?

6. **When** did the volcanic activity **end?**

7. Create a timeline for the key events of the Mount Pinatubo eruption.

FOCUSED QUESTIONS SEQUENCE **Social Studies**

The section of your textbook that discusses the work of archeologists emphasizes the **order** or **sequence** of the tasks associated with their work. The following questions will help you to follow the **sequence** of those tasks.

1. **Before** archeologists begin their "dig," what two tasks must be completed?

2. What are those two tasks called?

3. Who is involved when the dig or excavation actually starts?

4. What tasks are involved **as** they dig?

5. **When** an artifact is found, what happens?

6. What happens **after** all the artifacts are found?

7. Create a timeline for the key tasks that take place during an archeological dig.

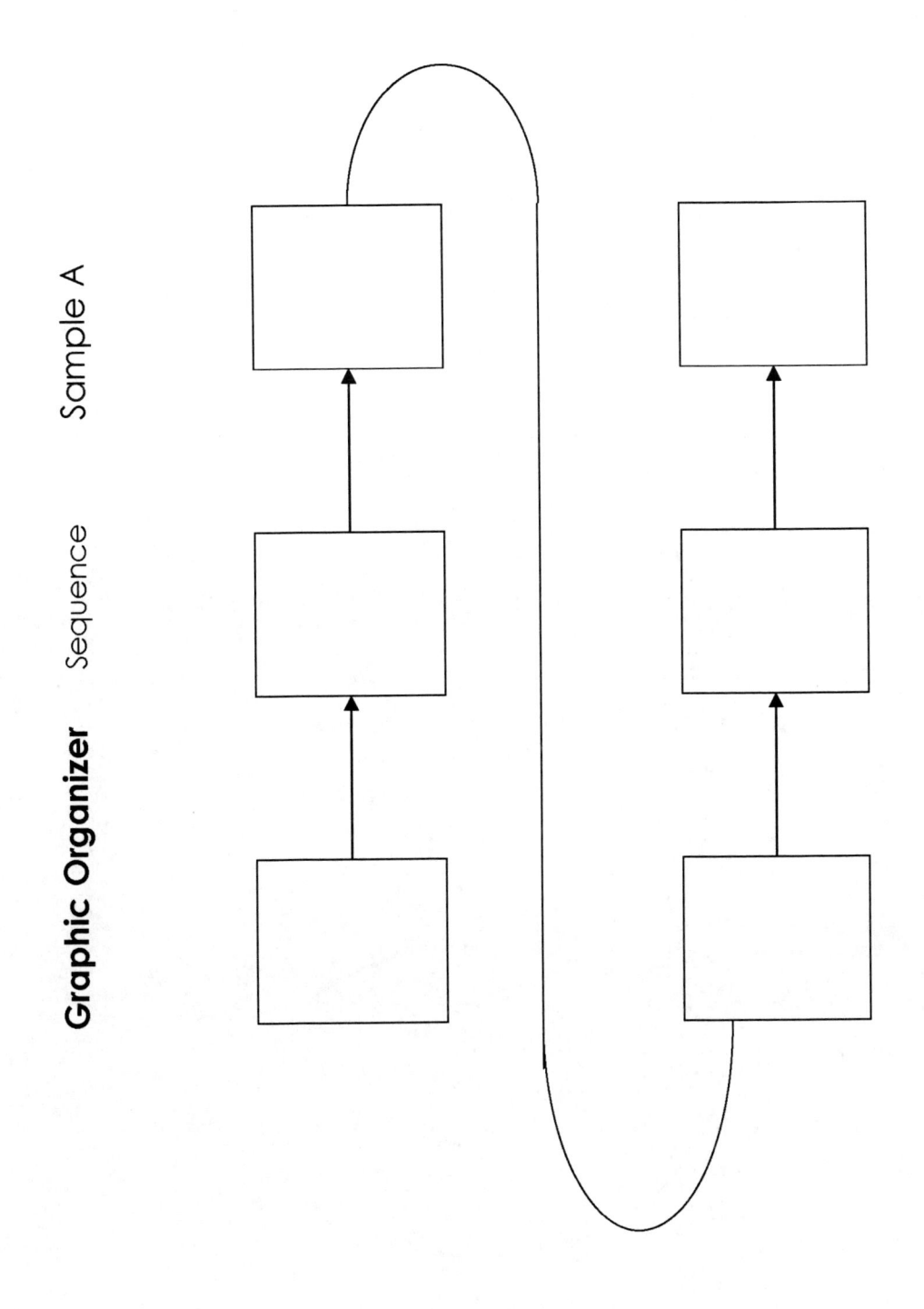

How Do I Connect Text Structure to
Help My Students Learn Content?

Graphic Organizer   Sequence   Sample A

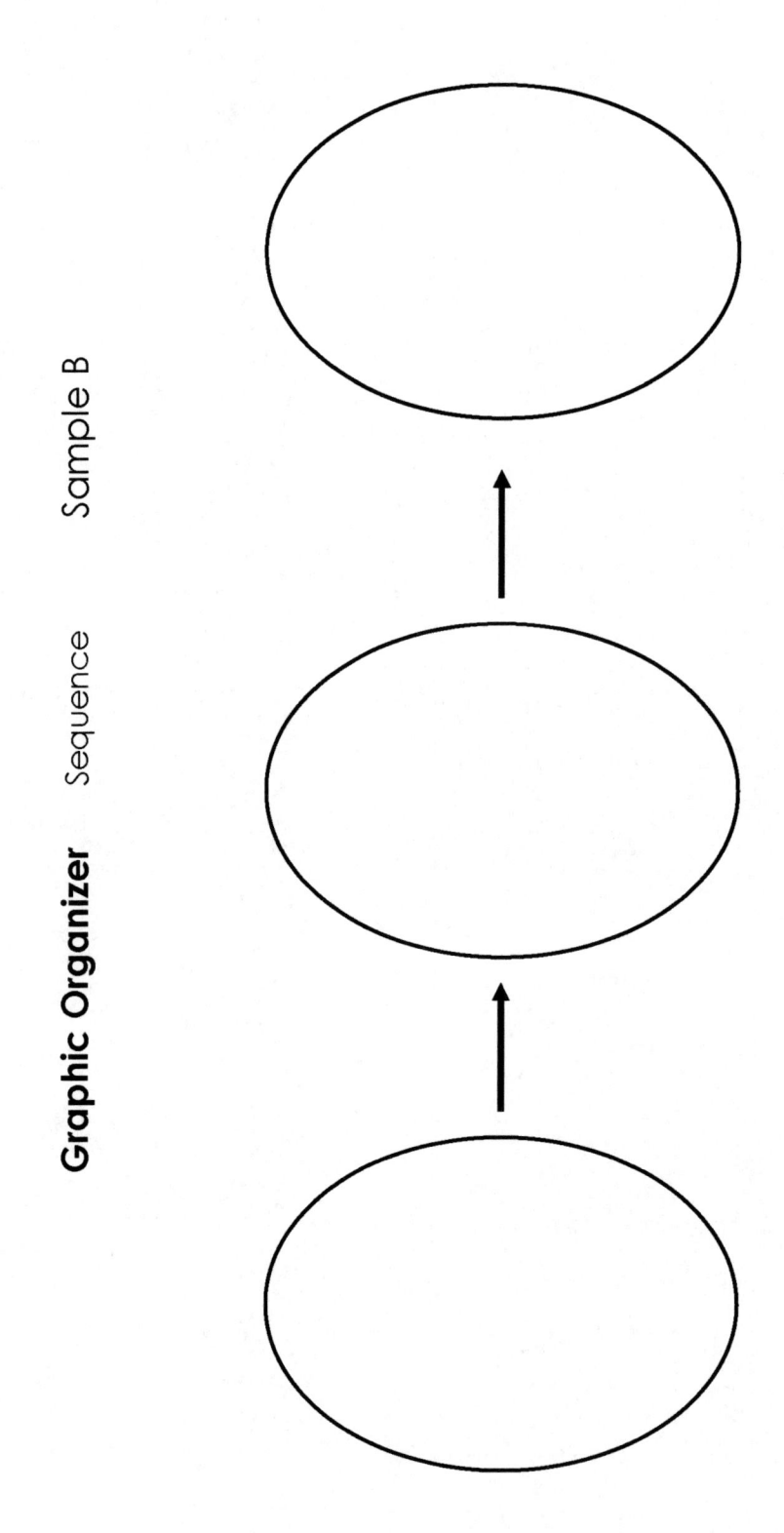

Graphic Organizer Sequence Sample B

How Do I Connect Text Structure to
Help My Students Learn Content?

Graphic Organizer   Sequence   Sample C

Graphic Organizer Sequence Social Studies

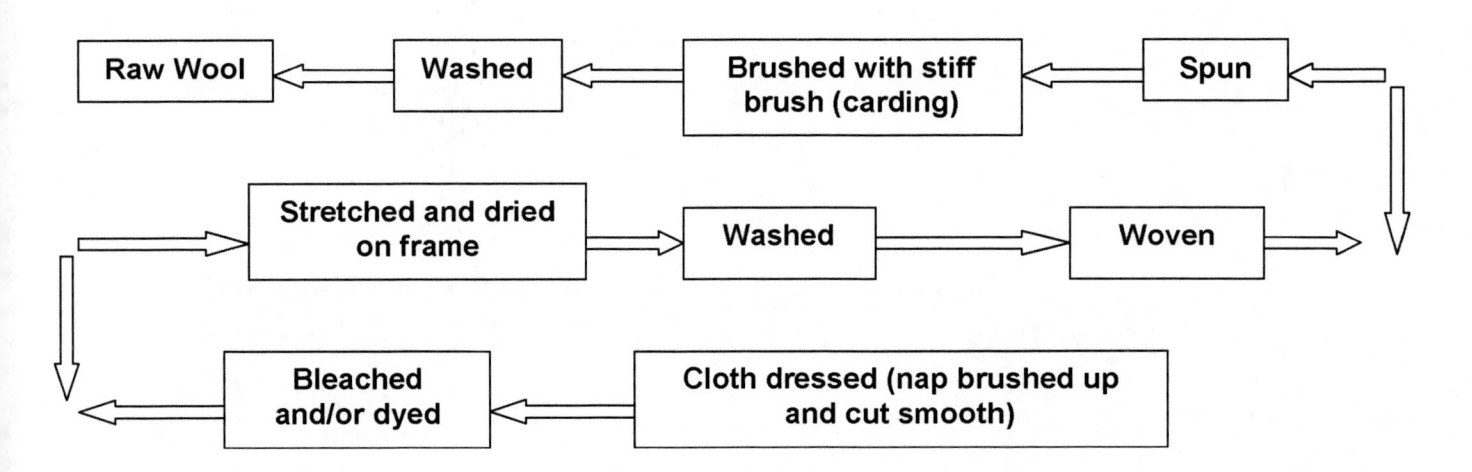

Raw Wool ← Washed ← Brushed with stiff brush (carding) ← Spun ←

→ Stretched and dried on frame → Washed → Woven →

← Bleached and/or dyed ← Cloth dressed (nap brushed up and cut smooth) ←

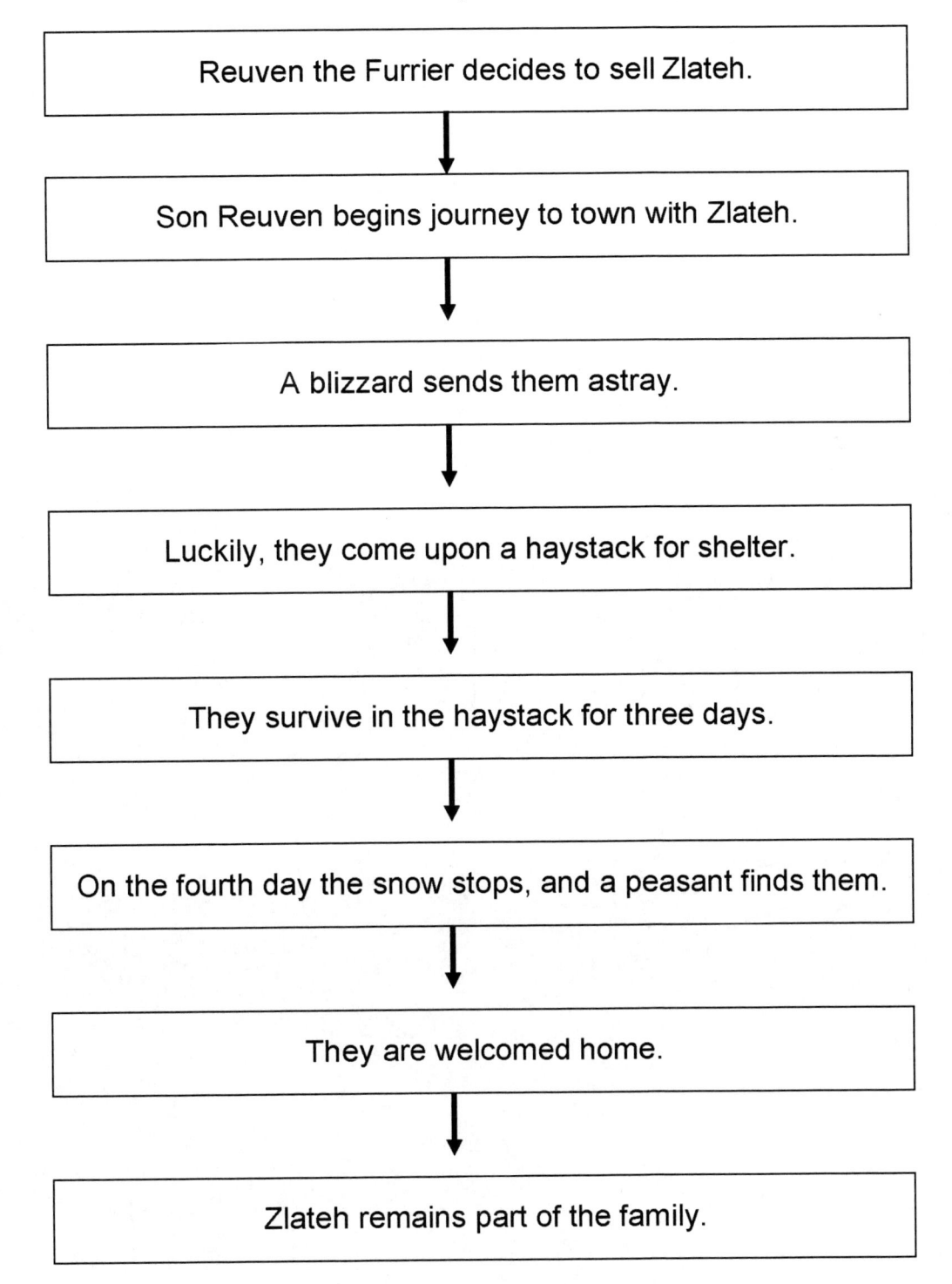

GRAPHIC ORGANIZER   SEQUENCE   English

Zlateh the Goat by Isaac Singer

- Reuven the Furrier decides to sell Zlateh.
- Son Reuven begins journey to town with Zlateh.
- A blizzard sends them astray.
- Luckily, they come upon a haystack for shelter.
- They survive in the haystack for three days.
- On the fourth day the snow stops, and a peasant finds them.
- They are welcomed home.
- Zlateh remains part of the family.

Graphic Organizer　Sequence　　Science

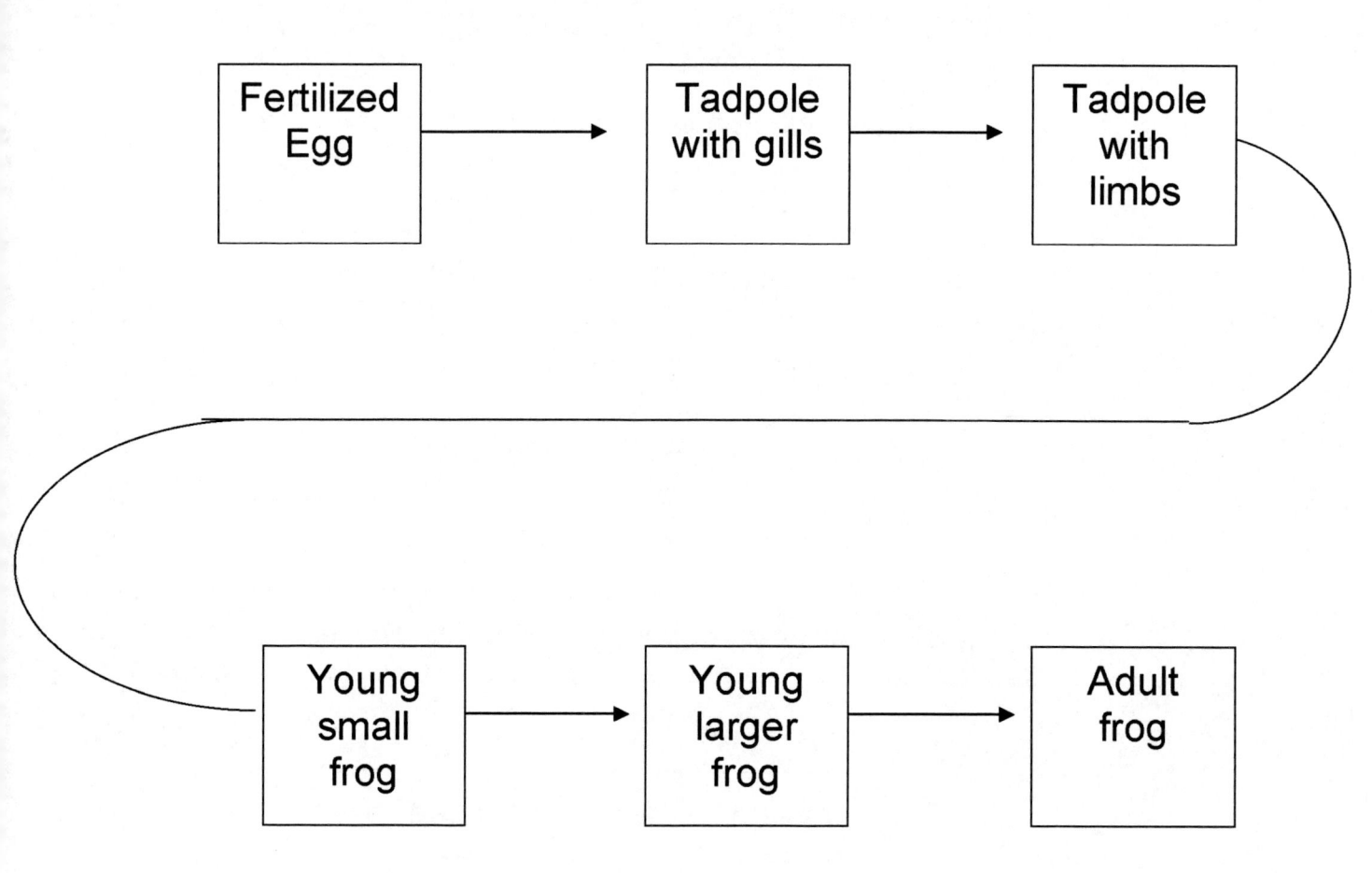

```
[Fertilized Egg] → [Tadpole with gills] → [Tadpole with limbs]
                                                    ↓
[Young small frog] → [Young larger frog] → [Adult frog]
```

THE COMPARISON/CONTRAST PATTERN

Writers use the compare/contrast pattern to show similarities and differences related to data, people, concepts, ideas, or events. Marzano and his colleagues (2001) say that comparing and contrasting might be considered to be the core of all learning. They offer specific guidelines for guiding students to compare and to contrast:

1. Point out directly and discuss similarities and differences in texts.

2. Have students identify similarities and differences independently because this activity enhances their understanding and use of knowledge.

3. Have students represent similarities and differences in graphic organizers. (We would add to this guideline the use of pattern guides and focused questions).

4. Provide students with practice in classifying, creating metaphors, and creating analogies.

Signal Words

You can share with your students certain *signal* words that alert them to the fact that authors are using the compare/contrast pattern in their writing. Here is a list of them.

Comparison/Contrast Signal Words

- on the other hand
- as well as
- in contrast to
- different from
- alternatively
- similarly
- by comparison
- while
- although
- yet
- as well as

You may want to give students practice in circling signal words. Note the example below.

Mass is a fundamental property of an object. It does not depend on where the object is. Weight, ⟨on the other hand,⟩ is the pull of gravity on an object. ⟨Unlike⟩ mass, weight depends on the distance between the object and the body that is exerting the pull. ⟨While⟩ weight is measured in units of force, mass is measured in units of force divided by units of acceleration.

Following are some examples of teaching compare/contrast with pattern guides, focused questions, and graphic organizers.

PATTERN GUIDE **COMPARE/CONTRAST** Science

To the Student: Use this Guide to help you to compare and contrast the different arthropods.

ARTHROPODS				
Points of Distinction	Crustaceans	Arachnids	Millipedes Centipedes	Insects
Habitat				
Number of body parts				
Number of legs				
Antennae				
Wings				
Reproduction				
Examples				
Importance to man				

PATTERN GUIDE   COMPARE/CONTRAST   English

To the student: Below is a guide to help you to compare and contrast Roland Merullo's "Two Heavens" that he presents in his memoir.

Points of Distinction	Revere	Exeter Academy
Neighborhoods		
Social Class		
Unique Landmarks		

How Do I Connect Text Structure to
Help My Students Learn Content?

Pattern Guide   Compare/Contrast   Physical Education

To the student: Your text chapter contrasts football, rugby, and soccer. The guide below is designed to help you to understand and remember how they are different.

Points of Distinction	Football	Rugby	Soccer
Number of players on team			
Size/shape of ball			
Size/shape of field			
System of scoring			

Focused Questions Compare/Contrast English

To the student: Your text includes two retellings of "Ant and Grasshopper," an *Aesop Fable*. One is retold in verse and the other is retold in prose. These questions will help you to compare and contrast the two retellings.

1. Are the characters in each retelling the *same* or *different*?

2. Is the moral in each retelling the *same* or *different*?

3. Were the retellings written at *similar* or *different* times?

4. Does the ant treat the grasshopper in *similar* or *different* ways in each retelling?

5. Which retelling provides the moral directly? Which one provides it indirectly?

Focused Questions Compare/Contrast
Science

1. Are oil and gas tapped in similar or different ways?

2. Do we have a greater supply of oil or gas?

3. What are the advantages and disadvantages of producing and using oil and gas? Make a chart to highlight the comparisons.

4. Are gas and oil renewable or nonrenewable?

Focused Questions Compare/Contrast   Social Studies

Crazy Horse and He Dog

1. How were the backgrounds of Crazy Horse and He Dog alike? How were they different?

2. How were the personalities of Crazy Horse and He Dog alike? How were they different?

3. How did they differ in the ways they met challenges?

4. How were the challenges each faced alike?

Reading to Learn: A Content Teacher's Guide

Graphic Organizer   Compare/Contrast   Sample A

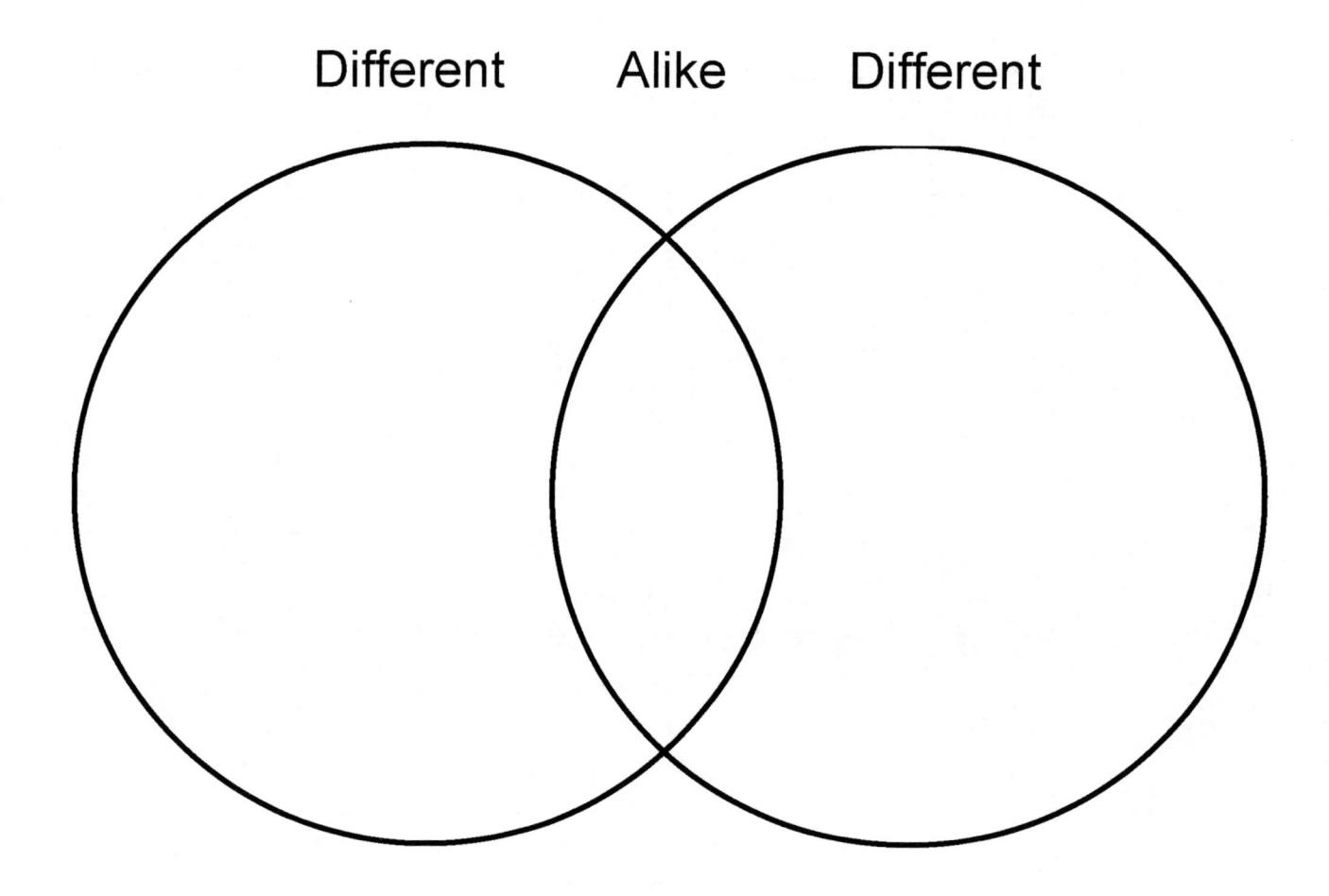

Different   Alike   Different

150

How Do I Connect Text Structure to
Help My Students Learn Content?

Pattern Guide Compare/Contrast   Sample B

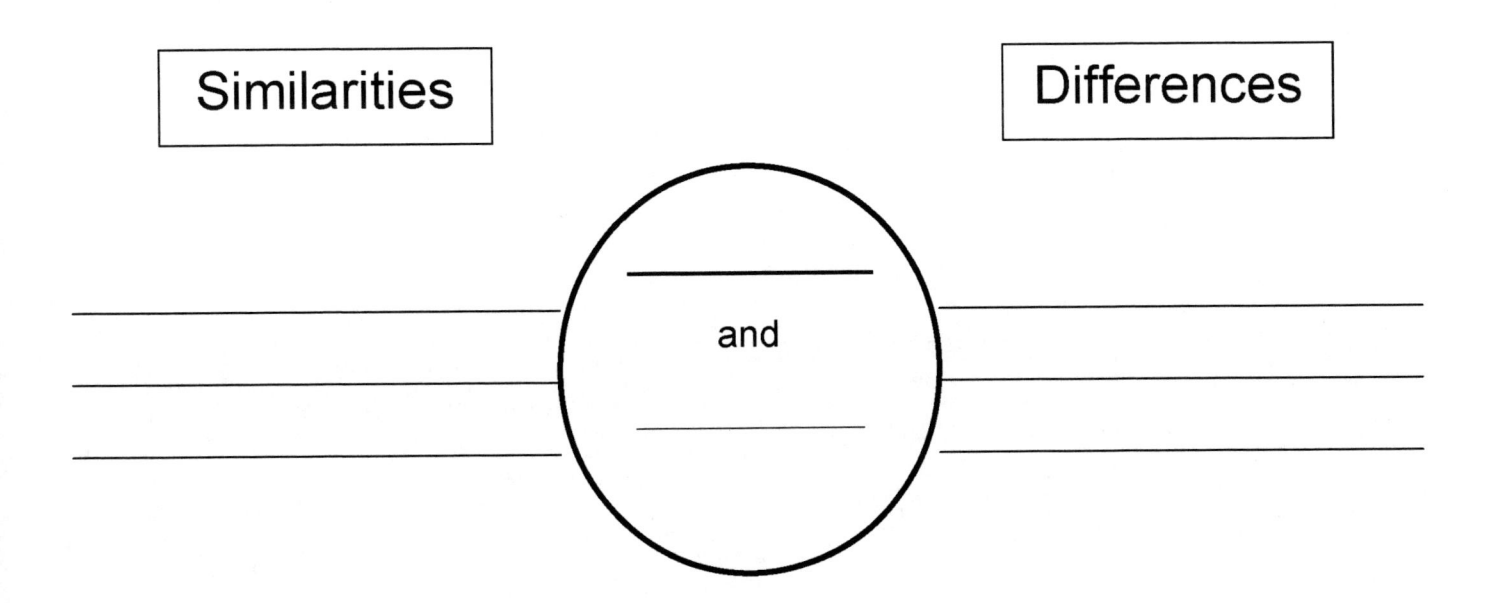

Similarities   Differences

_____
       and
_____

Reading to Learn: A Content Teacher's Guide

Graphic Organizer   Compare/Contrast   Sample C

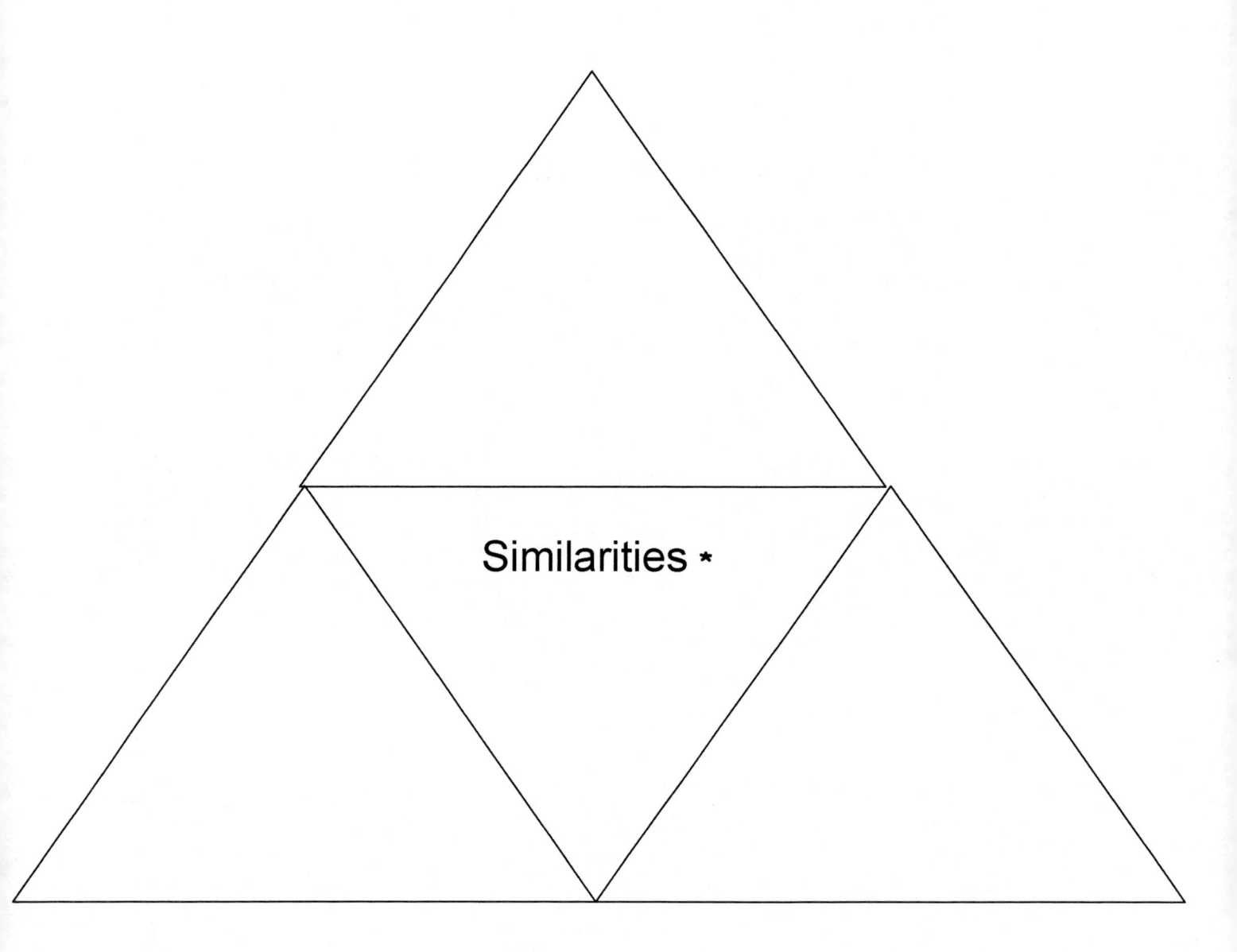

Similarities *

*repeat for differences

How Do I Connect Text Structure to
Help My Students Learn Content?

GRAPHIC ORGANIZER **COMPARE/CONTRAST** English

The Diary of Anne Frank

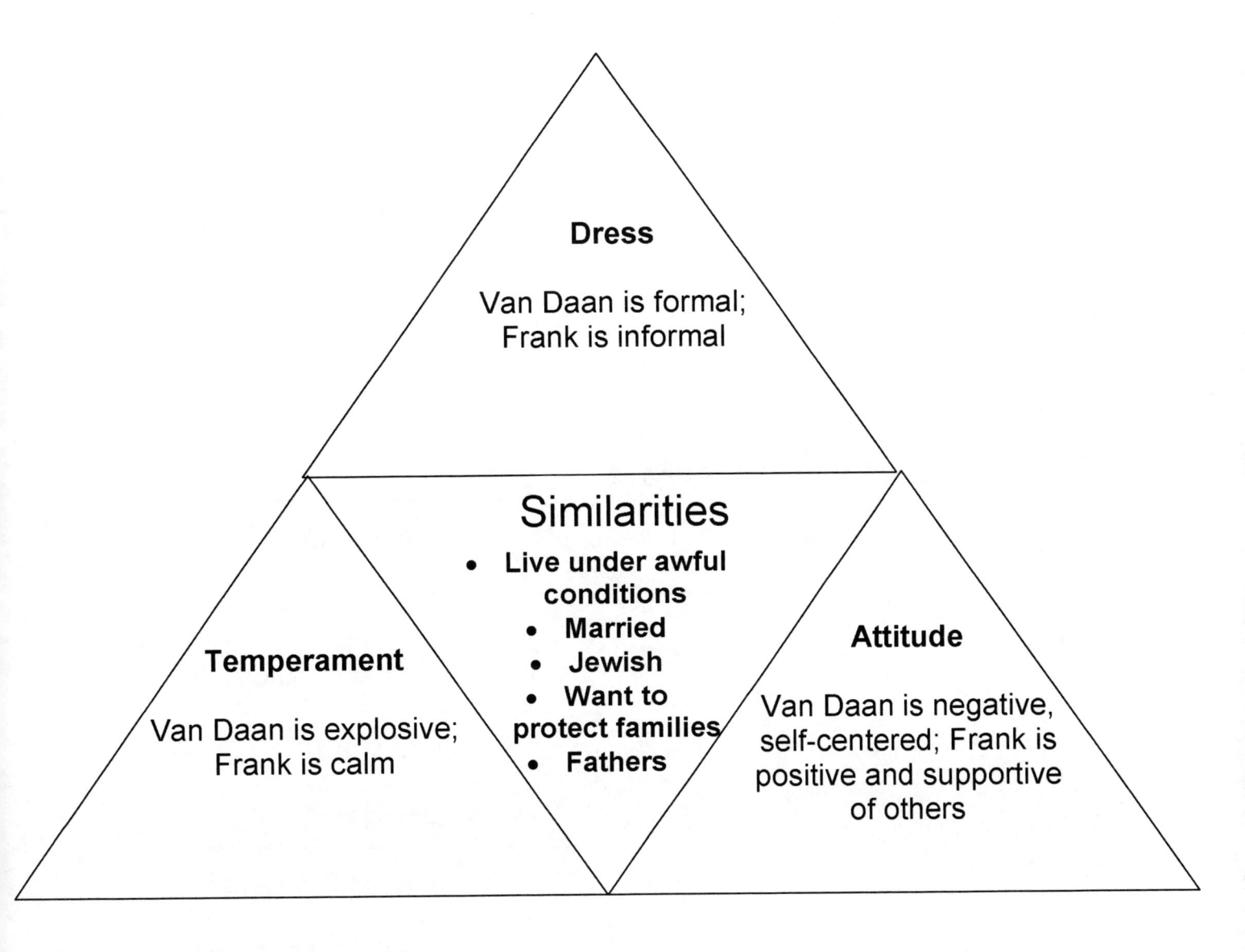

Dress

Van Daan is formal; Frank is informal

Similarities
- Live under awful conditions
- Married
- Jewish
- Want to protect families
- Fathers

Temperament

Van Daan is explosive; Frank is calm

Attitude

Van Daan is negative, self-centered; Frank is positive and supportive of others

Graphic Organizer Compare/Contrast Science

Similarities

- Severe storms
- Threaten people
- Cause damage and affect the environment

Tornadoes and Hurricanes

Differences

H: Lasts a week
T: Lasts a few minutes

H: Width of storm can be 300 miles
T: 100 to 600 meters

H: Can predict 2/3 days in advance
T: Can predict 20 minutes before or less

GRAPHIC ORGANIZER COMPARE/CONTRAST English

The Diary of Anne Frank

Similarities

- Live under awful conditions
- Married, fathers, Jewish
- Want to protect family

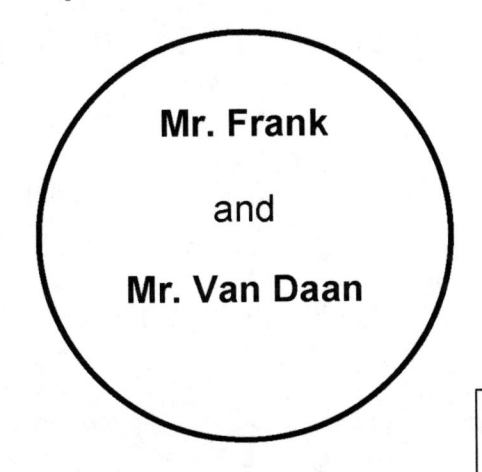

Mr. Frank and Mr. Van Daan

Differences

- Dress
- Temperament
- Attitude toward women

MATHEMATICS AND TEXT STRUCTURE

Because of the nature of mathematics, the patterns that emerge in the other content areas do not clearly emerge in mathematics textbooks. Rather, mathematics books are characterized by exposition, instructions, and exercises.

Math authors use *exposition* when they explain concepts and introduce new vocabulary. They use *instructions* when they tell readers to solve a problem or perform a task. They provide *exercises* to work out problems. These characteristics of math textbooks make them very different from other content area textbooks. Barton and Heidema (2000) say that math textbooks tend to follow a pattern used with guided discovery. They tell us that "In guided discovery, authors provide activities and questions through which students are supposed to discover the ideas or infer them on their own. Active participation in constructing meaning is essential. (However), Even students who are able to read the problem and understand its situational context still can have trouble identifying what the problem is asking them to do."

The authors go on to say that mathematics educators and the materials they use in the classroom approach problem solving as suggested by Polya (1957). This four-step plan follows along with some questions students can ask themselves to carry out each step.

1. *Understand the problem.*
   - Do I understand all the words use in the problem?
   - What am I asked to find or show?
   - Can I create a diagram to help me understand the problem?

2. *Devise a plan.*
   - What strategy should I use solve the problem?
   - What is the connection between the data and the unknown?
   - How is this problem like other ones I have solved?
   - Have I used all the data?
   - Can I restate the problem in my own words?

3. *Carry out the plan.*
   - Have I followed each step need to carry out my solution plan?
   - Can I prove that my answer is correct?

- If my original plan did not work, what is an alternative one?

4. *Look Back*
    - Did I check my results?
    - Can I derive the solution differently?
    - What worked?
    - What did not work?
    - Will I be able to use this strategy with other problems?

MATHEMATICS AND GRAPHIC ORGANIZERS

Mathematics teachers can use graphic organizers to help students summarize the main points of important concepts. Below are two examples related to the concepts of measurement and equations.

Example

MEASUREMENT

UNITS
- Metric: meter, cm, liter, gram, kg, Celsius
- Customary: foot, inch, mile, quart, ounce, pound, Fahrenheit
- Non-standard: pencils, paper clips, glasses

TOOLS
- ruler, tape measures
- scales
- cups
- clocks
- thermometer
- protractor

TYPES
- Length (1-dimension): width, height, perimeter, circumference
- Cover (2-dimensions): area, surface area
- Volume (3-dimensions): volume
- Other: Capacity, weight, mass, time, temperature, angle measure

FORMULAS
- Rectangle: $A = l * w$, $P = 2(l + w)$
- Circle: $A = \pi r^2$, $C = \pi * d$
- Sphere: $V = 4/3 \pi R^3$
- Cylinder: $V = \pi r^2 h$

EQUATIONS

SYSTEMS
- simultaneous equations
- consistent/inconsistent
- dependent/independent

UNKNOWNS/VARIABLES
- numerical
- degree
- dependent

NUMBER RELATIONS
- $2 \times 3 = 3 \times 2$
- $72 - 58 = 74 - 60$

DEGREE (GRAPHING)
- linear
- quadratic
- cubic

FORMULAS
- $A = l * w$
- $P = 2(l + w)$
- $C = 2\pi r$

Barton, M.L. and Heidema, C. *Teaching Reading in Mathematics.* Aurora, CO: Mid-continent Research for Education and Learning, 2000. Reprinted with permission of McREL.

STUDY SYSTEMS AND MATHEMATICS

Students may find that using study systems may help them follow the flow of ideas contained in mathematics textbooks. Two such systems are SQ3R (Robinson, 1970) and HEART (Santeusanio, 1990).

SQ3R has five steps:

> **S** – *Survey* or skim the problem to get a general idea.
>
> **Q** – *Questions* like: What facts are needed for solution? What is my plan for solving this problem?
>
> **R1** – *Read* to clarify the question, to identify the needed facts, and to determine the steps required to solve the problem.
>
> **R2** – *Recite* the answer.
>
> **R3** – *Review* to check the answer and reflect on other ways of solving the problem.

HEART has five steps:

> **H**ow much do I know from reading over this math problem?
>
> **E**stablish a purpose for completing the problem
>
> **A**sk yourself questions about the problem
>
> **R**ecord the steps involved in solving the problem
>
> **T**est yourself.

Here is an example of how HEART can be used in solving a problem. (Santeusanio, 1988)

> A living room is 16 feet by 20 feet. The rug, also rectangular, measures 12 feet by 15 feet. How many square feet of the floor remains uncovered by the rug?

How much do I know from reading over this problem?

> I know:
>
> - the living room is 16 feet by 20 feet
> - the living room is rectangular
> - the rung is rectangular
> - the rug is 12 feet by 15 feet
> - a portion of the room is not covered by the rug

Establish a purpose for completing the problem.

> My purpose is to find out how many square feet of the floor are not covered by the rug.

Ask yourself questions about the problem.
- Do I understand all the vocabulary (rectangular, measures, square feet)?
- What is my plan for computing the answer to this problem?

Record the steps to solving the problem.
- Draw a rectangle to represent the living room.
- Label the length and width.
- Draw in the rug.
- Label the length and width of the rug.
- Review my purpose
- Shade in the part of the floor that is not covered by the rug
- Solve the problem

Test yourself.
- Check your figures. Did I multiply and subtract accurately?
- Examine the solution carefully
- Check to see if the answer makes sense

Answer: 140 square feet are not covered by the rug

SUMMARY

In this chapter we reviewed the major ways authors organize their writing. Some challenges that face readers as they tackle text in the various organizational patters were highlighted as well as the role that *signal words* play in helping students to comprehend. For each of the patterns, models for teaching were presented including ones that focus on questions, pattern guides, and graphic organizers.

CHAPTER 7   **WHAT IS CRITICAL LITERACY?**

In Chapter 3 we identify "Self-Questioning" as an important reading strategy used by competent readers. They use self-questioning to "call up" their existing knowledge of a topic. They use it to examine the text and to monitor their understanding. And they use self-questioning to analyze the beliefs and motives behind the author's surface meaning. We call this particular use of self-questioning "critical literacy," the focus of this chapter.

While we use the term "critical literacy," others use terms like critiquing, persuading, evaluating, critical analysis, critical thinking, and critical reading. Educators may equivocate over the differences and similarities of these terms, but all would agree that it is important for students to have a healthy questioning attitude towards everything they read and hear.

When we encourage adolescents to interrogate the texts they read, they become aware of how language is used to persuade an audience. Annandale and her colleagues (2004) suggest that in order for readers to engage in critical literacy, they need to know how context affects the interpretation of language. An understanding of situational and socio-cultural contexts equips readers with knowledge that helps them to question authors and to deconstruct, evaluate and interrogate what they write. An awareness of the relationship between context and the interpretation of language provides a solid foundation for critical literacy. Below is a summary of Annandale and her colleagues' discussion of situational and socio-cultural context.

SITUATIONAL CONTEXT

An author's choice of language varies according to the context of the writing. Several factors influence this choice. These include the purpose of the communication, the topic under discussion, and the medium for sharing the communication such as textbooks, email, ads, and news reports.

Other important factors influencing choice of language are the roles and relationships between writers and readers. The relationship for textbooks is between "authority" and "student," whereas in a political speech it is between a candidate or supporter and voters. In an email, the relationship is often between colleague and colleague. Changing any of these factors will have an impact on the language used.

Some of these same factors influence how readers interpret a writer's intended meaning. For example, while authors have purposes for communicating, readers have purposes for reading their communications. While authors select topics, readers have various degrees of knowledge about them.

SOCIO-CULTURAL CONTEXT

To varying extents, all texts reflect the expectations and values of their respective social and cultural groups. Authors use language that reflects their beliefs, values and assumptions, especially as they relate to gender, ethnicity and status. These same factors influence how readers interpret and question what they read. Culture and language are strongly related.

Much writing, even traditional subject-matter textbooks, is intended to influence readers; thus, the writing is intentionally crafted and communicated, especially when the clear purpose of the writer is to persuade. The use of various forms of language reflects and shapes socio-cultural attitudes and assumptions, including variations of Standard English generally used in formal communication.

When an author writes a text, that writer's socio-cultural context will influence the type of language used. Likewise, when a reader engages in a text, that reader's view of the world, society and culture influences the interpretation and questioning of the text. Texts are not neutral. Each reader interprets and questions a text according to what he or she brings to that text. For example, an environmentalist and a mining engineer will interpret and question a report on Antarctica differently because they probably have a diverse set of values, beliefs and understanding about the topic.

Annandale and her colleagues (2004, Facilitator's Notes, *First Steps Reading*, 2nd edition) provide an exercise that nicely clarifies the role situational and socio-cultural context plays in critical literacy. We share it with you in the following:

Read the following statement: REFUSE TO BE PUT IN A BASKET.

Depending on the meaning we associate with the word "refuse," this statement can have two entirely different meanings. One meaning is *rubbish or trash*; another meaning is *resist*. Let's now look at the chart below to illustrate how interpreting and questioning this text will vary according to the meaning attached to "refuse."

REFUSE TO BE PUT IN A BASKET

	Meaning #1 *Rubbish or trash*	Meaning #2 *Resist*
Purpose	To instruct, to direct	To persuade
Subject Matter	Rules	Being free-spirited
Form	Sign	T-shirt, bumper sticker
Who or what role	School principal Fast-food manager	Nonconformist
Where/situation	School, park, restaurant	Protest/political Meeting On a wall
Questioning of text	"Will the trash be recycled?"	"Does the author think everybody should be a nonconformist?"

The two different readings and the two different meanings of the statement depend on where we place the emphasis in the first word, "refuse." If our meaning for "refuse" is *trash*, it can be assumed that the statement is a command or a direction from an authority in a particular place such as a school, public park, or fast-food restaurant. If our meaning for "refuse" is *resist*, then the statement takes on a more abstract, deeper meaning about not conforming to mainstream beliefs. The statement may be found on a bumper sticker or on a T-shirt.

Much hinges on where the statement is located, who wrote it, and the relationship between the writer and the reader. The situational aspects of the reading as well as the social and cultural perceptions of the writer and the reader, influence how the message is interpreted and questioned.

THE PERSUADING AUTHOR AND THE EVALUATING READER

Zwiers (2004) calls persuasion "tipping another person's scale to your side." A goal of writers and speakers is to convince their readers and listeners that the theory, idea, or opinion they put forth is the correct one. And their arguments are supported with reasons and evidence to give it weight. Such writers or speakers, including advertisers, politicians and academicians use a variety of devices to try to persuade their audience. Here is a review of some of them:

Analogy

Analogy is used when comparing an idea, theory, candidate, or hypothesis with another. Sometimes the comparison is extended too far in efforts to persuade.

Example: *The potential effects of our social security going bankrupt are like the great depression. People will be jumping out of windows.*

Association

Association is used when writers attempt to get readers to transfer the respect, admiration, or sympathy they have for one thing to the idea they are proposing. For example, an editorial writer might describe a day that a candidate for public office spent with his or her family on a picnic. The writer's goal is to have the readers associate their admiration for clean family living with the candidate's behavior and therefore vote for the candidate. Other types of associations include basic needs (food), economy (save or make money), space (neighborhood), love and belonging, and authority figures (Rank, 2005).

Bribery

This persuasive device is commonly used in advertising. Bonuses, free products, discounts and privileges are offered to readers/consumers.

Example: *Wash your car four times and get the fifth one free.*

Composition

Composition presentation is a common persuasive device. For example the language used can either be negative or positive. The ideas can be presented clearly or abstractly. The author can present many or few details. A writer can elect to use absolutes, qualifiers, metaphors and rhetorical exaggerations (Rank, 2005). Non verbal (see "The Persuading Illustrator" below) compositions include *visuals*, like shape, color and size, as well as *aural* elements like music or particular sounds.

Confusion

When writers use confusion they "make things so complex, so chaotic, that other people 'give up,' get weary, or overloaded. Confusion, whether caused by accidental error or deliberate deception, can hide or obscure potential harmful items. Chaos can be the accidental result of a disorganized mind, or the deliberate flim-flam of a con-man or the political demagogue, who then offers a 'simple solution' to the confused. Confusion can result from faulty logic, equivocation, circumlocution, contradictions, multiple diversions, inconsistencies, jargon, or anything which blurs clarity or understanding" (Rank, 2005).

Connotation

Connotation is when the meaning of a word or phrase goes beyond its explicit one. In persuasive writing, it is used to suggest a meaning that furthers the author's argument.

Example: *Where do you want to live when you retire? In the bitter, freezing cold of New England or in the warm ocean breezes of Florida?*

Diversion

The diversion device distracts focus or diverts attention away from key issues. Communicators make attacks, appeal to the emotions, evade difficult topics, and even may use humor to divert an audience's attention.

Euphemism

Euphemism is when a thought-to-be harsh word is replaced with a mild, indirect or vague one.

Example: *Although the value of the Jethroe Mutual Fund* plummeted *in value, the directors are optimistic about its future in the market.* (Notice how the tone changes with the replacement of the harsh word "plummeted".) *Although the value of the Jethroe Mutual Fund* declined, *the directors are optimistic about its future in the market.*

Exaggeration

Exaggeration is the use of sweeping, overstated remarks.

Example: *This new theory of treating cancer has been endorsed by just about every physician in the country.*

Figurative Language

Figurative language refers to using language not meant to be read literally. The understanding of figurative language is determined by a shared socio-cultural context.

Examples include similes: *She's as cute as a button.*; idioms: *It's raining cats and dogs.*; and hyperbole: *That linesman is as big as a house.*

Glittering Language

Glittering Language is when pleasant, agreeable words are used to arouse good feelings, approval, and respect for the position of the writer or speaker.

Example: *The food at our restaurant is succulent, the atmosphere is dreamy, and the service is friendly.*

Name Calling

Name Calling is when writers or speakers use disagreeable words to arouse anxiety, hate or disapproval. Usually little or no evidence is used to support a stated position that includes name calling.

Example: *If the government continues to cut taxes, our children will be utter failures in life and people will die unnecessarily because of cuts in police and fire protection.*

Omission

According to Rank (2005), "Omission is common since the basic selection/omission process necessarily omits more than can be presented. All communication is limited, slanted, or biased to include and exclude items. But, omission can also be used as a deliberate way of concealing." Politicians, for example, can be expected to omit information about scandalous activities of their own or questionable past associations.

Advertisers will omit any studies that do not support the value of their products. Writers present only one side of the issue or selectively quote others. Statistics are often misused or incorrectly interpreted. A science author eager to gain acceptance of his new theory on a particular topic is likely to include only the data that supports his theory. This technique is very evident in articles we read on nuclear energy, abortion, gay marriage, gun control, and other highly emotional issues.

Notice when you read the following passage how the writer seems to be in awe of Archie Jones. However, the writer omits the fact that Jones' two major rivals were injured and unable to compete.

Jones Blitzes Field

The brilliant Archie Jones yesterday emphasized his dominance over other sprinters in the southwest region when he won the Regional 100-metre summer sprint. Jones led from start to finish, leaving his opponents trailing in this wake.
(Annandale et. al. 2004)

Overgeneralization

Overgeneralization is the use of a statement that encompasses a wide group of people or several situations. Overgeneralization is not based on fact. Writers draw on people's desire to do what the great majority is doing and many people do not want to think they are out of step with the mainstream opinion.

Example: *It is pretty clear that all the parents in this district want the high school to implement block scheduling.*

Oversimplification

Oversimplification occurs when a simple and sometimes single statement is used to explain a situation that is the result of a number of complex and interwoven factors.

Example: *The Allies won World War II because of their dominance in the air.*

Personalization

Personalization involves adopting a tone of intimacy. Personal pronouns can affect the tone. (We must stay true to our beliefs and causes – the things that helped us to make this a great institution.) Commands can affect the tone. (Your country needs you!) And rhetorical questions can affect the tone. (Is the medication you are currently taking really helping you?)

Plain Folks

Writers associate their ideas with people "just like you and me" so that we will accept them.

Example: *Social security was set up for us plain folks who don't have lots of money. It is our insurance policy, so why tamper with it?*

Print Size and Font Selection

Choosing specific words to be printed in bold type, italics, color or in a larger font size often indicates points the author feels are important for the reader to notice. Different fonts can be used for different reasons. A handwriting font, for instance, may be used to suggest a familiar or informal relationship between the author and reader.

Quoting out of context

Quoting out of context to mislead or influence the reader can create bias. Authors often select a particular section of a written or spoken text and can use this section to present a different impression or point of view.

Example: *A theatre reviewer writes "The play is awkwardly written, but the actors do a terrific job of engaging the audience." However, the ad for the play only quotes the* reviewers opinion that "the actors do a terrific job of engaging the audience."

Repetition

Repetition is used to emphasize a point, either positively or negatively. Rank (2005) tells us that repetition is an easy and effective way to persuade. "People," he says, "are comfortable with the known, the familiar. As children we love to hear the same stories repeated: later, we have 'favorite' songs, TV programs, and so on. All cultures have chants, prayers, rituals, and dances based on repetition." George W. Bush used repetition effectively in the 2004 Presidential campaign continuously repeating the same message, particularly the claim that John Kerry "flip flopped" on many issues.

Sarcasm

Sarcasm relies heavily on a shared socio-cultural context to achieve the author's purpose. Sarcasm is scathing language that offends or ridicules a person or idea.

Example: *Maybe if the governor were not out of state partying, he would know what was going on here at home.*

Testimony

Quotes from experts or celebrities are used to create a positive association with a product or idea.

Example: *Join Robert Redford and Eric Clapton in supporting the environment. Keep our country beautiful and the air clear.*

Understatement

Understatement is used when the author tries to underplay someone else's position or opinion on a topic.

Example: *Lots of people think the New England Patriots are the best team in football because they won the Super Bowl. But if a few plays had gone the other way, the Philadelphia Eagles would have won and they would be considered the best.*

THE INTENSIFY/DOWNPLAY *SCHEMA* TECHNIQUES

Many of the devices we have shared with you play a major role in Hugh Rank's (2005) Intensify/Downplay *Schema* Techniques. Rank encourages students to recognize that writers and speakers manipulate communication to:

(1) intensify their own **good**

(2) intensity other's **bad**

(3) downplay other's **good**

(4) downplay their own **bad**

Everybody naturally engages in intensifying and downplaying communications. Applying the four-part schema to communications does not necessarily mean that one is making moral or ethical judgments about the communication. The schema helps students recognize their own efforts at language manipulation as well as the efforts of others.

Communicators *intensify* their own "goodness" or the "badness" of others by means of repetition, association, and composition (see above). On the other hand, they will *downplay* their own "badness" or the "goodness" of others by means of the devices of omission, diversion, and confusion (see above).

Below are some examples of how this schema can be applied to speeches and text like the 2004 nomination speeches of George W. Bush and John F. Kerry. Let's first look at some examples from Kerry.

1A. And in this journey, I am accompanied by an extraordinary band of brothers led by that American hero, Max Cleland. Our band of brothers doesn't march together because of who we are as veterans, but because of what we learned as soldiers.

   Intensify own good through association (American hero, band of brothers, veterans, soldiers)

1B. America can do better. And help is on the way. (Repeated five times.)

   Intensify own good through repetition

1C. I will be a commander in chief who will never mislead us into war. I will have a Vice President who will not conduct secret meetings with polluters to rewrite our environmental laws. I will have a Secretary of Defense who will listen to the best advice of our military leaders. And I will appoint an Attorney General who actually upholds the Constitution of the United States.

Intensify other's bad through repetition, "I will ..."

1D. Today our national security begins with homeland security. The 9-11 Commission has given us a path to follow, endorsed by Democrats, Republicans, and the 9-11 families. As President, I will not evade or equivocate; I will immediately implement the recommendations of that commission.

Downplay other's good (Creation of 9-11 Commission) through omission of the fact that Bush created the Commission

1E. Now I know there are those who criticize me for seeing complexities - and I do – because some issues just aren't all that simple. Saying there are weapons of mass destruction in Iraq doesn't make it so. Saying we can fight a war on the cheap doesn't make it so. And proclaiming mission accomplished certainly doesn't make it so.

Downplay own bad through diversion

Here are some examples from Bush's nomination speech.

2A. To create more jobs in America, America must be the best place in the world to do business. To create jobs, my plan will encourage investment and expansion by reducing federal spending, reducing regulation, and making the tax relief permanent. To create jobs, we will make our country less dependent on foreign sources of energy. To create jobs, we will expand trade and level the playing field to sell American goods across the globe.

Intensify own good through repetition ("To create jobs ...")

2B. Senator Kerry opposed Medicare reform and health savings accounts. He opposes legal and medical liability reform. He opposed reducing the marriage penalty, opposed doubling the child credit, opposed lowering income taxes for all who pay them.

Intensify other's bad through repetition (opposed)

2C In Northeast Georgia, Gainesville Elementary School is mostly Hispanic and 90 percent poor – and this year 90 percent of the students passed state tests in reading and math. The principal expresses the philosophy of his school this way: "We don't focus on what we can't do at this school; we focus on what we can do. And we do whatever it takes to get kids across the finish line." See, this principal is challenging the soft bigotry of low expectations. And this is the spirit of our education reform, and the commitment of our country: We will leave no child behind.

Intensify own good through association with schools, the Hispanic and the poor

2E. To be fair, there are some things my opponent is for. He's proposed more than two trillion dollars in federal spending so far, and that's a lot, even for a senator from Massachusetts. And to pay for that spending, he's running on a platform of increasing taxes – and that's the kind of promise a politician usually keeps.

Downplay other's good through confusion

Downplay own bad by omitting the names of countries that did not support the Iraq war

It bears repeating that when we ask students to use this *schema*, we are not asking them to make moral or ethical judgments about the commentators. And critically analyzing patterns of persuasion "doesn't tell us which side is 'right,' what charges are true, what supporting evidence is reliable, or what to do. But such basic pattern literacy does help us to sort out some very complex emotional arguments, to identify the examples, to recognize past history, and to define the key issues" (Rank, 2005).

THE PERSUADING ILLUSTRATOR

Illustrators use visual devices to try to influence readers. Here are some devices they use:

Amount of detail

Varying amounts of detail can be used to enhance and complement positions stated in a text. A single picture, for example, can be used to exaggerate a point or ridicule an opposing point of view. Such pictures frequently take the form of cartoons that appear on editorial pages of newspapers.

Artistic style

The artistic style refers to the way the illustrations are rendered. The style may tend towards the realistic or towards representational. In realistic art, subject and objects are portrayed with detailed accuracy, as they would be in real life. On the other hand, in representational art, the illustrator makes no attempt to make the art appear realistic. Each artistic style conveys a different message to the reader.

Color

Colors have symbolic meaning. Illustrators often choose them to create certain effects. For example, strong bold colors may indicate happiness or a positive image whereas darker, bland colors may indicate sadness or a negative image.

Composition and page design

The placement of visual elements on a page or in a text is another device illustrators use. Objects placed in the foreground tend to have more prominence than those in the background. Visual elements placed on the right-hand page have prominence over those on the left. Newspapers exploit prominence by increasing the cost of advertisements in that section of the page. An illustrator or book designer can also attract the reader's attention through the use of white spaces in the page design.

Medium

Medium refers to the material or technique an illustrator has used such as collage, charcoal, watercolors and photographs. The choice of medium by the illustrator can provide readers with clues about the message or purpose of the text. For example, photographs suggest a text is accurate and realistic.

Size

Illustrators may indicate that some characters or concepts are more important than others by making them larger. The relative sizes of visual elements may also change at different places in a text as different points are emphasized.

SUMMARY

In this chapter we answered the question, "What is Critical Literacy?" We reviewed the importance of situational and socio-cultural context in assisting students to interrogate their texts. We outlined specific devices that authors and illustrators use, noting that familiarizing your students with these devices, and an approach like the Intensify/Downplay *Schema*, will contribute to their success as they critically analyze text.

In the next chapter, we will share with you more approaches you can use to connect critical literacy to your content area.

CHAPTER 8   **HOW DO I CONNECT CRITICAL LITERACY TO MY CONTENT AREA?**

In this chapter we cover three areas related to critical literacy. First, we look at the teaching and learning practices that promote critical literacy. Next, we offer some general suggestions for teaching it. And finally, we share some specific activities to teach critical literacy.

TEACHING AND LEARNING PRACTICES

Annandale and her colleagues (2004) identify some teaching and learning practices that lend themselves nicely to critical literacy.

Familiarizing involves exposing your students to texts other than your regular textbook. These may come from newspapers and popular magazines such as *Time* and *Newsweek*, advertisements or journals, and special magazines related to your content area. Any number of critical literacy activities can be applied to these various resources.

Discussing is central to helping students become critical analyzers. The generic questions listed below will help you to conduct discussions.

Analyzing texts involves examining parts of the text to reveal the social and cultural values that are embedded in them. This can be accomplished by comparing similar texts. For example, students can compare:

- two versions of the same story or event.

- the way characters of groups of people are portrayed in different texts.

- the points of view, accuracy, validity, and currency of "factual" accounts.

Investigating a text can encompass finding out, analyzing, and questioning who has written the text, when, for what purpose, and how the author and/or illustrator has chosen to convey the message. This might include investigating who owns a magazine, sponsors a website, or whether the author has credibility in the field. Investigating also includes identifying the devices authors use to persuade their readers.

Innovating is amending an existing text or transforming a text by re-creating it in another genre, form, mode, medium, or format. This allows students to disrupt the reading of a text as they deconstruct and reconstruct parts of a text to reveal different perspectives. Innovations include substituting alternative words for those with excessively positive or negative connotations. It can also incorporate removing parts of a text, or adding parts such as a sequel or a postscript.

Simulating involves assuming the role of another person or group of people to interpret a text from a different viewpoint. The point of view may differ on the basis of culture, time, geography, age, gender, and the like.

Reflecting can be accomplished by promoting discussion about the different identities students may assume when reading a text. For example, students may see themselves as a supporter or non-supporter of a cause, a supporter or non-supporter of a state or political party, and take on the role of a member of a cultural or religious group. Students can reflect on the divided loyalties that characters or historical figures experience, confronting situations from their different identities.

Reflecting also involves the consideration of personal values that underpin students' responses to texts. When responses to reading are elaborated and substantiated, students can reflect on how their thinking is driven by their experiences, beliefs, and attitudes.

GENERIC QUESTIONS FOR CRITICALLY ANALYZING TEXTS

Use the following lists to choose and frame questions that will stimulate discussion. When answering these questions, have students substantiate, justify, and extend their answers.

WHAT

- is the text about?
- type of text is this?
- do you think the text means?
- is left out of the text?
- is valued or devalued?
- are the author's qualifications to write on this topic?
- extravagant expressions are used (*only, never, absolutely, always, unconditionally, every, completely, positively*) to support a point of view?
- are the policies of the author's publishing company?

WHY

- was it written?
- was it illustrated in particular ways?
- were certain phrases and words used?

WHEN

- was the text written?
- does the author explicitly give his opinion or thesis?

WHO

- wrote the text?
- was the text written for?

HOW

- do your values affect your interpretation of the text?
- does the author create his/her position?
- could the text have been written differently?
- does this text compare with similar texts you have read?
- does the author prove his/her assertion, thesis, or opinion?

- are other points of view treated, if at all, by the author?
- are quotations used to reflect the point of view of the person being quoted, or has the person been quoted out of context?
- up-to-date are studies to support the author's thesis?
- does the author use emotional language?

FIVE HABITS OF MIND

Deborah Meier (2003), founding principal of the Mission Hill School in Boston, and her colleagues approach the teaching of all the academic disciplines as well as the "stuff of ordinary life" through their Five Habits of Mind. The Habits are their definition of a well-educated person. These Habits can serve as a very helpful framework for critical literacy:

1. **Evidence**   How do you know what is true and what is false? What is the evidence? How sure can you be? What makes it credible to you?

2. **Viewpoint**   What would this look like if you stepped into another person's shoes? If you look at it from a different direction? If you had a different history or expectation? Empathy, imagination, and flexible thinking are required.

3. **Connections/Cause and Effect**   Do you discern a pattern of thinking? Have you seen anything like this before? What are the possible consequences?

4. **Conjecture**   Could it have been otherwise? Supposing that? What if? Imagination and knowledge of alternative possibilities are required.

5. **Relevance**   Does this matter? To whom? Who cares about this?

The individual habits do not stand separately, and their use differs depending on the content area being analyzed or real life situations and controversies like stem cell research.

PATTERN GUIDES

Our chapters on text structure provide you with many examples of pattern guides. You can create, in a relatively simple format, guides to help your students ferret out the important information when writers organize their material in a thesis-proof or opinion-reason pattern. The guide can also include space where your students can rate the quality of the reasons or proof the authors use to substantiate their arguments. A rating scale of 1 to 4 can be used to rate the quality of the proof. A rubric might be helpful to students as they make their judgments:

1. Author quotes several reliable experts and studies to support argument.
2. Author quotes a few reliable experts and studies to support arguments.
3. Author provides some reasons, but no experts and studies.
4. Author provides limited reasons to support argument.

Rate the Author's Argument!

Thesis/Opinion

_____

Reasons/Proof   **Rating**

1._____

2._____

3._____

4._____

5._____

Author's Conclusions

GRAPHIC ORGANIZERS

You can also ask your students to create their own graphic organizers to visually represent an author's position on a topic. Below is an example.

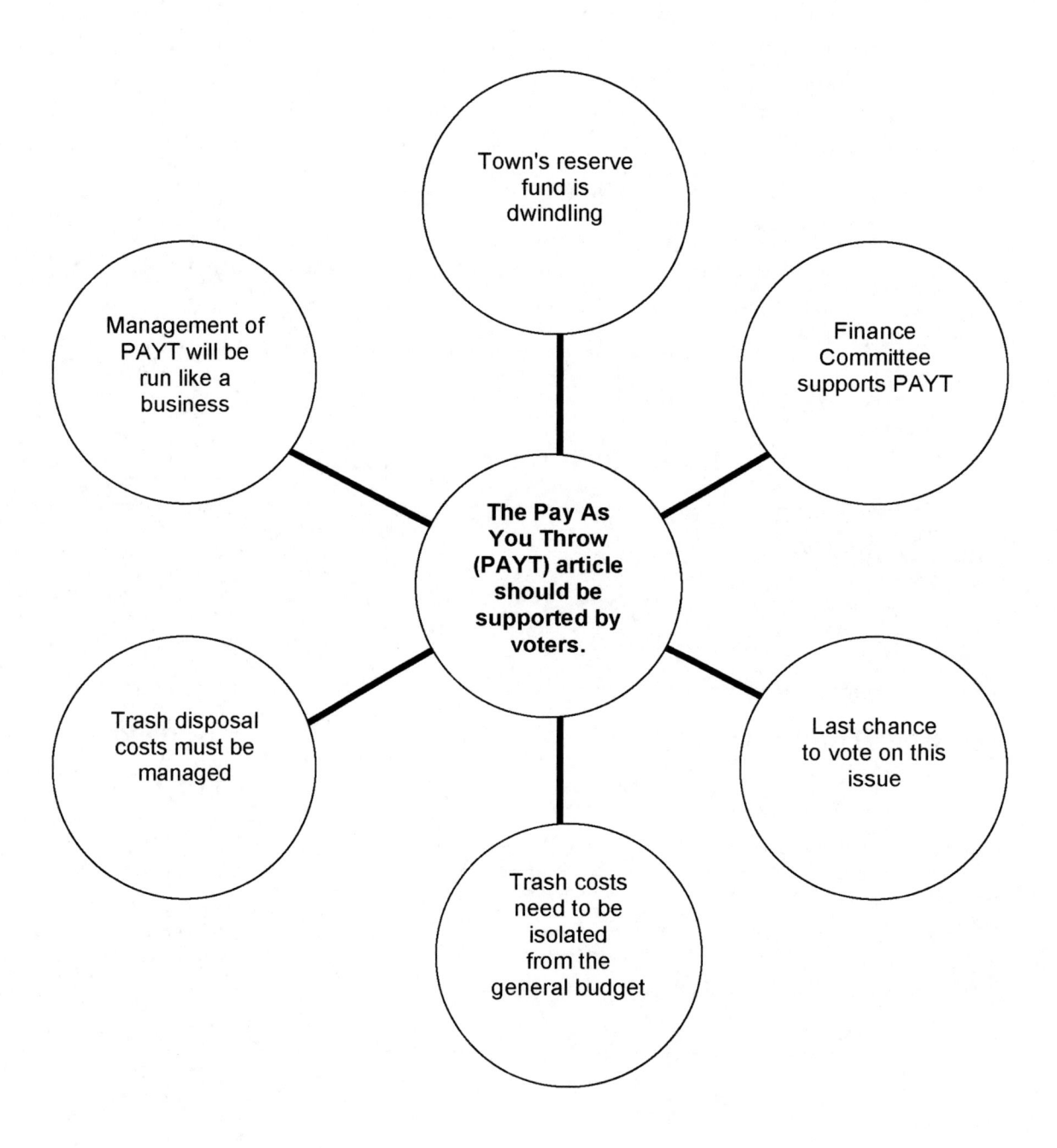

- **Center:** The Pay As You Throw (PAYT) article should be supported by voters.
  - Town's reserve fund is dwindling
  - Finance Committee supports PAYT
  - Last chance to vote on this issue
  - Trash costs need to be isolated from the general budget
  - Trash disposal costs must be managed
  - Management of PAYT will be run like a business

SPECIFIC ACTIVITIES

The specific activities for critically analyzing text are listed alphabetically and, as in Chapter 4, they tell **what** the activity is, **why** it benefits students, and **how** to use it.

CRITICIAL LENS

What is Critical Lens?

A Critical Lens is a student completed circular diagram that helps students to critically analyze what they read with respect to the point of view of the author(s). They analyze why the piece was written, what is valued and devalued in the piece, and how the piece could have been written differently.

Why Critical Lens Benefits Students

To succeed academically, students need to move beyond literally understanding main ideas and details to evaluating them (Zwiers, 2004). Having students use a Critical Lens is one way students can begin to make these evaluations. It helps them to discover that information presented by authors is rarely neutral in its orientation and that it inevitably reflects a particular view of the world. Effective readers are aware of the way that they can be positioned by authors to accept values and assumptions. Using a Critical Lens helps students to question aspects of the text with regard to bias, accuracy, and validity.

How to Use Critical Lens

1. Brainstorm with students some questions they might ask themselves as they critically reflect on what they read. This process should yield questions such as:

    - What is the viewpoint of the author?

    - What are the author's qualifications to write on the subject matter?

    - How convincing are the author's ideas?

    - What does the author do to support points of view presented?

- Why was the piece written?

2. Assign readings for the specific purpose of having students evaluate them. You may want to use readings students used in completing a Synthesis Journal.

3. Have students use the Critical Lens Quadrants (see below).

4. Discuss why using the Critical Lens Quadrants aids students' comprehension of text.

5. Have students use the Critical Lens Quadrants that follow

Critical Lens Chart

Text: _____   Author: _____

What is the Author's Point of View?	**What was this written?**
What is valued and devalued?	**How could this have been written differently?**

FACT/OPINION CONTINUUM

What is a Fact/Opinion Continuum?

A Fact/Opinion Continuum is a scale students use to make decisions regarding the extent to which a statement is a factual one vs. an opinionated one.

Why the Fact/Opinion Continuum Benefits Students

It is not always possible to categorize statements neatly into a fact category or an opinion category. Providing students with practice in placing statements on a continuum helps them to make decisions on whether a statement is *more* of a fact or *more* of an opinion.

How to use a Fact/Opinion Continuum

1. Prior to assigning a reading and a continuum to students, share with students some criteria they can use when trying to place statements on the continuum. Below is a recommended criterion.

Consider if the statement:

- comes from a believable authority.
- is substantiated by other evidence or other authorities.
- is reconcilable with what we know from personal experience.
- seems logical and reasonable.
- is generally endorsed by those you trust.
- is open to few or no exceptions.
- has been repeated often with little or no contradiction to this point.
- can be checked.

2. Assign a text related to your content area that includes both facts and opinions.

3. Copy the text and highlight the statements you want students to rate on the continuum.

4. Have students rate each of the statements on the continuum.

Below is a model Fact/Opinion continuum. Numbers 1 to 4 represents the extent to which the student rates the statement to be an opinion, and 5 to 8 represents the extent to which a student rates the statement to be a fact.

Fact/Opinion Continuum

OPINION　　　　　　　　　　　　FACT

1　　2　　3　　4　　5　　6　　7　　8

1. Have students share their ratings and ask them to justify their ratings.

2. Review with students the importance of differentiating facts from opinions.

FOUR CORNERS

What is Four Corners?

Four Corners is a small-group activity that involves four students reading a common text that lends itself to critical literacy. Students record their thoughts as they read and share them with others in the group. This activity is particularly good for critical literacy using the Intensify/Downplay *Schema*. Students read a common text, in this case advertisements and political statements are particularly good, with each student assigned one of the following tasks:

- Identify examples of Intensify own *good*
- Intensify other's *bad*
- Downplay own *bad*
- Downplay other's *good*

Why Four Corners Benefits Students

This activity provides students with an opportunity to discuss and share different points of view and differences in the way they critically analyze text.

How to Use Four Corners

1. Provide each group of four a large sheet of chart paper. This distribution gives each student a "corner" to record responses during individual reading.

2. Have students read the text individually.

3. Encourage students to periodically stop reading to record their responses in their corners.

4. Once they have read and responded, direct students to use the Four Corners chart as a stimulus for discussion about the text.

CHANGE THE POINT OF VIEW

What is Change the Point of View?

This activity has students identify the point of view of an author and consider how it would change if written from a different perspective.

Why Change the Point of View Benefits Students

This activity helps readers to discuss a text from more than one point of view, stimulating ideas about alternative interpretations.

How to Use Change the Point of View

1. Assign a text to students and ask them to determine from whose point of view it is written.

2. Have students identify sections of the text that led them to their conclusion.

3. Discuss whose point of view is *not* presented.

4. Arrange students in small groups and have them discuss a particular event from the reading from a different point of view. For example, male vs. female, Australian vs. American.

5. Ask students to create a reconstruction of the event from the point of view chosen.

6. Invite several groups to share their reconstructions, explaining aspects that need modification.

7. Review the value of considering text from a different point of view.

POSSIBLE PREDICTIONS

What is Possible Predictions?

This activity helps students to focus on how and why texts may be interpreted differently by different people. It also provides an opportunity for readers to discuss the decisions authors make and to speculate about possible alternatives.

Why Possible Predictions Benefits Students

By making comparisons between personal predictions and the text, and listening to justifications for these predictions, students understand that prior knowledge plays an important part in constructing meaning. The activity also provides an opportunity for readers to discuss the decisions authors make and to speculate about possible alternatives.

How to Use Possible Predictions

1. Have students read a text, stopping at a pre-selected point of view that is either a significant "crossroad" or offers a variety of options as to what might happen next.

2. Invite students to think about what they have read so far and to make a prediction of what actions, events and/or outcomes might happen next. Encourage them to supply reasons for their predictions.

3. Invite students to record their predictions on cards or sticky notes.

4. Collect predictions and group similar ones. As a whole class, discuss the reasons for the different predictions. Encourage students to refer to the text and/or to their prior knowledge when stating their reasons.

5. Have students continue reading, stopping at the next pre-select point where discussion and further predictions take place.

6. At appropriate points in the text have students compare their predictions with the author's actual content.

SPOT THE DEVICES

What is Spot the Devices?

In this activity, readers hunt for words, expressions, or images that have been used by the authors and/or illustrators in an attempt to position the reader.

Why Spot the Devices Benefits Students

This is a valuable activity because it gives students practice in identifying the devices authors and illustrators use to further a thesis or opinion.

How to Use Spot the Devices

1. Familiarize students with the devices listed in Chapter 7.
2. Select a text that has examples of the devices.
3. Have students highlight words, expressions, or images that have been chosen to position the reader.
4. Invite them to discuss the highlighted text pieces and devices used by the author and/or illustrator.
5. Encourage them to suggest alternative words, expressions, or images that would temper the impact, reverse its meaning, or change the audience appeal.

MULTIPLE TEXT APPROACH

What is the Multiple Text Approach?

This activity uses a number of texts that are linked by theme, topic, or issues so that readers can explore the way different authors have communicated their messages.

Why does the Multiple Text Approach Benefit Students?

This activity gives students the opportunity to compare different messages related to the same topic and to identify the devices used to position the reader.

How to use the Multiple Text Approach

1. Familiarize students with the devices discussed in Chapter 7.

2. Assign an appropriate reading from your content area.

3. Organize the class in groups of five or six.

4. Give each group a different text on the same topic, theme, or issue.

5. Have students read their allocated text, noting the key messages presented and the devices used by the authors.

6. Invite each group to report their findings to the rest of the class and use this information to make comparisons between the texts. Discuss how the devices used in each one influenced readers to take a particular point of view.

GREAT DEBATE

What is Great Debate?

Great Debate is an excellent culminating activity to be used at the completion of any unit of study or topic. It can be used in conjunction with the Multiple Text Approach as a way to compare texts and to consider different points of view.

Why Great Debate Benefits Students

This activity provides a framework for students to synthesize and critically respond to information from a range of sources or from a single text.

How to Use Great Debate

1. Create an open-ended statement directly related to the topic of study or to the texts used in your unit of study.

2. Organize students to work in groups identifying and listing information from the text that can provide affirmative or negative responses to the question or statement you have provided.

3. Invite students to then create personal position statements, including justifications, about the statement presented.

4. Provide time for students to share and compare personal position statements. The sharing of statements provides further assistance for students to draw conclusions and to consider different points of view.

CONCLUSION

The ability to critically analyze the written and spoken word is often cited by school districts as part of their mission statements. Yet, because high-stake tests permeate our middle and high schools, too little time is spent on critical literacy because it rarely is tested. This is because it is very difficult to construct and score tests of critical literacy.

Still, it behooves us to incorporate critical literacy in our classroom practices. The question raised by Weaver and Alvermann (2000) is worthy of your consideration: "A classroom within which children can learn to select valid criteria for evaluation of ideas, to take the risk of being wrong or misunderstood or out of the mainstream, and to value the contexts of others' lives – what better environment could we offer our (secondary) school children for the days they spend with us?"

CHAPTER 9

HOW DO I ASSIST MY STRUGGLING READERS?

At the beginning of this book we note that if you are a middle or a high school subject-matter teacher, you are not and should not be expected to also be a reading teacher. Rather, our goal is to offer you non-technical, easy-to-implement ways you can assist your students to access their textbooks so that their learning will increase in the subject(s) you teach. We trust we have achieved our goal.

Still, despite your best efforts in guiding your students' reading in your content areas, some of them will continue to struggle with the reading assignments you give them. So how do you help them? You could try teaching them yourself, if you have the time and inclination. Typically, such students are referred to the reading specialist and/or special education teacher(s).

If you do make referrals to them, we suggest you share your impressions of the students you are referring. One way to do this is by predicting the reading phase your students are in relative to the FIRST STEPS *Reading Map of Development* (Annandale et. al., 2004) that appears at the end of this book.

WHAT IS THE *READING MAP OF DEVELOPMENT*?

The *Reading Map of Development* (henceforth referred to as "The Reading Map") has six phases: Role Play, Experimental, Early,

Transitional, Proficient, and Accomplished. Chances are your struggling readers are performing in the experimental or early phase.

The typical reading behaviors of students are described for each phase. So you will want to read those behaviors carefully to determine which phase best matches what you have observed while teaching your struggling readers in your classroom. When you find the best match, you will have determined or at least predicted the current developmental reading phase for each of the students you are referring.

Now you have information about your students to share with the specialist(s). Your have the **phase name**. Below the phase name is a **global statement** that summarizes the general characteristics of the typical reader performing at that phase. The global statement also describes the student's beliefs about reading and the kinds of texts they generally read.

Below the global statement is a set of **key indicators**. These indicators describe very specific reading behaviors in four areas: use of text, contextual understanding, conventions, and processes and strategies. "Use of Text" relates to reading comprehension. "Contextual Understanding" relates to critical analysis. "Conventions" relates to vocabulary, features of text like its purpose and organization, and student understanding of semantic, syntactic and graphophonic cues. (These cues are discussed in Chapter 1). And finally "Processes and Strategies" relates to student ability to use and apply strategies in order to comprehend. In other words, how well does the student use the strategies we discuss in chapters three and four?

Below the key indicators is the **Major Teaching Emphases (MTEs)**. This guide provides what a teacher should emphasize in order to help the struggling reader advance to the next phase on the Reading Map. Together, these features help you to make informed, strategic decisions about how to support your students' reading development.

Here is a summary of what you will find in each phase on the Reading Map.

1. **The Phase Name.**

2. **The Global Statement:** Summarizes the general characteristics of the typical reading behaviors in that phase, the student's beliefs about reading and the types of texts with which students usually interact.

3. **The Indicators:** Statements of specific reading behaviors as they relate to the four sub-strands of reading: use of text, contextual understanding, conventions, and processes and strategies.

4. **The Major Teaching Emphases (MTEs):** Statements of suggested teaching priorities designed to support and challenge your students' current understanding of how to read.

HOW DO I USE THE READING MAP?

The purpose of the Reading Map is to link assessment, teaching, and learning in order to address the strengths and needs of your struggling students. As we note above, you need to read carefully the descriptions of the phases so you can **predict** where to place your struggling readers on the Reading Map. The descriptions are contained in the "Global Statements" and the "Indicators." This information, in concert with your professional judgment and the judgments of specialists in your school, allows you to make an "educated guess."

These predictions can then be used to begin selecting the Major Teaching Emphases (MTEs) from appropriate phases for your students. The MTEs will then guide the selection of teaching and learning experiences to improve your students' reading. Specialists should complete diagnostic tests and collect data on your struggling readers to confirm or amend your initial predictions.

Once the Major Teaching Emphases have been selected for your students, appropriate Teaching and Learning Experiences can be chosen. Many of the teaching activities highlighted in Chapter 3 can be used. If a specialist in your school has taken on the responsibility of working with your struggling readers, they are apt to have resource material to provide further support for the chosen MTEs. We also strongly recommend that they refer to the *First Steps Reading Resource Book*, which provides a wealth of teaching activities related to the MTEs at all phases. (This book is available from STEPS Professional Development, the publisher of this text and contains more information on the Reading Map.)

WHAT IS AN APPROPRIATE TEACHING MODEL FOR MY STRUGGLING READERS?

Whether you or a specialist on your staff takes on the responsibility for teaching reading strategies to your struggling readers, we suggest using a *scaffold approach.* (Note: in the following discussions, references to "you" mean the content area teacher *and/or* a specialist.) By this we mean that the instructor provides students with strategic leads, prompts and support by modeling, sharing, guiding and conferencing with the students. The aim is for these students to become proficient readers in all their content areas and to become independent readers. This *scaffold* approach is described in the next section.

A Scaffold Approach

A long-term goal for all your students, struggling readers in particular, is that they can select and use strategies flexibly and independently during any reading event. The use of a reading strategy rarely happens in isolation, but often involves the interaction of a number of strategies such as connecting, predicting and inferring all at once. It is important that students be introduced to a variety of strategies and to understand how they work together. However, it is appropriate to teach an individual reading strategy and have students practice it over time.

As you plan your sessions for teaching specific reading strategies, we suggest you use an approach suggested some time ago by Pearson and Gallagher (1983). It is called *The Gradual Release of Responsibility* Model (See Figure 9.1.)

The use of this framework helps you plan for the direct teaching of reading strategies and its application to the content areas.

The framework involves first working with students in a supportive or scaffold context where you have a high degree of control. At this point you are working with students in their "zone of proximal development" (Vygotsky, 1978). This activity means you are helping students use strategies to succeed when they could not succeed alone. As students become more skilled in using the strategy, you "gradually release" your control of the learning over to the students, who now are more independent and can take responsibility for their own learning.

How Do I Assist My Struggling Readers?

	Modeled Reading	**Joint Reading**	**Guided Reading**	**Independent Reading**
Role of the Teacher	The teacher demonstrates and explains the reading strategy being introduced. This is achieved by thinking aloud the mental processes used when using the strategy.	The teacher continues to demonstrate the use of the strategy with a range of texts inviting students to contribute ideas and information.	The teacher provides scaffolds for students to use the strategy. Teacher provides feedback.	The teacher offers support and help as necessary.
Role of the Student	The students participate by actively attending to the demonstrations.	Students contribute ideas and begin to practice the use of the strategy in whole-class situations.	Students work with help from the teacher and peers to practice the use of the strategy using a variety of texts.	The students work independently to apply the strategy in contexts across the curriculum.

Degree of Control (vertical axis on left)

Figure 9.1 Teaching Reading Strategies using a Scaffolded Approach

Figure 9.1 identifies four effective teaching practices to facilitate the gradual release of responsibility. These practices are modeling, sharing, guiding and applying.

Let's look at each of these practices that make up the *Scaffold Approach* to teaching reading strategies to struggling readers.

Modeled Reading

Modeling is the most significant step when teaching any reading strategy. It is essential to conduct regular, short teaching sessions that involve modeling and thinking aloud how an effective reader makes use of a particular strategy.

When you introduce a new reading strategy through modeling, you articulate what is happening inside your head. This acknowledgment makes the strategy evident to your struggling reader. Thinking aloud is a vital part of the modeling process. Plan for multiple demonstrations of how to use the strategy and why it is beneficial.

Modeling sessions need to be well planned and thought out. You need to think through what will be modeled and where in the text that might happen. Spontaneous modeling sessions can confuse your students.

As you plan, consider the following questions:

1. How do I use this strategy in my own reading?
2. How does this strategy help me become a more efficient reader?
3. What is important for students to know about this strategy?
4. Which texts are most appropriate to model this strategy?
5. Where in this text can I demonstrate the use of the strategy?
6. What language will best describe my thinking? encouragement

As you plan, we strongly suggest you use the *Strategy Demonstration Plan* we introduced to you in Chapter 2. Here it is again.

STRATEGY DEMONSTRATION PLAN

Strategy to be introduced:
_____

When and why it is useful

Key points to model

Text selected

Pages to be used

Language to describe my thinking

Now it is time to teach the strategy. We suggest you follow these steps:

- Introduce the name of the strategy.
- Explain what it means.
- Explain why it's useful and how efficient readers use it.
- Explain that modeling involves times when the text is being read and times when thinking is being described. Alert students that when you are looking up, you are thinking about what you are doing as you read and when you are looking down, you are reading the text aloud.
- Begin reading text to students, stopping at selected places to think aloud. Use precise, accurate language to describe the thinking while demonstrating the use of the selected strategy.
- Invite students to discuss their observations of the demonstration. Asking them to respond to the question *"What did you notice?"* helps.

Joint Reading Sessions

Joint Reading Sessions provide the opportunity for you and your students to think through texts together. It is also a time when you can continue to demonstrate the use of the selected strategy. The major difference between the Modeled Reading Sessions and Joint Reading Sessions is that your students are now invited to contribute ideas and information during these demonstrations.

It is beneficial to use a variety of informational and literary texts for continuing demonstrations during Joint Reading Sessions. As your students begin sharing their use of the strategy, you and your students can construct strategy charts. These charts, created over time, document how to make use of a particular strategy. An alternative to using the charts is to have students create a "Strategy Notebook" where the same type of information can be documented.

Planning and Conducting Joint Reading Sessions

Prior to conducting Joint Reading Sessions, consider these questions:

1. What aspects of the strategy do I need to further demonstrate?
2. Which texts should I use?
3. What language will I use?
4. How can I involve the students in the demonstration?

Here is how to conduct the Joint Reading Session.

- Re-introduce the strategy and invite students to explain it.

- Ask students to explain why it is useful and how effective readers use it.

- Begin reading text to students. Stop at selected places to think aloud and demonstrate the use of the strategy. Use precise, accurate language to describe your thinking.

- Invite students to make use of the strategy throughout the demonstration and to share their thinking.

- Provide constructive feedback and positive comments about students' use of the strategy.

- Summarize different ways that individuals made use of the strategy.

Guided Reading Sessions

Guided Reading Sessions provide your students with the opportunity to practice the strategies with a variety of texts. In Guided Reading Sessions you provide scaffolds as your students practice the strategy. It is important to provide ongoing feedback and support as students move toward taking responsibility for the use of the strategy.

Many activities, linked to particular strategies, are appropriate for Guided Reading Sessions. They are provided in chapter 4. The activities are designed to provide students with the opportunity to practice the strategy. Activities can be completed in oral or written form. Students can work in small groups or as pairs to share a text and complete the activity.

Consider the following questions as you plan your Guided Reading Sessions.

1. Which strategy do my students need to practice?

2. Have I provided multiple demonstrations?

3. Have I provided many opportunities for Joint Reading Sessions where students and I have discussed and used the strategy?

4. What texts do I want the students to use to practice the strategy?

5. What is the most effective way for the students to record their work?

6. How should I group students?

7. How will I provide feedback to the students during the activity?
8. How will I provide the opportunity for students to reflect on and to share their learning after completing the activity?

Here is how to conduct a Guided Reading Session.

- Select texts to be used for both demonstration and independent student use.
- Re-introduce and discuss the strategy.
- Model the use of the strategy using a selected practice activity.
- Provide time for students to work with partners or in small groups.
- Provide time for students to complete the activity.
- Provide constructive feedback and support.
- Encourage students to share completed activities.
- Encourage students to reflect on the use of the strategy.

Independent Reading Sessions

Now it is time for your students to work independently and to apply the strategy. You can continue to talk about and to demonstrate the application of any strategies when sharing texts from across the curriculum. Ongoing modeling of how and when strategies can be applied and how they assist readers to identify unknown words and comprehend text will encourage your students to use strategies beyond planned classroom activities.

In summary, as you teach the strategies, your role is to provide opportunities for students to:

- observe a variety of "strategy" demonstrations
- hear the thinking behind the use of each strategy
- contribute ideas about the use of strategies
- practice the use of strategies
- receive feedback and support on the use of strategies from the teacher and peers
- read and practice the use of the strategies independently and with a range of texts
- apply the strategies to their subject matter texts.

Research on Teaching Strategies

After Davis and her colleagues (2004) reviewed the research of teaching strategies, they compiled the following guidelines.

1. Focus on a few well-taught, well learned strategies.

2. Make reading instruction and strategies adaptable to the learner's level of expertise.

3. Create a learning environment that reinforces the usefulness of reading.

4. Give students opportunities to use their knowledge and discover new information.

5. Build opportunities for practice and feedback into the instruction, using the scaffold approach.

6. Help students understand how and when to use the strategies.

SUMMARY

We know that your classrooms probably contain some students who are having difficulty reading your textbook(s). These students need reading strategies directly taught to them. Someone must provide them with plenty of structure and support. If you are a content area teacher, you are not the one responsible for the direct, explicit teaching of reading strategies. Typically these readers are referred to a specialist. However if you, the content-area teacher, have the time and inclination, you can try to do this type of direct teaching yourself. Regardless of who takes on the responsibility, we offered a way to meet the needs of your struggling students.

First, we suggested that you become familiar with The Reading Map of Development and try to predict the particular phase at which your struggling students are performing. Then, we suggested using a *Scaffold Approach* to teach specific reading strategies. Finally, we walked you through the planning and teaching of modeled reading, joint reading and guided reading. The successful completion of these aspects of the *Scaffold Approach* will lead your students to a point where they will work independently applying the strategy to their content area textbooks.

CHAPTER 10   **HOW DO I EVALUATE TEXTBOOKS?**

The verdict is in: "guilty." A distinguished jury of scholars and associates from scholarly organizations has found textbook publishers "guilty" on the charge of producing inadequate textbooks for middle and high school students. According to Chester Finn (2004), "liberals, conservatives, independent scholars, and academic review panels alike share a surprising unanimity about the deplorable state of today's textbooks." Let's look at some of the reasons "jurors" rendered a guilty verdict.

On textbooks in general

"[The books] are sanitized to avoid offending anyone who might complain at textbook-adoption hearings in big states, they are poorly written, they are burdened with irrelevant and unedifying content, and they reach for the lowest common denominator. As a result of all this, they undermine learning instead of building and encouraging it" (Ravitch, 2004).

"The painful truth is that today's textbooks fail students – and are directly implicated in the poor showing that U.S. youngsters make in international achievement tests. It takes little imagination to see that student ignorance and disinterest are nurtured by boilerplate writing and chock-a-block, narrative-deprived textbooks. Not surprisingly, these glorified encyclopedias make poor nighttime-reading companions. Today's textbooks are incoherent, overloaded with splashy graphics and nifty exercises, devoid of controversy, whimsy, and wonderment – and about as exciting to read as the Federal Register" (Whitman, 2004).

On science textbooks

"[They] are written in an impersonal, seemingly objective tone, which ignores the readers' needs. The style seldom offers invitations to the reader to access or 'check-in' with his or her prior knowledge about the topic. Textbook authors write as if the reader has as much prior knowledge as they have; and, they assume that readers are familiar with the style and structure of expository writing" (Ulerick, 2000).

After reviewing 12 of the most popular middle school science textbooks used in the United States, AAAS, the American Association for the Advancement of Science, (2000) has concluded that the books are replete with errors and fail to have acceptable levels of accuracy.

After reviewing the 10 most popular high school biology textbooks, AAAS (2000) found a plethora of facts in them, but little explanation about the underlying scientific importance related to the facts. Dr. Jo Ellen Roseman, director of the study notes that "While most contain the relevant content on heredity and natural selection, for example, they don't help students to learn it or help teachers to teach it. On topics such as cells and matter and energy transformations, information is presented piecemeal. In addition, the textbooks fail to convey the coherence among key ideas in biology or their connections to ideas in physical science, mathematics, and technology."

On middle school physical science textbooks

"According to the criteria we set forth, none of the 12 most popular middle-school physical science texts was acceptable. The committee was particularly concerned with scientific accuracy, and with good reason. Mass and weight were often confused. The speed of light was first timed in 1926, according to one text. Isaac Newton's first law was often incorrectly stated. Many of the errors involved sloppy use of language. We regularly saw 'speed,' 'velocity,' and 'acceleration' confused" (Hubisz, 2003).

On world history textbooks

"[They] have abandoned narrative for a broken format of competing instructional activities. American Textbook Council reviewers repeatedly objected to anti-historical devices designed to spur the interest of students that reflect, in fact, editorial degradation of history.

For reviewers, the widespread lack of authorial voice, disappearance of narrative structure, and confusing randomness of subject were universal concerns" (Sewall, 2004).

On history books

"There seems to be something in the very nature of today's [history] textbooks that blunts the edges of events and strips from the narrative whatever is lively, adventurous, and exciting. In part, this happens because so much needs to be covered and compressed in the texts; in part, it is due to the lack of an authorial voice and the ability to express wonderment, humor, outrage, or elation" (Ravitch, 2004).

On literature anthologies

"Unlike the fusty classics, contemporary writing is particularly prized in literature anthologies, in large measure because the National Council of Teachers of English has adopted the position that literature must be relevant to high school students and "include" them. Captain Ahab, Heathcliffe, Hester Prynne, and Miss Haversham are all so old, from such a different era, that they are hard for teenagers to 'relate' to – or so the theory goes. This narrow, functional view of literature seems counterproductive, at least if the aim is to stimulate young people's imaginations and taste for reading" (Whitman, 2004).

On mathematics books

Although AAAS (2000) recognizes the availability of a few excellent middle-grade mathematics textbook series and cites some that do a satisfactory job on number and geometry skills and helping students to develop and use mathematical ideas, they also note serious weaknesses. One was that there are no popular commercial textbooks among the best rated. They found most of the 13 textbooks reviewed to be weak in their instructional support for students and teachers. They offer little development in sophistication of math ideas from grades 6 to 8, and they provide students with little or no purposes for learning math.

On the effects of the state textbook adoption system

"This dysfunctional system constrains the textbook options available to schools and teachers, constrains what authors and publishers can put in their books, constrains the normal functioning of supply and demand, and contributes to the educational mediocrity enshrined in so many of the books that survive this archaic and bizarre process" (Finn, 2004).

On the weight of textbooks

"These door-stoppers – which average 750-1100 pages in length – are so heavy that the Consumer Product Safety Commission has warned that an 'overweight backpack' phenomenon may be sending thousands of children to emergency rooms with back and neck injuries. In 2003, more than half-a-dozen states considered legislation to limit the size and weight of textbooks – surely a dubious moment in publishing history" (Whitman, 2004).

On textbook production

"[They] are hurriedly put together by teams of hack writers from 'development houses,' known in the el-hi world as 'chop shops.' Publishers are preoccupied with scrubbing textbooks of any reference that adoption panels in California and Texas might object to, while at the same time scrambling to add state-endorsed keywords, figures from history, and visual aids to ensure their spots on the adoption lists of those states. They have managed to turn out textbooks with more pages but less content. The explanation has to do with the powerful incentives that publishers face to produce quantity rather than quality" (Whitman, 2004).

Given the apparent deplorable state of textbooks, why do they still permeate classrooms across the country? Finn (2004) says one reason is that many teachers have a poor background in the subjects they are assigned to teach. For them, it is a huge challenge to put textbooks aside, plan their own courses, and collect their own instructional materials. In addition, says Finn, "They may also lack the time or wherewithal. And, especially when teaching core subjects for which students and schools will be held accountable, they are likely to be pressed by principal, department head, or district curriculum director to use 'approved' textbooks that are supposedly attuned to applicable standards and aligned with the tests by which progress will be gauged."

Even teachers who are knowledgeable in the subjects they teach apparently also rely heavily on textbooks. Whitman (2004) cites a survey of teachers across all grade levels showing that about 80 percent of them use textbooks and that nearly half of their classroom time is spent using them. According to Whitman, this co-sponsored survey by the National Education Association and the Association of American Publishers indicates that 80 to 90 percent of classroom and homework-time assignments are textbook-driven or textbook-centered.

In consequence, we have a situation whereby classrooms are full of poor textbooks which teachers use almost exclusively for instruction. The reality of this scenario makes what we have shared with you in this book all the more important. Confronted with poorly created, designed, and sometimes inaccurate textbooks, students need your help in navigating their way through them. Consistent reinforcement of how to go about reading the texts is essential. And at the beginning of each course, you can take your students on a textbook journey. We offer the following "Text Quest" to guide your journey.

THE TEXT QUEST

When you complete a Text Quest with your students, you take a "trip" with them through the different sections of the text. Such a familiarity will help your students cope with some of the "road hazards" associated with their textbooks.

- Begin your Text Quest with the book's **cover**. Review the title and, if there is one, the subtitle. Analyze it. Does the title indicate any particular slant or emphasis?

- Go to the **title page.** Check out the names of the authors. What are their affiliations? Are they qualified to write a text on this topic? If the text provides no information, "Google" them. Who published the book? Is it a reputable publisher?

- Turn to the **copyright** page. When was the book published? What is the significance of the date?

- Read the **preface.** What ideas about the book do the authors share with you? Why was the book written? Who is the intended audience? How is the book organized? Do the authors suggest how readers should approach the text? Do the authors reveal their philosophical position on their subject? If the book is a revision, what makes this newer edition different from the previous one? Do the authors acknowledge the help of others in the writing of the book? (Sometimes this is a separate section.) Who are they and of what significance is their contributions?

- Turn to the **table of contents.** How many chapters are in the book? How long are they? What do the chapter titles tell you about the book and the way it is organized? What are some of the topics covered?

- Sample a **chapter.** Read the **introduction** carefully. What is in it, and how is this information helpful? Are new terms highlighted and/or defined? Then jump to the **summary**. Why does reading the summary at this point make sense? Skim over the chapter by reading the **bold-faced headings**. What do they tell you? Are **visuals** like charts, graphs, photographs, sidebars, and drawings included? How will they add to your understanding of the chapter? Are there questions at the end of the chapter? Why is reading them before studying the chapter a help to you?

- Now jump to the end of the book where the **index** appears. How does the listing of names, topics, and events help you to determine their importance? Which ones do the authors pay most attention to? How will knowing this help you?

Alternatives to Textbooks

Despite their widespread use, many teachers do make use of other forms of print when they teach. These are usually available in the school library and include newspapers, reference books, journals, manuals, legal documents, novels, biographies, memoirs, and the like. Teachers have found many successful ways to integrate these resources with the main textbook.

We agree with Daniels and Zemelman's (2004) suggestions on "balancing" content area reading. Students, they say, should have some choice of what they read in class, and these readings should include material they *can* read. And some of these materials should be "quick reads" that can be located on the internet. The "classics" typically taught in English classes should be supplemented with contemporary young adult literature. And primary sources like speeches and diaries should be among the materials available for students to read.

If you are inclined to create a classroom library in your room, we recommend you review their suggestions on setting one up. They also provide a valuable annotated bibliography of "Great Books for Middle and High School" tied to various content areas.

Textbook Evaluation Form

While we support and encourage alternatives to using traditional textbooks, the reality is that you probably are using one in your classroom. We offer the following checklist to evaluate your current textbook. It can also be used should you have the opportunity to choose a new text.

TEXT BOOK EVALUATION FORM

NAME OF TEXT _____

AUTHORS _____

DATE OF PUBLICATION _____

Scoring Key: 4 = excellent   3 = good   2 = fair   1= poor

LAYOUT

Table of Contents is clear and logical   _____

Index and glossary are clear and functional   _____

Print is pleasing to the eye with adequate
 "white space"   _____

Overall layout is interesting and engaging   _____

AVERAGE LAYOUT SCORE _____

STRUCTURE

Chapter summaries do, if fact, summarize   _____

Chapters have a consistent,

Easy-to-follow structure   _____

Chapter headings are appropriate   _____

Sub-headings connect well to chapter headings   _____

Headings and subheadings are well placed   _____

Paragraphs are well written with clear main ideas   _____

AVERAGE STRUCTURE SCORE _____

GRAPHICS

Number of graphics is suitable for the chapter   _____

Captions clearly explain the graphic   _____

Graphics are used to further explain content of text   _____

Graphics are free of bias (gender, race, culture etc.)   _____

AVERAGE GRAPHICS SCORE _____

VOCABULARY

Key words are highlighted in the text   _____

Key words are defined   _____

Examples clearly illustrate the meaning of key words   _____

Examples are relevant to students' background   _____

AVERAGE VOCABULARY SCORE _____

SYNTAX

Sentence structure is easy to follow   _____

Unnecessary complex sentence structure is avoided   _____

Pronoun references are easy to follow   _____

AVERAGE SYNTAX SCORE _____

CONTENT

New content is related to students' background   _____

Content encourages higher-level thinking   _____

Stereotyping is avoided   _____

Content is accurate and up-to-date   _____

Content supports other resources used in your class   _____

Language is appropriate for your students   _____

References and bibliographies included and helpful   _____

Pagination is easy to follow   _____

AVERAGE CONTENT SCORE

END OF CHAPTER MATERIAL

Questions reflect important content   _____

Questions require students to think beyond the literal level   _____

Activities are relevant to the text   _____

AVERAGE END OF CHAPTER SCORE

PHYSICAL ASPECTS

Size and weight of text are appropriate for your students   _____

Font and style is age-appropriate   _____

Binding, pages, and cover are durable   _____

Text is appealing to students   _____

Page layout is uncluttered and balanced   _____

AVERAGE PHYSICAL ASPECTS SCORE

Average LAYOUT score _____

Average STRUCTURE score _____

Average GRAPHICS score _____

Average VOCABULARY score _____

Average SYNTAX score _____

Average CONTENT score _____

Average END OF CHAPTER score _____

Average PHYSICAL score _____

AVERAGE OVERALL SCORE FOR TEXT

NARRATIVE COMMENTS

SUMMARY

This chapter reviewed that a rather deplorable quality of textbooks are currently available to teachers and students. We presented a guide, "The Text Quest," to help your students explore their textbooks, regardless of their quality. We briefly reviewed some alternatives to textbooks and concluded with a Textbook Evaluation Form designed to help you to evaluate the current and future textbooks available for use in your classroom.

APPENDIX

Bibliography   B1

Adolescent Literacy: A Position Statement for the Commission on Adolescent Literacy of the International Reading Association

A Call to Action: What We Know About Adolescent Literacy and Ways to Support Teachers in Meeting Students' Needs. A Position/Action Statement from the National Council of Teachers of English Commission on Reading

The Fifteen Key Elements of Effective Adolescent Literacy Programs from *Reading Next – A Vision for Action and Research in Middle and High School Literacy: A Report to Carnegie Corporation of New York*

Overview of the FIRST STEPS® *Reading Map of Development*

BIBLIOGRAPHY

Aikman, C. (1997). Main idea: Writers have always used it. *Journal of Adolescent & Adult Literacy, 41,* 190-195.

American Association for the Advancement of Science (2000). Big Biology books fail to convey big ideas reports AAAS's Project 2061. On line at: www.project2061.org/about/press/pr00627.htm

American Association for the Advancement of Science. (2000). Heavy books light on learning: Not one middle grades science text rated satisfactory by AAAS Project 2061. Online at: www.project2061.org/newsinfo/research/textbook/articles/heavy2.htm

American Association for the Advancement of Science. (2000). Middle grades mathematics textbooks, a benchmark-based evaluation. Online at: www.project2061.org/tools/textbook/matheval/devault.htm

Anderson, V., & Hidi, S. (1988/89). Teaching students to summarize. *Educational Leadership, 46,* 26-28.

Anderson, R. C. Pearson, P. D. (1984). A schema-theoretic view of basic processes in reading. In P. D. Pearson (Ed.) *Handbook of reading research.* (pp. 255-291) Elmsford, NY: Longman.

Annandale, K., Bindon, R., Handley, K., Johnston, A., Lockett, L., & Lynch, P. (2004). *First Steps Literacy 2nd Edition Reading: Facilitator's notes.* Salem, MA: STEPS Professional Development.

Annandale, K., Bindon, R., Handley, K., Johnston, A., Lockett, L., & Lynch, P. (2004). *First Steps Literacy 2nd Edition Reading Map of Development.* Salem, MA: STEPS Professional Development.

Applebee, Arthur N. et. al. (Senior Consultants) *The Language of Literature* (2001). Evanston, Illinois: McDougal Littell.

Armbruster, B. L., & Anderson, T. H. (1984). Studying. In P. D. Pearson, R. Barr, L. Kamil and Mosental, P. B. (Eds.), *Handbook of Reading Research* (Vol. 1, pp. 657-679). New York: Longman.

Armento, B. J., Cordova, J. M., Klore, A., Nash, J. J., Ng, Salter, F. Wilson, C. L., Wilson, L. E. & Wixson, K. L. (1999) *A Message of Ancient Days*. Boston: Houghton Mifflin.

Aulls, M. (1981). Developmental considerations for reading research: Applications to good and poor reader research. In M. Kamil & Bowwick, M. (Eds.), *Directions in reading: Research and instruction*. Washington, DC: National Reading Conference, 1981. (pp. 83 – 91).

Baker, L. (1991). Metacognition, reading, and science education. In C. M. Santa & Alvermann, D. E. (Eds.) *Science learning: Processes and applications*. Newark, DE: International Reading Association (pp. 12-13).

Baker, L., & Brown, A. (1984). Cognition Monitoring in reading. In J. Flood (Ed.) *Understanding reading comprehension*. Newark, DE: International Reading Association (pp 21-44).

Baron, M. & Heidema, C. (2000). Teaching reading in mathematics. Aurora, CO: Mid-continent Research for Education and Learning.

Bartlett, Brendan J. (1978). *Top-level structure as an organizational strategy for recall of classroom text*. Ph.D dissertation, Arizona State College.

Baumann, J. F. (1986). The direct instruction of main idea comprehension ability. In J. F. Baumann (Ed.), *Teaching main idea comprehension* (pp. 133 – 178). Newark, DE: International Reading Association.

Beck, I.L, Omanson, R.C., & McKeown, M.G. (1982). An instructional redesign of reading lessons: Effects on comprehension. *Reading Research Quarterly*, 17 (4), 462-481.

Block, C. (1993). Strategy instruction in a student-centered classroom. *Elementary School Journal*, 94 (2), 137-153.

Block, C.C. (2001). Teaching students to comprehend non-fiction. *California Reader*, 21 (2), 1-12.

Block, C.C., Gambrell, L.B., & Pressley, M. (Eds.) (2002). *Improving comprehension instruction: rethinking research, theory and classroom practice*. San Francisco: John Wiley and Sons.

Bransford, J., Stein, B., Vye, N., Franks, J., Auble, P., Mezynski, K. and Perfetto, G. (1982). Differences in approaches to learning: An overview. *Journal of Experimental Psychology*, 111, 390-398.

Brown . J. & Cambourne, B. (1987). *Read and retell*. Portsmouth, N.H.: Boynton/Cook

Brown, A.L. & Day, J. D. (1983). Macrorules for summarizing texts: The development of expertise. *Journal of Verbal Learning and Verbal Behavior*, 22, 1-14.

Brown, R. (2002). Self-directed comprehension instruction for middle schoolers. In Block, C. C. & Pressley, M. *Comprehension instruction research-based best practices.* New York: The Guilford Press.

Burke, J., Klemp, R. & Schwartz, W. (2002). *Reader's Handbook.* Wilmington, MA: Great Source.

Byer, B. K. (2001). Developing a scope and sequence for thinking skills instruction. In A. L. Costa (Ed.) *Developing minds: A resource book for teaching thinking, 3rd ed.* Alexandria, VA: Association for Supervision and Curriculum Development.

Chambliss, M. J. (1995). Text cues and strategies successful readers use to construct the gist of lengthy written arguments. *Reading Research Quarterly, 30* (4), 778-807.

Ciardiello, A. V. (2002). Helping adolescents understand cause/effect text structure in social studies. *The Social Studies*, 93, 31-36.

Coolidge, O. (1977). *Greek Myths:* Boston: Houghton-Mifflin.

Cote, N. and Goldman, S. (1999). Building representations of informational text: Evidence from children's think-aloud protocols. In H.Van Oostendorp and S. Goldman (Eds.), *The construction of mental representations during reading* (pp. 169-193). Hillsdale, NJ: Erlbaum.

Daniels, H. & Zemelman S. (2004). Subjects matter. Portsmouth, NH: Heinemann.

Davis, D., Kushman, J., & Spraker, J. (2004). Improving adolescent reading: Findings from research. Portland, OR: Northwest Regional Educational Laboratory.

Dickson, S. H., Simmons, D. C. & Kameenui, E. J. U. (1995). Text Organization and its relation to reading comprehension: A synthesis of the research. Synthesis of research technical report #17, National Center to Improve the Tools of Educators, U.S. Office of Special Education.

Durrell, D. (1956). Improving reading instruction. New York: Harcourt, Brace & World.

Ehri, L.C. (1991). Development of the ability to read words. In R. Barr, Kamil, M.L. Mosenthal, P. B. & Pearson P. D. (Eds.), *Handbook of reading research* (Vol. 2, pp. 383 – 417). White Plains, NY: Longman.

Faber, J. E., Morris J. D., & Lieberman, M. G. (2000). The effects of note taking on ninth grade students' comprehension. *Reading Psychology,* 21: 257-270.

Finn, Jr., C. E. "Foreword" in Whitman, D. The mad, mad world of textbook adoption (2004). Washington, D.C. Thomas B. Fordham Institute.

Flavell, J. H. (1981). Cognitive monitoring. In P. Dickson (Ed.) *Communication skills.* Orlando, FL: Academic Press.

Flood, J. & Lapp, D. (2000). Reading comprehension instruction for at-risk students: research- based practices that can make a difference. In D. W. Moore., Alvermann, D. E., Hinchman, K. A. (Eds.). *Struggling adolescent readers,* Newark, Delaware: International Reading Association.

Gambrell, L.B., & Bales, R. J. (1986). Mental imagery and the comprehension-monitoring performance of fourth-and fifth-grade poor readers. *Reading Research Quarterly,* 21, 454 – 464.

Gambrell, L. B., & Javitz, P.B. (1993). Mental imagery, text illustrations, and children's story comprehension and recall. *Reading Research Quarterly,* 21, 264 – 273.

Gambrell, L. B. & Koskinen, P.S., (2002). Imagery: a strategy for enhancing comprehension. In Block, C. C. & Pressley, M. *Comprehension instruction research-based best practices.* New York: The Guilford Press.

Goldman, S. R. & Rakestraw, J. A. (2000). Structural aspects of constructing meaning from text. In Kamil, M. L., Mosenthal, P. B., Pearson, P.D., & Barr, R. (Eds.) *Handbook of Reading Research, Vol. II.* Mahwah, NJ: Earlbaum.

Graves, M., & Graves, B. (2003). *Scaffolding reading experiences: Designs for students' success* (2nd Ed.) Norwood, MA: Christopher-Gordon.

Greaney, K. T., & Tunmer, W. E. & Chapman, J. W. (1997). Effects of rime-based orthographic analogy training on the word recognition skills of children with reading disability. *Journal of Educational Psychology,* 89, 645 – 651.

Great Source Education Group (2002) *ScienceSaurus.* Wilmington, MA: Great Source.

Hakim, J. (2003). *All the people.* New York: Oxford University Press.

Herber, H. (1970) Teaching reading in the content areas. Englewood Cliffs, NJ: Prentice-Hall.

Heilman, A., W., Blair, T. R. & Rupley, W. H. (2002). *Principles and practices of teaching reading* (10th Ed.). Upper Saddle River, NJ: Merrill Prentice Hall.

Hergenhahn, B. R. & M. H. Olson (2004). *An Introduction to Learning Theories* (7th Ed.). Upper Sadler River, New Jersey: Prentice-Hall.

Holmes, B.C. (1983). The effect of prior knowledge on the question answering of good and poor readers. *Journal of Reading Behaviour*, 15 (4), 1 – 18.

Hubisz, J. (2003). "Middle-school texts don't make the grade" Online at: www.aip.org/pt/vol-56/iss-5/p50.html

Hyerle, D. (1996). *Visual tools for constructing knowledge.* Alexandria, VA: Association for Supervision and Curriculum Development.

Kaplan, A. & A. Petroni-McMullen, (1998). *Math on Call.* Wilmington, MA: Great Source.

Keene, E. O. & Zimmerman, S. (1997). *Mosaic of thought: Teaching comprehension in a reader's workshop.* Portsmouth, NH: Heinemann.

King, A. (1992). Comparison of self-questioning, summarizing and notetaking review as strategies for learning from lectures. *American Educational Research Journal*, 29, 303-323.

Langer, J. A. (1981). From theory to practice: A pre-reading plan. *Journal of Reading*, 25, 152-156.

Leslie, L., & Calhoon, A. (1995). Factors affecting children's reading of rimes: Reading ability, word frequency and rime neighbourhood size. *Journal of Educational Psychology*, 87, 576 – 586.

Marzano, R. J. (1988). *Dimensions of thinking: A framework for curriculum and instruction.* Alexandria, VA: Association for Supervision and Curriculum Development.

Meier, D. (2003). Mission hill school's habits of mind. Retrieved March 11, 2005, from www.missionhillschool.org

Meyer, B. J. F. (1975). *The organization of prose and its effects on memory.* Amsterdam: North Holland.

Meyer, B. J. F., Brandt, D. M. and G. J. Bluth. (1980). Use of top-level structure in text: key for reading comprehension of ninth-grade students. *Reading Research Quarterly.* 16: 72-103.

Marzano, R. J. Pickering, D. J. & Pollock, J. E. (2001). *Classroom instruction that works: research-based strategies for increasing student achievement.* Alexandria, Virginia: Association for Supervision and Curriculum Development.

McAlexander, P & Burrell, K. (1996). *Helping students "get it together" with synthesis journals.* Paper presented at the annual conference of the National Association of Developmental Education. Little Rock, Arkansas.

Morris, A. & Stuart-Dore, N. (1989). *Learning to learn from text.* North Ridge: NSW.

Morrison, E. S. (1997) *Science plus*. Austin, Texas: Holt, Rinehart and Winston.

National Reading Panel (NRP). (2000). *Teaching children to read: An evidence-based assessment of the scientific research literature on reading and its implications for reading instruction.* Washington, DC: National Institute of Child Health and Human Development and U.S. Department of Education.

Nokes, J. D. & Dole, J. A. (2004). Helping adolescent reader through explicit strategy instruction. In Jetton, T. L. & Dole, J. A. *Adolescent literacy research and practice*. New York: Guilford Press.

O'Donnell, A. M. & Dansereau, D. F. (1992). Scripted cooperation in student dyads: A method for analysing and enhancing academic learning and performance. In R. Hertz-Lazarowitz & N. Miller (eds.) *Interaction in cooperative groups: The theoretical anatomy of group learning* (pp. 12—141), New York: Cambridge University Press.

Ogle, D. (1986). The K-W-L: A teaching model that develops active reading of expository text. The Reading Teacher, 39, 564 – 576.

Paris, S. G., Lipson, M., & Wilson, K. K. (1994) Becoming a strategic reader. In R. B. Rudell, M. R. Rudell & H. Singer (Eds.) *Theoretical models and process of reading* (4th ed.) Newark, DE: International Reading Association.

Paris, S.G., Wasik, B.A. & Turner, J.C. (1991). The development of strategic readers. In R. Barr, M. L. Kamil, P. B. Mosenthal, & P. D. Pearson (Eds.), *Handbook of reading research* (Vol 2, pp. 609 – 640). New York: Longman.

Pearson, P. D. & Gallagher, M. C. (1983). The instruction of reading comprehension. *Contemporary Educational Psychology.* 8: 317-344.

Polka, G. (1957). How to solve it. Garden City, NY: Doubleday and Co., Inc.

Pressley, M. & Afflerbach, P. (1995). *Verbal protocols of reading: The nature of constructively responsive reading.* Hillsdale, NJ: Erlbaum.

Pressley, M. & Wharton-McDonald, R. (1997). Skilled comprehension and its development through instruction. *School Psychology Review,* 26 (3), 448 – 466.

Rank, H. (2005). *Persuasive Analysis.* Retrieved March 11, 2005 from: http://webserve.govst.edu/users/grank/index.html

Raphael, T. E. (1982) Teaching children question-answering strategies. The Reading Teacher, 36, 186-191.

Raphael, T. E. (1986) Teaching question-answer relationships, revisited. The Reading Teacher, 39, 516-522.

Ravitch, D. (2004). A consumer's guide to high school history textbooks. Washington, D.C. Thomas B. Fordham Institute.

Ravitch, D. (2004). "Introduction" in Whitman, D. The mad, mad world of textbook adoption. Washington, D.C. Thomas B. Fordham Institute.

Readence, J.E., Bean, T.W., & Baldwin, R.S. (1995). Content Area Reading: An integrated approach (5th ed.) Dubuque, IA: Kendall/Hunt.

Rhoder, C. (2002). Mindful reading: Strategy training that facilitates transfer. *Journal of Adolescent and Adult Literacy.* 46, 498-512.

Rosenshine, B., & Meister, C. (1994). Reciprocal teaching: A review of the research. *Review of Educational Research,* 64, 479 – 530.

Rosenshine, B., Meister, C. & Chapman, S. (1994). Reciprocal teaching: A review of the research. *Review of Educational Research,* 64, 479-530.

Ryder, R. J., & Graves, M. F. (1980). Secondary students' internalisation of letter-sound correspondences. *Journal of Educational Research,* 73, 172 – 178.

Sadowski, M. & Paivio, A. (1994). A dual coding view of imagery and verbal processes in reading comprehension. In R. B. Ruddell, M. R. Ruddell, & H. Singer (Eds.), *Theoretical models and processes of reading* (4th ed.) Newark, DE: International Reading Association.

Santeusanio, R. P. (1988). Study skills and strategies. Circle Pines, Minnesota: American Guidance Services, Inc.

Santeusanio, R. P. (1990). Content area reading and study. In Hedley, C., Houtz, J. & Baratta, A. (Eds.) *Cognition, Curriculum, and Literacy.* Norwood, NJ: Ablex.

Schoenbach, R., Greenleaf, C. L., Cziko, C. & Hurwitz, L. (2000). *Reading for understanding: A guide to improving reading in middle and high school classrooms.* San Francisco: Jossey-Bass.

Scruggs, T. E. and M. A. Mastropieri (1990). Current approaches to science education: Implications for mainstream education of students with disabilities. *Remedial and Special Education, 14,* 15-24.

Sewall, G. T. (2004) "World History Textbooks, a Review". New York: American Book Council.

Sinatra, G.M., Brown, K. J., & Reynolds, R. E. (2002). Implications of cognitive resource allocation for comprehension strategies instruction. In Block, C. C. & Pressley, M. *Comprehension instruction research-based best practices*. New York: The Guilford Press.

Scruggs, T. E. and M. A. Mastropieri (1990). Current approaches to science education: Implications for mainstream education of students with disabilities. *Remedial and Special Education, 14,* 15-24.

Slater, W. H., Graves, M. F. & G. L. Piche (1985). Effects of structural organizers on ninth grade students' comprehension and recall of four patterns of expository text. *Reading Research Quarterly, 20,* 189-202.

Slater, W. H. (2004). Teaching English from a literacy perspective. In Jetton, T. L. & Dole, J. A. (Eds.). *Adolescent literacy research and practice*. New York: The Guilford Press.

Slater, W. H., & Horstman, F. R. (2002). Teaching reading and writing to struggling middle school and high school students: The case for reciprocal teaching. *Preventing School Failure,* 46(4), 163-166.

Stahl, S. A. & Fairbanks, M. M. (1986). The effects of vocabulary instruction: A model-based meta-analysis. *Review of Educational Research,* 56 (1), 72-110.

Taylor, B. M. (1980). Children's memory for expository text after reading. *Reading Research Quarterly* 15, 399-411.

Taylor B. M. & Beach, R. W. (1984). The effects of text structure instruction on middle-grade students' comprehension and production of expository prose. *Reading Research Quarterly, 19,* 134-136.

Tierney, R. J., & Cunningham, J. W. (1984). Research on teaching reading comprehension. In P. D. Pearson (Ed.), *Handbook of reading research* (pp. 609 – 654). White Plains, NY: Longman.

Trabasso, T. & Bouchard E. (2002). Teaching readers how to comprehend text strategically. In Block, C. C. & Pressley, M. *Comprehension instruction research-based best practices*. New York: The Guilford Press.

Ulerick, S. L. (2000). "Using Textbooks for Meaningful Learning in Science", one of a series of papers in the *Research Matter to the Science Teacher* series. Columbus, MO: The National Association for Research in Teaching.

Vacca, R. T. & J. L. Vacca (2004). *Content Area Reading* (8th edition). Boston: Allyn & Bacon.

Van den Broek, P. & Kremer, K.E. (2000). The mind in action: What it means to comprehend during reading. In B. M. Taylor, M. F. Graves, & P van den Broek (Eds.), *Reading for meaning: Fostering comprehension in the middle grades* (pp. 1 – 31). New York: Teachers College Press.

Vygotsky, L. S. (1978). *Mind in society.* Cambridge, MA: MIT Press.

Weaver, D. and D. Alvermann (2000). Critical thinking and discussion. In Wood, K. D. and T. S. Dickinson (Eds.), *Promoting Literacy in Grades 4-9,* Boston.

Wenglinsky, H. (2001). *Teacher classroom practices and student performance: How schools can make a difference.* Retrieved June 18, 2004, from http://www.ncrel.org/gap/library/text/teachersmake.htm

Westwood, P. (1995). Teachers' beliefs and expectations concerning students with learning difficulties, *Australian Journal of Remedial Education,* 27 (2) pp 19 – 21.

Whitman, D. (2004). The mad, mad world of textbook adoption Washington, D.C. Thomas B. Fordham Institute.

Winograd, P. N., & Bridge, C. A. (1986). The comprehension of important information in written prose. In J.F. Baumann (Ed.), *Teaching main idea comprehension* (pp. 18 – 48). Newark, DE: International Reading Association.

Wittrock, M. C. (1974). Learning as a generative process. *Educational Psychologist.* 11: 87-95.

Wittrock, M. C. (1990). Generating processes of comprehension. *Educational Psychologist* 24 (4), 345-376.

Zwiers, J. (2004). *Developing academic thinking skills in grades 6-12.* Newark, DE: International Reading Association.

David W. Moore
Thomas W. Bean
Deanna Birdyshaw
James A. Rycik

Adolescent literacy: A position statement

for the Commission on Adolescent Literacy of the International Reading Association

Adolescents deserve more

Carol Minnick Santa, President
International Reading Association

I want to thank members of the International Reading Association's Commission on Adolescent Literacy for the development of this position paper, which was approved by the Association's Board of Directors in May 1999. Ironically, the Board approved this statement in the aftermath of the shattering violence at Columbine High School in Colorado—a vivid and horrible testimony to the ever-deepening crises in adolescent literacy. If only these young men had been touched by a book or a teacher, or had felt more connected with their school, perhaps none of this would have happened. As teachers and parents, we have to do things differently.

This position statement is a start. We must begin with a clear message about what adolescents deserve. Adolescents are being shortchanged. No one is giving adolescent literacy much press. It is certainly not a hot topic in educational policy or a priority in schools. In the United States, most Title I budgets are allocated for early intervention—little is left over for the struggling adolescent reader. Even if all children do learn to read by Grade 3, the literacy needs of the adolescent reader are far different from those of primary-grade children. Many people don't recognize reading development as a continuum. Moreover, schools have worked hard to reduce class size for children in grades K–3, while at the same time we have watched a steady increase in class size as children progress through school. Reading specialists have become history in too many middle and high schools.

I speak for the Association's Board of Directors as we unanimously endorse the powerful messages in this document. We hope it will provide you with a tool for becoming a stronger advocate for the adolescents in your neighborhood school, your community, your state or province, and your country.

A day in the literacy lives of Nick and Kristy Araujo

"Hey, Nick, wake up!" Nick Araujo felt his friend Adam's punch in the arm, jolting him out of his daydream in fourth-period English at Polytechnic High. Mr. Potter, his teacher, had assigned Charles Dickens's *A Tale of Two Cities*, a really ancient book that Nick's dad said he had to read years ago. Today they were supposed to take an essay test on the book. They never talked about what they read, and, anyway, Nick was preoccupied with thoughts about the new virtual bass fishing game he'd read about in his *North American Fisherman* magazine.

Fortunately, the video he'd watched of *A Tale of Two Cities* got him through the essay test ordeal, then it was on to psychology class. Mr. Jackson was great. He knew how to make any topic interesting, and his class seemed more like a television talk show than school. Nick struggled with reading, but he loved watching movies, and he was able to use his vast knowledge of cinema in this class. Yesterday they had talked about a film of people meeting on the Internet, and today's discussion was about why some people create false identities in Internet chat rooms.

As the final bell rang, Nick headed out to his small truck in the parking lot. He was off to the gym to lift some weights. At least he didn't have to work today; there was lots of time for the assignment from his history class. That teacher just dumped work on them without any idea of what she wanted. Nick was supposed to write a five-paragraph essay about a famous person. That was all the instruction Mrs. Nathan provided. Maybe his hotshot sister, Kristy, could help.

"No, Nick," Kristy said, when he got home. "I have to practice my serves for volleyball, and I have to study for a science test. I hate science. All we do is read the book, and then he gives us a test. I don't have time to do your homework, too!"

"There goes Kristy again," Nick thought. It was hard to be the brother of a straight-A seventh grader who was a star athlete too. Nick plunked down on the couch and turned on the *Legend of Zelda* video game. Off into the world of Hyrule. "Hey, Kristy, I need to know what *dispel* means for this game."

"I don't know. Figure it out or go look it up in the dictionary yourself!"

Nick looked it up, then passed into the Zora domain.

"Mom, what famous person should I do my essay on?"

"You like hunting, Nick. How about Daniel Boone or Davy Crockett? They're famous people who hunted."

Nick headed into the family room, where the computer was, to search the Internet for some information on famous hunters. Of course Kristy was hogging the computer again. She was probably in a chat room with her friends or writing her secret diary. Or she was playing that geography game again. "Kristy's idea of fun looks like work to me," Nick thought.

"Hey, Kristy, I thought you had to study. It's my turn."

Kristy bounced out of the room, grabbing a copy of *Chicken Soup for the Teenage Soul*. Time for a quick story before tackling her boring science assignment.

She read the section of her textbook on mitosis and meiosis and dutifully outlined it. Mr. Taylor didn't care if they understood it; they only needed to memorize key parts for the test. She finished quickly, then went outside and hit volleyballs against a wall.

Meanwhile, Nick printed out a biography on Davy Crockett and headed into the kitchen to help his mom with a quick microwave dinner.

After dinner, Kristy went back on the computer to begin her assignment for language arts class.

She loved to search the Internet. They had read Mildred D. Taylor's *Roll of Thunder, Hear My Cry*, and her assignment was to research events during the Great Depression that might have affected Cassie's life. There was sure to be a lively discussion tomorrow in class, and Kristy wanted to be prepared. She enjoyed Mrs. Mangrum's class.

Nick disappeared upstairs to compose his essay while talking to his girlfriend, Jennifer, on the phone. Kristy finished her work for language arts class and settled down to watch her favorite series on television. Then it was time for bed and a few minutes of reading *Teen People* magazine.

Nick fell asleep, sprawled on his bed with his nearly completed essay scattered on his bedroom floor.

This fictional account of Nick and Kristy's day illustrates how adolescents read and write amid conditions they and their families, friends, schools, and society establish. To be sure, Kristy and Nick's day only hints at the actual literacy practices of the more than 20,000,000 students currently enrolled in U.S. middle and high schools. Adolescents use print—and learn how to use print—in countless ways.

Despite the prevalence of literacy in adolescents' lives, educational policies, school curricula, and the public currently are neglecting it. For instance, state and federal funding for middle and high school reading programs in the United States has decreased. Fewer and fewer schools are able to hire reading specialists who work with individual students and help teachers of all subjects be more effective teachers of reading. The limited number of reading education courses required for preservice middle and high school teachers often does not sufficiently prepare them to respond to the escalating needs of adolescent learners.

This position statement developed by the International Reading Association Commission on Adolescent Literacy (CAL) calls for the literacy of adolescents to be addressed directly and effectively. We begin by responding to questions that bring into the open some common misconceptions.

Questions and answers about adolescent literacy

Shouldn't adolescents already be literate?

As the story of Nick and Kristy's day indicates, adolescents generally have learned a great deal about reading and writing, but they have not learned all they need. For instance, the 1998 Reading Report Card produced by the National Assessment of Educational Progress (NAEP) showed that a majority of U.S. adolescents (approximately 60%) can comprehend specific factual information. Yet few have gone beyond the basics to advanced reading and writing. Fewer than 5% of the adolescents NAEP assessed could extend or elaborate the meanings of the materials they read. The NAEP writing assessments have indicated that few adolescents could write effective pieces with sufficient details to support main points.

Adolescents entering the adult world in the 21st century will read and write more than at any other time in human history. They will need advanced levels of literacy to perform their jobs, run their households, act as citizens, and conduct their personal lives. They will need literacy to cope with the flood of information they will find everywhere they turn. They will need literacy to feed their imaginations so they can create the world of the future. In a complex and sometimes even dangerous world, their ability to read will be crucial. Continual instruction beyond the early grades is needed.

Couldn't the problem be solved by preventing reading difficulties early on?

Reading success in the early grades certainly pays off later, but early achievement is not the end of the story. Just as children pass through stages of turning over, sitting up, crawling, walking, and running as they develop control of their bodies, there are developmental stages of reading and writing. During the preschool and primary school years, children learn how written language can be used for purposes such as telling stories and recording facts, how print is arranged on a page, and how letters and sounds combine to form words. These are major accomplishments, but they are only the first steps of growth into full literacy.

When all goes well, upper grade youth increase their reading fluency and adjust their reading speed according to their reasons for reading. They discern the characteristics of different types of fiction and nonfiction materials. They refine their tastes in reading and their responses to literature. Middle and high school students build on the literacy strategies they learned in the early grades to make sense of abstract, complex subjects far removed from their personal experiences. For Nick, Kristy, and other adolescents, the microscopic realm explained in a science book and the French Revolution depicted in *A Tale of Two Cities* can be strange worlds described in alien words.

The need to guide adolescents to advanced stages of literacy is not the result of any teaching or learning failure in the preschool or primary years; it is a necessary part of normal reading development. Guidance is needed so that reading and writing develop along with adolescents' ever increasing oral language, thinking ability, and knowledge of the world.

Even with the best instruction early on, differences magnify as students develop from year to year. Today's adolescents enter school speaking many different languages and coming from many different backgrounds and experiences, so their academic progress differs substantially. Some teens need special instruction to comprehend basic ideas in print. Others need extensive opportunities with comfortable materials so they learn to read smoothly and easily. And almost all students need to be supported as they learn unfamiliar vocabulary, manage new reading and writing styles, extend positive attitudes toward literacy, and independently apply complex learning strategies to print.

Why isn't appropriate literacy instruction already being provided to adolescents?

Exemplary programs of adolescent literacy instruction certainly exist, but they are the exception because upper grade goals often compete with reading development. Elementary schools traditionally emphasize mathematics and literacy instruction, but middle and secondary schools generally shift attention to other matters.

Middle school programs often emphasize an expanded range of student needs: physical, emotional, and social, as well as academic. Although literacy growth might be recognized as important, many schools do not include reading instruction in the curriculum for all students. Language arts teachers often have sole responsibility for guiding students' reading growth while still being held accountable for covering a literature program, teaching grammar, offering personal advisory programs, and so on.

High school teachers often feel a great responsibility to impart knowledge about subjects such as science or history in which they are expert. This focus on subject matter is supported by the typical organization of high schools with the faculty assigned to separate departments and the day divided among separate subjects. Many teachers come to believe that teaching students how to effectively read and write is not their responsibility. Without intending to do so, they might send subtle messages that adolescents' continued growth in reading and writing is incidental.

So is there a solution?

There are no easy answers or quick fixes. Adolescents deserve nothing less than a comprehensive effort to support their continued development as readers and writers. A productive first step is for all involved in the lives of adolescents to commit themselves to definite programs of literacy growth. The CAL recommends the following principles as touchstones for such programs.

What adolescents deserve: Principles for supporting adolescents' literacy growth

1. Adolescents deserve access to a wide variety of reading material that they can and want to read.

The account of Kristy and Nick's day shows adolescents reading inside- and outside-of-school print such as textbooks, paperbacks, magazines, and Web sites. Yet national assessments provoke concern about the amount of such reading among adolescents. For instance, the 1996 NAEP findings indicate that about one quarter of the tested adolescents reported daily reading of five or fewer pages in school and for homework. As students grow older, the amount of time they read for fun declines. About one half of the tested 9-year-old students reported reading for fun on a daily basis, whereas only about one quarter of the 17-year-old students reported doing so. Literacy research and professional judgment support at least four reasons for providing adolescents access to inside- and outside-of-school reading materials they can and want to read.

- *Time spent reading is related to reading success.* If students devote some time every day reading connected text, their word knowledge, fluency, and comprehension tend to increase. Reading continuously for a brief part of each day is a small investment for a large return.
- *Time spent reading is associated with attitudes toward additional reading.* Students who habitually read in the present tend to seek out new materials in the future. These students are on the way to lifelong reading.
- *Time spent reading is tied to knowledge of the world.* Combining materials such as textbooks, library books, paperbacks, magazines, and Web sites provides full accounts of phenomena, new vocabulary, and up-to-date information. These materials permit readers to expand and strengthen their grasp of the world.
- *Reading is a worthwhile life experience.* Readers can find comfort and delight in print. Vicariously stepping into text worlds can nourish teens' emotions and psyches as well as their intellects.

Providing opportunities to achieve the outcomes just listed is accomplished through a network of educators, librarians, parents, community members, peers, policy makers, technology providers, and publishers. These groups affect middle and high school students' access to wide reading by shaping the following elements:

- *Time.* An often overlooked—yet essential—component of access to reading is the time available for it. Adolescents deserve specific opportunities to schedule reading into their days.
- *Choice.* Choosing their own reading materials is important to adolescents who are seeking independence. All adolescents, and especially those who struggle with reading, deserve opportunities to select age-appropriate materials they can manage and topics and genres they prefer. Adolescents deserve classroom, school, and public libraries that offer reading materials tied to popular television and movie productions; magazines about specific interests such as sports, music, or cultural backgrounds; and books by favorite authors. They deserve book clubs, class sets of paperbacks, and personal subscriptions to magazines.
- *Support.* Time and choice mean little if there is no support. Support includes actions such as bringing books to the classroom, arousing interest in them, orally reading selections, and fostering student-to-student and student-to-adult conversations about what is read. Adolescents deserve these supports so they will identify themselves as readers and take advantage of the times and choices that are offered.

2. Adolescents deserve instruction that builds both the skill and desire to read increasingly complex materials.

Kristy and Nick Araujo tackled their assignments with a few basic reading and writing strategies. Outlining text passages and looking up an unfamiliar word like *dispel* in the dictionary are some of strategies Nick and Kristy used in their studies. However, these teens will need to expand their strategies to handle increasingly complex material now and in the future. In addition, Nick's history as a struggling reader indicates he will need extra help if he is to grasp future concepts successfully. Adolescents need well-developed repertoires of reading comprehension and study strategies such as the following:

- questioning themselves about what they read;
- synthesizing information from various sources;
- identifying, understanding, and remembering key vocabulary;
- recognizing how a text is organized and using that organization as a tool for learning;
- organizing information in notes;
- interpreting diverse symbol systems in subjects such as biology and algebra;
- searching the Internet for information;
- judging their own understanding; and
- evaluating authors' ideas and perspectives.

Many teaching practices are available for supporting adolescent learners as they apply strategies to complex texts. For example, teachers who introduce some of the technical vocabulary students will encounter in a chapter help reduce comprehension problems, and students help themselves by independently previewing passages and discerning the meanings of unfamiliar words. Study-guide questions and statements that prompt students from literal understandings to higher order ones also foster comprehension. When teachers inform students while the guides are being phased out, adolescents can appropriate for themselves the thinking strategies the guides stimulated.

Middle and secondary schools where reading specialists work with content area teachers in the core areas of science, mathematics, English, and social studies show great promise. For example, a reading specialist's work with a social studies teacher to map ideas during a unit on the Aztec, Inca, and Mayan cultures can become the basis for teaching students to map ideas as an independent study strategy. The CAL recommends that content area teachers and reading specialists work together to effectively support adolescents' development of advanced reading strategies.

Developing students' advanced reading skills is insufficient if adolescents choose not to read. Unfortunately, students' attitudes toward reading tend to decline as they advance into the middle grades, with a particularly disturbing impact on struggling readers like Nick. Attitudes toward reading contribute to reading achievement.

Caring teachers who act on adolescents' interests and who design meaningful inquiry projects address motivational needs. For example, Kristy was excited about independently researching events of the Great Depression that affected Cassie's life in *Roll of Thunder, Hear My Cry*. Based on her experiences in this class, Kristy knew she would have an attentive audience for discussing her research and a considerate teacher supporting and evaluating her demonstration of knowledge. Mrs. Mangrum regularly fostered discussions of multicultural literature, and she expressed sincere interest in her students' wide ranging cultural and ethnic differences, learning styles, and needs for respect and security. In addition to having the whole class read and talk about one particular novel, Mrs. Mangrum provided students access to various books for self-selected reading on their own. She gleaned books from her own classroom collection, students' recommendations, and a close working relationship with her school librarian. Adolescents deserve classrooms like Mrs. Mangrum's that knowingly promote the desire to read.

3. Adolescents deserve assessment that shows them their strengths as well as their needs and that guides their teachers to design instruction that will best help them grow as readers.

National-level mandates on education such as Goals 2000 and the reauthorization of the Elementary and Secondary Education Act in the United States require that states develop standards for instruction and assess student achievement of the standards. In some states these measures are being used to determine the type of diploma students receive and whether or not students will even graduate. Although state assessments are useful in monitoring the achievement of standards, they rarely indicate specific teaching-learning experiences that foster literacy development.

Adolescents deserve classroom assessments that bridge the gap between what they know and are able to do and relevant curriculum standards; they deserve assessments that map a path toward continued literacy growth. For instance, when Nick began writing his essay about a famous person, he did not seem clear about the expected standards. He probably would have benefited from understanding how writing this particular essay connected with the world beyond the classroom. He could have used lessons on how to accomplish expectations. He might have benefited from examining papers that reflected the expected standards. And he could have profited from a rubric or scoring guide that clearly articulated the standards for evaluation.

Conferring with his teacher and classmates about how his efforts fit curriculum standards also might have promoted Nick's writing. During such conferences he would have opportunities to assess his own writing, set specific goals, and decide on strategies for achieving his goals. Further, Nick would benefit from maintaining a record of his efforts in something like a portfolio to help gauge his reading and writing growth and plan appropriate actions. Emphasizing relevance and self-improvement in classroom assessment encourages adolescents to invest themselves in learning. It helps them understand how to control the rate and quality of their own literacy growth.

Effective assessments are crucial for students who come from environments that differ from Kristy and Nick's. Using tests simply to determine which students will graduate or which type of diploma students will receive especially disadvantages adolescents from homes where English is not the first language or where poverty endures. It wrongs those most in need of enriched educational opportunities.

In sum, the CAL believes that adolescents deserve classroom assessments that
- are regular extensions of instruction;
- provide usable feedback based on clear, attainable, and worthwhile standards;
- exemplify quality performances illustrating the standards; and
- position students as partners with teachers evaluating progress and setting goals.

4. Adolescents deserve expert teachers who model and provide explicit instruction in reading comprehension and study strategies across the curriculum.

Like masters with apprentices, expert teachers immerse students in a discipline and teach them how to control it. Expert teachers engage students with a novel such as *Roll of Thunder, Hear My Cry* in Kristy's language arts class or a topic such as the presentation of self in Nick's psychology class. Then they teach reading, writing, and thinking strategies that enable students to explore and learn about subject matter. Reading and subject matter teachers often collaborate to provide such instruction.

If Kristy's teacher, Mrs. Mangrum, were teaching self-questioning as a strategy, she might first take a chapter of *Roll of Thunder, Hear My Cry* and model queries such as "What became clear to me?" and "I wonder why Cassie didn't complain to her teacher about the school bus driver running them off the road." Mrs. Mangrum would explain how she arrived at answers to her questions, thinking through the process aloud. She would explicitly demonstrate how to ask and answer productive questions during this stage of instruction.

Next Mrs. Mangrum and Kristy's class might produce questions and answers collectively, again thinking aloud. At first they might stay with the chapter Mrs. Mangrum began with, or they might move to another. Together the students and teacher would explain and comment on what they were doing. Additionally, Mrs. Mangrum might provide written guides for students to question themselves, exploring and experimenting with the strategy on their own. She also might design small-group assignments that encourage students to reflect on self-questioning, sharing how they used it and difficulties they overcame.

Eventually Mrs. Mangrum would expect Kristy and her classmates to apply self-questioning on their own. She would remind students to question themselves while reading other novels and passages later in the year. Throughout this cycle of instruction, she would have students assess how well they were accomplishing the strategy.

Research on expert teachers has produced an image of decision makers effectively orchestrating classroom life. Expert teachers help students get to the next level of strategy development by addressing meaningful topics, making visible certain strategies, then gradually releasing responsibility for the strategies to the learners. Adolescents deserve such instruction in all their classes.

5. Adolescents deserve reading specialists who assist individual students having difficulty learning how to read.

In the early 1900s standardized tests in the United States revealed large numbers of adolescents reading well below expectations. This finding sparked many educators and members of the public to develop programs for adolescents that included remedial instruction in reading classes and modified instruction in regular subject-matter classes. Federally funded programs to compensate for the effects of poverty on achievement later were instituted for reading, writing, and mathematics instruction.

National-level data continue highlighting the presence of adolescents like Nick with reading needs. For instance, 13% of fall 1989 first-year higher education students in the United States were enrolled in courses devoted specifically to remedial reading. The high school dropout rate, which is related to literacy difficulties, was 11% in 1993. Race, ethnicity, and economic status continue to be strongly associated with reading achievement. Although the number of secondary schools that assist adolescents who struggle with reading is declining, most schools still provide programs. These include widely varying provisions such as special education classes, after-school tutoring, and content reading integration.

Reading difficulties do not occur in a vacuum. Adolescents' personal identities, academic achievement, and future aspirations mix with ongoing difficulties with reading. Because literacy promises to enhance individuals as well as society, adolescents struggling with reading deserve assistance by professionals specially prepared in reading. The CAL recommends services that include the following:

- providing tutorial reading instruction that is part of a comprehensive program connected with subject matter teachers, parents, and the community;
- structuring challenging, relevant situations in special reading classes and in subject matter classrooms where students succeed and become self-sufficient learners;
- assessing students' reading and writing—and enabling students to assess their own reading and writing—to plan instruction, foster individuals' control of their literacy, and immediately support learners when progress diminishes;
- teaching vocabulary, fluency, comprehension, and study strategies tailored to individuals' competencies;
- relating literacy practices to life management issues such as exploring careers, examining individuals' roles in society, setting goals, managing time and stress, and resolving conflicts; and
- offering reading programs that recognize potentially limiting forces such as work schedules, family responsibilities, and peer pressures.

6. Adolescents deserve teachers who understand the complexities of individual adolescent readers, respect their differences, and respond to their characteristics.

Adolescents demonstrate substantial differences. In the Araujo family, Nick's interests in film and the outdoors differed from Kristy's preferences for athletics and teen culture. Nick tended to struggle with and avoid school-based reading and writing tasks; Kristy generally excelled with and enthusiastically approached them.

Viewing members of one family in relation to another calls attention to additional differences. Factors such as family heritage, language, and social and economic position contribute to the variation that students regularly display during reading and writing activities.

Differences also are apparent when individuals are considered one at a time. Nick often was preoccupied in one class, English, but highly engaged in another, psychology. Kristy hated how her science teacher conducted class but enjoyed language arts. Nick and Kristy probably acted slightly differently from day to day in all their classes depending on what was happening in their personal worlds.

Adolescents deserve classrooms that respect individuals' differences. To promote respect, teachers encourage the exchange of ideas among individuals. They regularly set up paired, small-group, and whole-class arrangements so that everyone can have his or her voice heard. Believing that everyone has something to offer, they organize instruction so students of diverse backgrounds share their insights into course topics. One of the reasons Kristy eagerly researched the Great Depression was that she anticipated a productive discussion the next day.

Respectful classrooms are safe enough for students to take risks when expressing themselves publicly. No rudeness, put-downs, or ugly remarks are allowed. Learners address others courteously and expect courteous treatment in turn. They disagree without being disagreeable, contesting others' ideas without personal insults.

Respectful classrooms also display positive expectations. Teachers believe that students who are taught appropriately can meet rigorous standards. They acknowledge conditions outside of class that might interfere with learning, but they inspire teens to be resilient and take charge of their lives. Learning failures are unacceptable.

Along with respect, individual adolescents deserve teachers who respond to their characteristics. Responsive teachers address the mandated curriculum while engaging students in self-expression. To illustrate, Nick's five-paragraph report on a famous person could be extended several ways. Nick could inquire into Davy Crockett through interviews, library materials, and textbooks as well as through the Internet. He could enrich his investigation by examining legendary aspects of Crockett or he could look at Crockett's role as an icon of individualism. Nick could supplement his essay by representing Crockett through a poem, poster, Readers Theatre, or skit. Teachers often limit such choices to manageable options, but they offer choices and supports for accomplishing them.

In sum, adolescents deserve more than a centralized, one-size-fits-all approach to literacy. They deserve teachers who establish productive conditions for learning; move into individuals' worlds with respect, choice, and support; and move out to allow growth.

7. Adolescents deserve homes, communities, and a nation that will support their efforts to achieve advanced levels of literacy and provide the support necessary for them to succeed.

For adolescents, growing in literacy means being continually stretched. Because of this, adolescents deserve all the support they can get, not only from school but from their families, communities, and the nation.

Parents play an important role. They help adolescents extend and consolidate their literacy by engaging them in discussions about what they read, responding sincerely to the ideas they write, and making printed materials available. Parents become partners with educators in supporting their adolescents' growth.

Members of the local community often are partners with adolescents. Libraries, religious groups, and after-school programs are centers for community workers and volunteers to assist adolescents with homework, tutor individuals with learning difficulties, and initiate book discussion groups. Businesses become partners with schools by providing mentors and role models as well as funds for buying books and recognizing achievements.

Adolescents preparing for the 21st century deserve new forms of collaboration among educators. Community colleges, technical schools, and universities can offer input and assistance. Professional organizations working together and exploring relationships among reading, writing, and learning may lead to new educational directions. The educational community can demonstrate that adolescent literacy is important.

The many dimensions of adolescent literacy are addressed best in school reform and restructuring that place the growth of students at the center of every activity. Environments of high expectations, inquiry, and decision making encourage students to refine the reading and writing abilities they have and take the risks necessary to grow. Adolescents deserve new perspectives on what it means to know a subject and to display that knowledge. Surface changes to schools involving scheduling and required courses are not enough to fully support adolescents' advanced reading and writing.

Finally, the CAL believes that the literacy achievement of adolescents cannot grow to new levels without changes in governmental policy. Emphasizing the achievement of early readers has not produced adolescents who read and write at high levels of proficiency. Adolescents deserve increased levels of governmental support. This includes appropriate funding for intervention services in the upper grades, the point in most comparisons at which children in the United States perform less well. School libraries can be the center of efforts to encourage wide reading, but for decades they have seen a steady decline in funding. Governmental support also involves exerting leadership to mobilize initiatives among parents and local communities.

Government can support ongoing staff development for helping students grow in literacy as they grow in content knowledge. Furthermore, government can support literacy research concentrating on the upper grades where literacy proficiencies are less well understood than those at the lower grades.

A commitment to growth

Public and educational attention long has been focused on the beginnings of literacy, planting seedlings and making sure that they take root. But without careful cultivation and nurturing, seedlings may wither and their growth become stunted. We, as members of the International Reading Association Commission on Adolescent Literacy, urge policy makers, administrators, business people, community members, parents, and educators to commit themselves to supporting adolescents' literacy in the ways presented in this position statement. Adolescents deserve enhanced opportunities to grow into healthy, strong, and independent readers and writers.

SUGGESTED READINGS
Shouldn't adolescents already be literate?
Berliner, D.C., & Biddle, B.J. (1995). *The manufactured crisis: Myths, fraud, and attacks on America's public schools.* Reading, MA: Addison-Wesley.
Campbell, J.R., Voelkl, K.E., & Donahue, P.L. (1998). *Report in brief: NAEP 1996 trends in academic progress* (Publication

No. 98-530). Washington, DC: National Center for Education Statistics.
Graham, P.A. (1981). Literacy: A goal for secondary schools. *Daedalus, 110*(3), 119–134.
Kibby, M.W. (1995). *Student literacy: Myths and realities*. Bloomington, IN: Phi Delta Kappa Educational Foundation.
National Assessment of Educational Progress. (1999). *NAEP 1998 reading report card for the nation and the states* [Online]. Available: http://www.ed.gov/NCES/NAEP.

Couldn't the problem be solved by preventing reading difficulties early on?

Chall, J.S. (1983). *Stages of reading development*. New York: McGraw-Hill.
Gee, T.C., & Rakow, S.J. (1991). Content reading education: What methods do teachers prefer? *NASSP Bulletin, 75*, 104–110.
Schumm, J.S., Vaughn, S., & Saumell, L. (1992). What teachers do when the textbook is tough: Students speak out. *Journal of Reading Behavior, 24*, 481–503.
Smith, F.R., & Feathers, K.M. (1983). The role of reading in content classrooms: Assumption vs. reality. *Journal of Reading, 27*, 262–267.
U.S. Department of Education, National Center for Education Statistics. (1997). *The condition of education, 1997* (NCES 97-388). Washington, DC: U.S. Government Printing Office.
Wells, M.C. (1995). *Literacies lost: When students move from a progressive middle school to a traditional high school*. New York: Teachers College Press.

Why isn't appropriate literacy instruction already being provided to adolescents?

Alvermann, D., & Moore, D. (1991). Secondary school reading. In R. Barr, M.L. Kamil, P. Mosenthal, & P.D. Pearson (Eds.), *Handbook of reading research* (Vol. II, pp. 951–983). White Plains, NY: Longman.
O'Brien, D., Stewart, R., & Moje, E.B. (1995). Why content literacy is difficult to infuse into the secondary school: Complexities of curriculum, pedagogy, and school culture. *Reading Research Quarterly, 30*, 442–463.
Oldfather, P., & Thomas, S. (1998). What does it mean when high school teachers participate in collaborative research with students on literacy motivations? *Teachers College Record, 99*, 647–691.
Perrone, V., & Traver, R. (1996). Secondary education. In J. Sikula, T.J. Buttery, & E. Guyton (Eds.), *Handbook of research on teacher education* (2nd ed., pp. 392–409). New York: Macmillan.
Romine, B.G.C., McKenna, M.C., & Robinson, R.D. (1996). Reading coursework requirements for middle and high school content area teachers: A U.S. survey. *Journal of Adolescent & Adult Literacy, 40*, 194–198.
Vacca, R. (1998). Let's not marginalize adolescent literacy. *Journal of Adolescent & Adult Literacy, 41*, 604–609.

Adolescents deserve access to a wide variety of reading material that they can and want to read

Anderson, R.C., Wilson, P.T., & Fielding, L.G. (1988). Growth in reading and how children spend their time outside of school. *Reading Research Quarterly, 23*, 285–303.
Campbell, J.R., Voelkl, K.E., & Donahue, P.L. (1998). *Report in brief: NAEP 1996 trends in academic progress* (Publication No. 98-530). Washington, DC: National Center for Education Statistics.
Cone, J.K. (1994). Appearing acts: Creating readers in a high school English class. *Harvard Educational Review, 64*, 450–473.
Fielding, L.G. (1994). Independent reading. In A. Purves (Ed.), *Encyclopedia of English studies and language arts* (Vol. I, pp. 613–613). New York: Scholastic/National Council of Teachers of English.
Fielding, L., & Roller, C. (1992). Making difficult books accessible and easy books acceptable. *The Reading Teacher, 45*, 678–687.
Ivey, G. (1998). Discovering readers in the middle level school: A few helpful clues. *NASSP Bulletin, 82*(600), 48–56.
Nell, V. (1988). *Lost in a book: The psychology of reading for pleasure*. New Haven, CT: Yale University Press.
Rosenblatt, L.M. (1978). *The reader, the text, the poem: The transactional theory of the literary work*. Carbondale, IL: Southern Illinois University Press.
Worthy, J., Moorman, M., & Turner, M. (1999). What Johnny likes to read is hard to find in school. *Reading Research Quarterly, 34*, 12–53.

Adolescents deserve instruction that builds both the skill and desire to read increasingly complex materials

Bean, T.W., Valerio, P.C., & Stevens, L. (1999). Content area literacy instruction. In L.B. Gambrell & L.M. Morrow (Eds.), *Best practices in literacy instruction* (pp. 175–192). New York: Guilford.
Bond, G.L., & Bond, E. (1941). *Developmental reading in high school*. New York: Macmillan.
Brozo, W.G., & Simpson, M.L. (1999). *Readers, teachers, learners: Expanding literacy across the content areas* (3rd ed.). Upper Saddle River, NJ: Merrill.
Irvin, J.L. (1998). *Reading and the middle school student: Strategies to enhance literacy* (2nd ed.). Boston: Allyn & Bacon.
McCombs, B.L., & Barton, M.L. (1998). Motivating secondary school students to read their textbooks. *NASSP Bulletin, 82*(600), 24–33.
McKenna, M., Ellsworth, R.A., & Kear, D. (1995). Children's attitudes toward reading: A national survey. *Reading Research Quarterly, 30*, 934–957.
Weinstein, C.E., & Mayer, R.E. (1986). The teaching of learning strategies. In M.C. Wittrock (Ed.), *Handbook of research on teaching* (3rd ed., pp. 315–327). New York: Macmillan.

Adolescents deserve assessment that shows them their strengths as well as their needs and that guides their teachers to design instruction that will best help them grow as readers

Bauer, E.B. (1999). The promise of alternative literacy assessments in the classroom: A review of empirical studies. *Reading Research and Instruction, 38*, 153–168.
Darling-Hammond, L., Ancess, J., & Falk, B. (1995). *Authentic assessment in action: Studies of schools and students at work*. New York: Teachers College Press.
Hansen, J. (1998). *When learners evaluate*. Portsmouth, NH: Heinemann.

Mitchell, R., Willis, M., & The Chicago Teachers Union Quest Center. (1995). *Learning in overdrive: Designing curriculum, instruction, and assessment from standards.* Golden, CO: North America Press.

Olson, L. (1999). Making every test count: Testing raises a host of concerns. *Education Week, 18*(17), 11–20.

Pearson, P.D. (1998). Standards and assessments: Tools for crafting effective instruction? In J.L.F. Osborn (Ed.), *Learning to read* (pp. 264–288). New York: Guilford.

Stiggins, R.J. (1997). *Student-centered classroom assessment* (2nd ed.). Upper Saddle River, NJ: Merrill.

Tierney, R.J., & Clark, C. (with Fenner, L., Herter, R.J., Simpson, C.S., & Wiser, B.). (1998). Theory and research into practice: Portfolios: Assumptions, tensions, and possibilities. *Reading Research Quarterly, 33,* 474–486.

U.S. Department of Education. (1996). *Guidance on standards, assessment, and accountability.* Washington, DC: Author.

Wiggins, G.M., Jr. (1998). *Understanding by design.* Alexandria, VA: Association for Supervision and Curriculum Development.

Adolescents deserve expert teachers who model and provide explicit instruction in reading comprehension and study strategies across the curriculum

Alvermann, D.E., & Phelps, S.F. (1998). *Content area reading and literacy: Succeeding in today's diverse classrooms* (2nd ed.). Boston: Allyn & Bacon.

Borko, H., & Putnam, R.T. (1996). Learning to teach. In D.C. Berliner & R.C. Calfee (Eds.), *Handbook of educational psychology* (pp. 673–708). New York: Macmillan.

Gall, M.D., Gall, J.P., Jacobsen, D.R., & Bullock, T.L. (1990). *Tools for learning: A guide to teaching study skills.* Alexandria, VA: Association for Supervision and Curriculum Development.

Pearson, P.D., & Fielding, L. (1991). Comprehension instruction. In R. Barr, M.L. Kamil, P.B. Mosenthal, & P.D. Pearson (Eds.), *Handbook of reading research* (Vol. II, pp. 815–860). White Plains, NY: Longman.

Rosenshine, B., & Meister, C. (1992). The use of scaffolds for teaching higher-level cognitive strategies. *Educational Leadership, 50,* 26–33.

Symons, S., Richards, C., & Greene, C. (1995). Cognitive strategies for reading comprehension. In E. Wood, V.E. Woloshyn, & T. Willoughby (Eds.), *Cognitive strategy instruction for middle and high schools* (pp. 66–87). Cambridge, MA: Brookline.

Vacca, R.T., & Vacca, J.L. (1999). *Content area reading: Literacy and learning across the curriculum* (6th ed.). New York: Longman.

Weinstein, C.E., & Hume, L.M. (1998). *Study strategies for lifelong learning.* Washington, DC: American Psychological Association.

Adolescents deserve reading specialists who assist individual students having difficulty learning how to read

Allen, J. (1995). *It's never too late: Leading adolescents to lifelong literacy.* Portsmouth, NH: Heinemann.

Anderson, V., & Roit, M. (1993). Planning and implementing collaborative strategy instruction for delayed readers in grades 6–10. *The Elementary School Journal, 94,* 121–138.

Barry, A.L. (1997). High school reading programs revisited. *Journal of Adolescent & Adult Literacy, 40,* 524–531.

Davidson, J., & Koppenhaver, D. (1993). *Adolescent literacy: What works and why* (2nd ed.). New York: Garland.

Kos, R. (1991). Persistence of reading difficulties: The voices of four middle school students. *American Educational Research Journal, 28,* 875–895.

Mehan, H., Hubbard, L., & Villanueva, I. (1996). *Constructing school success: The consequences of untracking low achieving students.* New York: Cambridge University Press.

Moore, D.W., Readence, J.E., & Rickelman, R.J. (1983). An historical exploration of content area reading instruction. *Reading Research Quarterly, 18,* 419–438.

U.S. Department of Education, National Center for Education Statistics. (1997). *The condition of education, 1997* (NCES 97-388). Washington, DC: U.S. Government Printing Office.

O'Brien, D. (1998). Multiple literacies in a high-school program for "at-risk" adolescents. In D.E. Alvermann, K.A. Hinchman, D.W. Moore, S.E. Phelps, & D.R. Waff (Eds.), *Reconceptualizing the literacies in adolescents' lives* (pp. 27–49). Mahwah, NJ: Erlbaum.

Roller, C.M. (1996). *Variability not disability: Struggling readers in a workshop classroom.* Newark, DE: International Reading Association.

Rose, M. (1989). *Lives on the boundary: The struggles and achievements of America's underprepared.* New York: Free Press

Adolescents deserve teachers who are trained to understand the complexities of individual adolescent readers, respect their differences, and respond to their characteristics

Beane, J.A. (1990). *A middle school curriculum: From rhetoric to reality.* Columbus, OH: National Middle School Association.

Diamond, B.J., & Moore, M.A. (1995). *Multicultural literacy: Mirroring the reality of the classroom.* White Plains, NY: Longman.

Dias, P.X. (1992). Literary reading and classroom constraints: Aligning practice with theory. In J.A. Langer (Ed.), *Literature instruction* (pp. 131–162). Urbana, IL: National Council of Teachers of English.

Finders, M.J. (1998/1999). Raging hormones: Stories of adolescence and implications for teacher preparation. *Journal of Adolescent & Adult Literacy, 42,* 252–263.

Hynds, S. (1997). *On the brink: Negotiating literature and life with adolescents.* New York: Teachers College Press.

Marzano, R.J. (1992). *A different kind of classroom.* Alexandria, VA: Association for Supervision and Curriculum Development.

National Middle School Association. (1992). *This we believe: Developmentally responsive middle level schools.* Columbus, OH: Author.

Rief, L. (1992). *Seeking diversity.* Portsmouth, NH: Heinemann.

Adolescents deserve homes, communities, and a nation that will support their efforts to achieve advanced levels of literacy and provide the support necessary for them to succeed

Alvarez, M. (1998). Adolescent literacy: Are we in contact? In E. Sturtevant, E.J. Dugan, P. Linder, & W. Linek (Eds.), *Literacy and community* (20th yearbook of the College

Reading Association, pp. 2–10). Commerce, TX: College Reading Association.

Anders, P. (1998). The literacy council: People are the key to an effective program. *NASSP Bulletin, 82*(600), 16–23.

Epstein, J.L. (1995). Creating school/family/community partnerships: Caring for the children we share. *Phi Delta Kappan, 76,* 701–712.

Graham, P.A. (1992). *SOS: Sustain our schools.* New York: Hill & Wang.

Humphries, J.W., Lipsitz, J., McGovern, J.T., & Wasser, J.D. (1997). Supporting the development of young adolescent readers. *Phi Delta Kappan, 79,* 305–311.

Moore, D.W. (1996). Contexts for literacy in secondary schools. In D.J. Leu, C.K. Kinzer, & K.A. Hinchman (Eds.), *Literacies for the 21st century: Research and practice* (45th yearbook of the National Reading Conference, pp. 15–46). Chicago: National Reading Conference.

National Association of Secondary School Principals. (1996). *Breaking ranks: Changing an American institution.* Reston, VA: Author.

Newmann, F.M. (1996). *Authentic achievement: Restructuring schools for intellectual quality.* San Francisco: Jossey-Bass.

Related resources from IRA

Books

Reading for Meaning: Fostering Comprehension in the Middle Grades

Barbara M. Taylor, Michael F. Graves,
Paul van den Broek, Editors

Reading comprehension is of great concern to many Americans, as evidenced by the mandate in most states today for graduation standards in reading and for assessment aligned to those standards. In *Reading for Meaning,* leading scholars and researchers provide a broad overview of current educational and psychological research about effective strategies for teaching reading comprehension to middle grade students. This rich collection offers practitioners, researchers, and literacy specialists a valuable resource for improving reading comprehension at the middle school level. (Available November 1999)

©1999 US$19.95 Order number **9135-574**

Popular Culture in the Classroom: Teaching and Researching Critical Media Literacy (Literacy Studies Series)

Donna E. Alvermann, Jennifer S. Moon,
Margaret C. Hagood

This book addresses the importance of developing within children and adolescents a critical awareness of the social, political, and economic messages emanating from the different forms of popular culture. The authors explain the term *critical media literacy* and the different cultural resources each author brings to the book, then consider the issues surrounding the selection and introduction of popular culture texts for use in critical media literacy lessons and provide examples of teaching strategies they have used to engage students in these lessons. The authors also give a detailed analysis of how children's and adolescents' identities are constructed through the media, and synthesize where the field is and needs to go in researching critical media literacy. Consider the possibilities involved in teaching critical media literacy using popular culture, and explore what such teaching might look like in your classroom. (March 1999 Book Club selection)

©1999 US$21.95 Order number **245-574**

Teaching Literacy Using Information Technology: A Collection of Articles From the Australian Literacy Educators' Association

Joelie Hancock, Editor

Rapid changes and advancements in technology are raising questions for teachers, librarians, and administrators about how to integrate these changes into the curriculum and the classroom. *Teaching Literacy Using Information Technology* provides valuable insight into the pros and cons of instituting and using information technology (IT) in the classroom. Learn how to establish acceptable-use policies for principals and administrators, select and purchase appropriate software and CD-ROM products, coordinate computer access among students, train teachers, and maintain parents' cooperation and involvement. This book is an excellent source of background information about technology use and practical advice for teachers. (January 1999 Book Club selection)

©1999 US$19.95 Order number **198-574**

Language Study in Middle School, High School, and Beyond

John S. Simmons, Lawrence Baines, Editors

The contributors to this book believe that language should be the central focus for study in the reading and language arts classroom and that gaining mastery over language can be stimulating, enlightening, and enjoyable. The text presents 10 diverse viewpoints on language study in the middle school and secondary school that are divided into the following areas: studying language through literature and the arts, using writing and speaking to study language, language use in different academic settings, and emerging trends in language study. All the chapters recommend that language study can be connected to students' lives in visceral as well as rational ways. (February 1998 Book Club selection)

©1998 US$29.95 Order number **182-574**

On the Brink: Negotiating Literature and Life With Adolescents

Susan Hynds

This book is a chronicle of one teacher's struggle to implement a constructivist approach to teaching English in a culturally diverse urban middle school. Teachers will recognize the struggles of their own adolescent students in Hynds's careful studies of these young readers and writers. *On the Brink* makes an argument for an activist, social constructivist approach, without minimizing the difficulties faced by teachers of literature as they attempt to negotiate the complicated social, cultural, and political arena of their own classroom. (November 1997 Book Club selection)

©1997 US$20.95   Order number **9102-574**

Envisioning Literature: Literary Understanding and Literature Instruction

Judith A. Langer

This book offers new ways of thinking about literature instruction and its contribution to students' learning. Langer focuses her theory of literature instruction on creating "literate communities" in the classroom and developing a reader-based pedagogy for all students. Filled with the words of students and teachers and rich with narratives of actual classroom experiences in elementary, middle, and high schools in urban and suburban communities, *Envisioning Literature* provides both strong theory about teaching literature and real examples that provide a context for change. (January 1996 Book Club selection)

©1995 US$17.95   Order number **159-574**

Guiding Readers Through Text: A Review of Study Guides

Karen D. Wood, Diane Lapp, James Flood

Study guides are useful tools for enhancing instruction at any grade level and in any content area. This practical book discusses why and how study guides help students comprehend text, while emphasizing the most effective ways to use these guides in the classroom. Complete descriptions of different types of study guides along with examples from a wide variety of lessons in primary through secondary grades, will help teachers select the best guides for their purpose. (August 1992 Book Club selection)

©1992 US$13.50   Order number **374-574**

Responses to Literature: Grades K–8

James M. Macon, Diane Bewell, MaryEllen Vogt

A practical tool for teaching students how to respond to literature, this book provides 10 classroom activities that encourage students to think more as they read and to focus on the literary elements of a story. Each activity is preceded by a concise description that includes the purpose of the activity and the grade level it addresses, as well as a completed chart. Reproducible blank charts also are provided. Activities are classroom tested, may be tailored to fit each literature selection, and may be used with small or large groups. (December 1990 Book Club selection)

©1990 US$5.95   Order number **474-574**

Prereading Activities for Content Area Reading and Learning (second edition)

David W. Moore, John E. Readence, Robert J. Rickelman

This book describes a wealth of prereading activities and strategies designed to help teachers make the unfamiliar and often unappealing material of textbooks understandable to students. The authors feature ideas teachers can apply in the classroom, strategies for making students independent learners, and a chapter on writing. (December 1988 Book Club selection)

©1988 US$10.95   Order number **233-574**

Booklists

Magazines for Kids and Teens (revised edition)

Donald R. Stoll, Editor

This is an easy-to-use guide to publications covering almost every conceivable interest of children and teens. It contains more than 200 listings that parents, teachers, librarians, and young people can choose from—complete with descriptions and ordering information. In a How-to-Use section the editor assists readers in selecting magazines to explore, and indexes to age and grade levels, subjects, and a list of magazines that publish readers' works also are included. Copublished with the Educational Press Association of America. (July 1997 Book Club selection)

©1997 US$15.95   Order number **243-574**

More Teens' Favorite Books: Young Adults' Choices 1993–1995

This book is an indispensable resource for anyone trying to get reluctant teenagers to read. The books on this annotated list are selected by the toughest critics around—the teens themselves. Over 4,000 ballots are cast annually to select just 30 books to be named as IRA's Young Adults' Choices. This valuable resource for teachers, librarians, parents, and young readers includes a new section titled Reading for Pleasure. Featured in the section are veterans of the struggle to get young people reading—teachers. You'll discover ways teachers are motivating teens to read for fun, promoting free-choice reading. (September 1996 Book Club selection)

©1996 US$9.95   Order number **149-574**

Young Adults' Choices

The books on this list are selected by young adult readers as the ones they consider the most enjoyable and informative. Titles are chosen by students in middle schools and high schools across the United States. Complete bibliographic data and annotations are supplied for each title. *Young Adults' Choices* is a project of IRA's Literature for Adolescents Committee.

Order number **9107-574**

10 copies	US$6.00
100 copies	US$45.00
500 copies	US$170.00

Parent Booklets

"Books Are Cool!" Keeping Your Middle-School Student Reading

Order number **1030-574**

Parents, Teens, and Reading: A Winning Combination

Order number **1031-574**

1–24 copies	US$2.00 each
25–99 copies	US$1.75 each
100+ copies	US$1.50 each

Ordering information

To order these materials (IRA members deduct 20% before adding shipping charges), contact: Order Department, International Reading Association, 800 Barksdale Road, Box 8139, Newark, DE 19714-8139, USA. Telephone: 302-731-1600. Fax: 302-731-1057. For credit card orders, call toll free (United States/Canada only) 800-336-READ, ext. 266.

A Report to Carnegie Corporation of New York

READING NEXT

A VISION FOR ACTION AND RESEARCH IN MIDDLE AND HIGH SCHOOL LITERACY

ALLIANCE FOR
EXCELLENT EDUCATION

About Carnegie Corporation of New York

Carnegie Corporation of New York was created by Andrew Carnegie in 1911 to promote "the advancement and diffusion of knowledge and understanding." As a grantmaking foundation, the Corporation seeks to carry out Carnegie's vision of philanthropy, which he said should aim "to do real and permanent good in the world." The Corporation's capital fund, originally donated at a value of about $135 million, had a market value of $1.8 billion on September 30, 2003. The Corporation awards grants totaling approximately $80 million a year in the areas of education, international peace and security, international development, and strengthening U.S. democracy.

About the Alliance for Excellent Education

The Alliance for Excellent Education is a national policy, research, and advocacy organization that works to help make every child a high school graduate—to prepare them for college, have success in life, and be contributing members of society. It focuses on the needs of the millions of secondary school students (those in the lowest achievement quartile) who are most likely to leave school without a diploma or to graduate unprepared for a productive future.

Based in Washington, D.C., the Alliance's audience includes parents, teachers and principals, and students, as well as the federal, state, and local policy communities, education organizations, the media, and a concerned public. To inform the national debate about education policies and options, the Alliance produces reports and other materials, makes presentations at meetings and conferences, briefs policymakers and the press, and provides timely information to a wide audience via its biweekly newsletter and regularly updated website, www.all4ed.org.

The Authors

Gina Biancarosa is an advanced doctoral student at the Harvard Graduate School of Education, where she received a Larsen Fellowship and is a Spencer Research Training Grant Alternate. She has been an adjunct professor at Boston College, where she taught two undergraduate courses on reading and the language arts required for undergraduate early childhood and elementary education majors. She coauthored the report *Adolescent Literacy: What Do We Know and Where Do We Go from Here?* with Catherine Snow, and the book *Afterschool Education: Approaches to an Emerging Field* with Gil Noam.

Dr. Catherine Snow is the Henry Lee Shattuck Professor of Education at the Harvard Graduate School of Education. Snow has recently chaired two national panels: the National Academy of Sciences committee that prepared the report *Preventing Reading Difficulties in Young Children*, and the RAND Reading Study Group that prepared *Reading for Understanding: Toward an R&D Program in Reading Comprehension*. Her current research activities include a longitudinal study of language and literacy skills among low-income children who have been followed for fifteen years since age three; following the language development of young children participating in the Early Head Start intervention; studying the vocabulary development of first- and second-language learners; and considering aspects of transfer from first to second language in the domains of language and literacy. Snow has also written about bilingualism and its relation to language policy issues such as bilingual education in the United States and in developing nations, and about testing policy. She is currently involved in efforts to improve middle school literacy outcomes, in partnership with other Boston-area researchers and the Boston Public Schools.

Additional copies of this report can be ordered from the Alliance for Excellent Education at

1201 Connecticut Avenue, NW
Suite 901
Washington, DC 20036
(202) 828-0828

or can be downloaded from our website, www.all4ed.org.

Permission for reproducing excerpts from this report should be directed to the Alliance for Excellent Education.

A Report to Carnegie Corporation of New York

THE FIFTEEN KEY ELEMENTS OF EFFECTIVE ADOLESCENT LITERACY PROGRAMS

To establish a list of promising elements of effective adolescent literacy programs, the panel considered elements that had a substantial base in research and/or professional opinion. After considerable discussion, they determined a list of fifteen critical components. (See Table 1.) Literature supporting these elements is cited in Appendix A.

In an ideal world, schools would be able to implement all fifteen elements, but the list may also be used to construct a unique blend of elements suited to the needs of the students they serve. This report treats each element as a distinct entity, but it is important to recognize that the elements are often synergistically related, and the addition of one element can stimulate the inclusion of another. The elements should *not* be seen simply as isolated elements in an inventory of potential elements, but rather as a group in which elements have a dynamic and powerful interrelationship. For instance, it is difficult to implement text-based collaborative learning (Element 4) without a classroom library of diverse texts (Element 6). We expect that a mixture of these elements will generate the biggest return. It remains to be seen what that optimal mix is, and it may be different for different subpopulations of students.

> **THE OPTIMAL MIX**
>
> In the medical profession, treatment needs to be tailored to an individual patient's needs; at times, more than one intervention is needed to effectively treat a patient. Similarly, educators need to test mixes of intervention elements to find the ones that work best for students with different needs.

Table 1. Key Elements in Programs Designed to Improve Adolescent Literacy Achievement in Middle and High Schools

Instructional Improvements	Infrastructure Improvements
1. Direct, explicit comprehension instruction	10. Extended time for literacy
2. Effective instructional principles embedded in content	11. Professional development
3. Motivation and self-directed learning	12. Ongoing summative assessment of students and programs
4. Text-based collaborative learning	13. Teacher teams
5. Strategic tutoring	14. Leadership
6. Diverse texts	15. A comprehensive and coordinated literacy program
7. Intensive writing	
8. A technology component	
9. Ongoing formative assessment of students	

Two Categories of Elements: Instruction and Infrastructure

The list of elements is divided into two sections: instructional improvements and infrastructural improvements. While the instructional improvements can have a tremendous impact, it is important to realize that they would be more effective if they were implemented in conjunction with infrastructural supports. Furthermore, the instructional improvements are unlikely to be maintained or extended beyond the original intervention classrooms if these infrastructural factors are not in place. Despite the clear advantage of linking instructional improvements to infrastructural improvements, the list prioritizes instructional improvements because of our focus on the individual learner as the unit of intervention and analysis and on improved instruction as the most important element influencing student outcomes.

Improving the overall school climate is undeniably a critical factor in improving adolescent literacy, and school reorganization and reform efforts have helped dramatically in this area. However, it too often happens that the climate improves with little or no impact on achievement. For the biggest returns, stakeholders must invest in school reform, with an eye toward curricular improvement. That is, structure and infrastructure changes should be determined by curricular and instructional considerations. Too frequently, changes in school structure (for example, block scheduling, small schools, and so on) have been adopted without *first* carefully considering curricular and instructional implications.

The list of the fifteen key elements begins with instruction and then focuses on infrastructure that will support the instructional improvements. Improving instruction, whether done by an entire school or a single teacher, can have dramatic effects on student achievement. However, improving school infrastructure to better support literacy teachers and students *in addition to instructional improvement* will reap the biggest rewards. Ultimately, change can be top down, bottom up, or middle in, but truly effective change must include considerations of both instruction *and* infrastructure.

Instructional Elements

Direct, explicit comprehension instruction

Effective adolescent literacy interventions must address reading comprehension. A number of excellent approaches have been shown to be effective in middle and high school contexts, but no one approach is necessarily better than another; the ideal intervention will tap more than one comprehension instructional approach. Possible approaches include

- *comprehension strategies* instruction, which is instruction that explicitly gives students strategies that aid them in comprehending a wide variety of texts;

- *comprehension monitoring and metacognition instruction*, which is instruction that teaches students to become aware of how they understand while they read;

- *teacher modeling*, which involves the teacher reading texts aloud, making her own use of strategies and practices apparent to her students;

- *scaffolded instruction*, which involves teachers giving high support for students practicing new skills and then slowly decreasing that support to increase student ownership and self-sufficiency; and

- *apprenticeship models*, which involve teachers engaging students in a content-centered learning relationship.

> **DIRECT, EXPLICIT COMPREHENSION INSTRUCTION: AN EXAMPLE**
>
> **Reciprocal Teaching** is a **scaffolded approach** to teaching **comprehension strategies**. It was designed for youth at any grade level, typically scoring in the thirty-fifth percentile or below on standardized reading measures, with the aim of teaching them to actively process the text they read in small groups. The **teacher models** four critical strategies: *questioning, clarifying, predicting,* and *summarizing*. The teacher then transfers responsibility for implementing the strategies to students by having them work in small groups. Students either take turns using each strategy or lead discussions by using all four strategies, in the latter case becoming the "teacher." By taking turns using each of the strategies with a series of texts, children learn to independently and flexibly apply the strategies on their own.
>
> **Questioning** poses questions based on a portion of a text the group has read, either aloud or silently.
>
> **Clarifying** resolves confusions about words, phrases, or concepts, drawing on the text when possible.
>
> **Summarizing** sums up the content, identifying the gist of what has been read and discussed.
>
> **Predicting** suggests what will next happen in or be learned next from the text.
>
> Source: Palincsar and Herrenkohl, 2002.

Note, too, that these approaches are not listed in order of importance and have been utilized by effective readers long before they were ever dubbed and defined as "strategies" or "metacognition."

> *From age ten, [Benjamin] Franklin was largely a self-taught reader (he had a tutor for a year). To improve his reading comprehension, he copied passages, made short summaries, rewrote passages, turned essays into rhyming verse and other games, and avidly discussed what he read with peers. [Frederick] Douglass was also briefly tutored but then forbidden to read. Forced to learn on his own, he too invented reading and writing exercises, summarized passages, played word games, and practiced giving speeches and responding to issues in debate. (Trabasso and Bouchard, 2002, p. 177)*

Many of the existing instructional options utilize more than one of these approaches. Whatever approach is utilized, teachers should teach these approaches explicitly by explaining to students how and when to use certain strategies. Teachers should also explain why they are teaching particular strategies and have students employ them in multiple contexts with texts from a variety of genres and subject areas.

Effective Instructional Principles Embedded in Content

This element has two forms. The first form applies to the language arts teacher. When instructional principles are embedded in content, the language arts teacher does not simply teach a technique (such as outlining) as an abstract skill, but teaches it using content-area materials. Students should receive instruction and then practice their new skills using these materials. Too often reading and writing instruction focuses solely on literature and does not promote the transfer of the skills into the context of content-area materials. Furthermore, learning from reading in content-area texts requires skills that are different than the skills needed to comprehend literature. Language arts teachers need to expand their instruction to include approaches and texts that will facilitate not only comprehension but also learning from texts.

The second form of this element applies to subject-area teachers. When instructional principles are embedded in content, subject-area teachers provide or reinforce instruction in the skills and strategies that are particularly effective in their subject areas. This instruction should be coordinated with the language arts teachers, literacy coaches, and other subject-area teachers. The idea is not that content-area teachers should become reading and writing teachers, but rather that they should emphasize the reading and writing practices that are specific to their subjects, so students are encouraged to read and write like historians, scientists, mathematicians, and other subject-area experts. Additionally, it is important that all subject matter teachers use teaching aids and devices that will help at-risk students better understand and remember the content they are teaching. The use of such tools as graphic organizers, prompted outlines, structured reviews, guided discussions and other instructional tactics that will modify and enhance the curriculum content in ways that promote its understanding and mastery have been shown to greatly enhance student performance—for all students in academically diverse classes, not just students who are struggling.

DIRECT, EXPLICIT COMPREHENSION INSTRUCTION: A SECOND EXAMPLE

Reading Apprenticeship puts the teacher in the role of content-area expert, and late-middle and high school students are "apprenticed" into the reasons and ways reading and writing are used within a "discipline" (subject area) and the strategies and thinking that are particularly useful in that discipline. In reading apprenticeship classrooms, *how* we read and *why* we read in the ways we do become part of the curriculum, accompanying a focus on *what* we read.

Rather than offering a sequence of strategies, reading apprenticeship is focused on creating classrooms where students become active and effective readers and learners. To accomplish this, teachers are encouraged to plan along four dimensions: *social, personal, cognitive,* and *knowledge-building.*

The *social* dimension focuses on establishing and maintaining a safe and supportive environment, where all members' processes, resources, and difficulties are shared and collaboration is valued.

The *personal* dimension focuses on improving students' identities and attitudes as readers and their interest in reading. It also promotes self-awareness, self-assessment, metacognition, and ownership.

The *cognitive* dimension is where students are given the reading tools and strategies they need to read like experts in the discipline.

The *knowledge-building* dimension focuses on building content and topic knowledge and knowledge of a discipline's typical text structures and styles.

The main tactic is that of metacognitive conversations that make the invisible aspects of these dimensions visible and open for discussion.

Source: Jordan, Jensen, and Greenleaf, 2001.

Motivation and Self-Directed Learning

This element addresses the need to promote greater student engagement and motivation. As students progress through the grades, they become increasingly "tuned out," and building student choices into the school day is an important way to reawaken student engagement. This is critical, because competency in reading is necessary but insufficient by itself to engender better academic performance. Students need to be self-regulating not only to become more successful academically, but also to be able to employ their skills flexibly long after they leave school.

> **EFFECTIVE INSTRUCTIONAL PRINCIPLES EMBEDDED IN CONTENT: AN EXAMPLE**
>
> **The Strategic Instruction Model (SIM)** provides teachers with an array of *Content Enhancement Routines* to enable them to teach complex curriculum content in ways that make it easier to understand and remember difficult subject matter. For example, there are routines that help teachers show how lesson or unit content is organized as well as to help them clearly explain the important features of a new concept. Additionally, SIM provides an array of targeted strategies to help students learn and deal with a variety of academic tasks. There are four reading strategies: the *Word Identification Strategy*, the *Visual Imagery Strategy*, the *Self-Questioning Strategy*, and the *Paraphrasing Strategy*.
>
> The ***Word Identification Strategy*** helps students to break down multi-syllabic words using three simple syllabication rules and a knowledge of roots, prefixes, and suffixes.
>
> The ***Visual Imagery Strategy*** helps students create "mental movies" of narratives they read in order to increase comprehension.
>
> The ***Self-Questioning Strategy*** helps students determine a motivation for reading by getting them to create questions about the material they will be reading, form predictions about what the answers will be, and locate their answers in the text.
>
> The ***Paraphrasing Strategy*** helps students summarize the text stating the main idea and major details in their own words.
>
> Source: Center for Research on Learning, 2001.

One way that motivation and engagement are instilled and maintained is to provide students with opportunities to select for themselves the materials they read and topics they research. One of the easiest ways to build some choice into the students' school day is to incorporate independent reading time in which they can read whatever they choose. Yet this piece of the curriculum is often dropped after the primary grades. Providing students with additional choices, such as research and writing topics, further stimulates motivated and engaged students. However, self-regulation is only developed when students are given choices *and* the instructional support and aids needed to succeed at their chosen tasks.

Another way to better engage students in literacy and learning is to promote relevancy in what students read and learn. As a first step, teachers need to "tune in" to their students' lives in order to understand what they find relevant and why. Then teachers can begin to redesign instruction so that it is more obviously relevant to students.

Text-Based Collaborative Learning

Another element is text-based collaborative learning, which means that when students work in small groups, they should not simply discuss a topic, but *interact with each other around a text*. This text might be assigned or self-selected reading, or it might be essays that the students are writing. The former case involves designing learning opportunities for pairs or small groups of students that are similar to the book clubs or literature circles implemented in primary grades. Learning is decentralized in these groups because the meaning drawn from a text or multiple texts is negotiated through a group process. In addition, such an approach is not limited to the language arts classroom, but can be implemented in subject-area classes and with students who have a wide range of abilities. For instance, students might read different texts about the Underground Railroad—each at his or her own reading level—and then present the ideas (rather than the plots) to the circle. A similar approach can be used in any subject area, even math, by having students work together on the same problem or on a set of similar problems. The important aspect of this approach is that teachers provide scaffolding for engagement at every ability level in the class and promote better oral language and content-area skills by giving the students concrete problems to discuss or solve. Such an approach requires that the teacher provide instruction about how to use time effectively, which means assigning roles within each group, at least initially, to ensure effective implementation.

TEXT-BASED COLLABORATIVE LEARNING: AN EXAMPLE

Questioning the Author engages upper elementary students in whole-class or small-group discussions of texts (including nonfiction) aimed at improving their comprehension and critical-thinking skills. Through guiding "queries" (open-ended questions without clear right answers) teachers get children to literally question the author's purpose and choices; students eventually come to regard the text as fallible and as a source of information about the author's thinking. Notable in these discussions is the degree to which children are engaged in trying to comprehend the text. The technique also gets children to voice their confusions as they arise without fear of being regarded as "stupid" for not understanding, as in the following example, where a small group of fourth-grade students discusses a passage about hermit crabs that includes the line "As the crab grows, it changes its shell for a larger one."

> Michael: Maybe it's growing or something. It said it's changing its shell for a larger one. But do they take it off?
>
> Nicole: They get them off with their claws.
>
> Terrence: They exchange them.
>
> Investigator: So, what are you saying isn't clear?
>
> Michael: How could they change one shell? I mean, I thought it stuck to the body.
>
> Nicole: But they get bigger, too.
>
> Michael: I know, but when they grow I thought the shell grows with them.
>
> Nicole: It's like people. Do you keep your clothes on and when you get bigger you break out of them?
>
> Terrence: As the crab grows, the shell breaks and it exchanges for another. It wants a larger shell as it gets bigger than it is now.
>
> Michael: It's like clothes, putting it on.

Source: McKeown, Beck, and Worthy, 1993, pp. 564–65.

Strategic Tutoring

Some students require or would benefit from intense, individualized instruction. This is particularly true of the student who struggles with decoding and fluency, but is also true of students requiring short-term, focused help. Such students should be given the opportunity to participate in tutoring, which need not occur only during the school day. Furthermore, through approaches detailed above, instruction in general education classes should be differentiated to allow students access to important content. Tutoring is referred to as strategic in this element to emphasize that while students may need tutorial help to acquire critical curriculum knowledge, they also need to be taught "how to learn" curriculum information. Hence, within strategic tutoring sessions, tutors teach learning strategies while helping students complete their content assignments. The goal of strategic tutoring is to empower adolescents to complete similar tasks independently in the future.

Diverse Texts

This element involves providing students with diverse texts that present a wide range of topics at a variety of reading levels. Whether teaching reading and writing or a subject area, teachers need to find texts at a wide range of difficulty levels. Too often students become frustrated because they are forced to read books that are simply too difficult for them to decode and comprehend simultaneously. Learning cannot occur under these conditions. Texts must be below students' frustration level, but must also be interesting; that is, they should be high interest and low readability. Given the wide range of reading and writing abilities present in almost any middle or high school classroom, this means having books available from a wide range of levels on the same topic. The term "diverse texts" is also used to indicate that the material should represent a wide range of topics. Topical diversity in any classroom (or school) library affords students more choices for self-selected reading and research projects. The range of topics should include a wide variety of cultural, linguistic, and demographic groups. Students should be able to find representatives of themselves in the available books, but they should also be able to find representatives of others about whom they wish to learn. High-interest, low-difficulty texts play a significant role in an adolescent literacy program and are critical for fostering the reading skills of struggling readers and the engagement of all students. In addition to using appropriate grade-level textbooks that may already be available in the classroom, it is crucial to have a range of texts in the classroom that link to multiple ability levels and connect to students' background experiences.

> **WRITING REMEDIATION NEEDED**
>
> More freshmen entering degree-granting postsecondary institutions take remedial writing courses than take remedial reading courses (NCES, 2003b).

Intensive Writing

Effective adolescent literacy programs must include an element that helps students improve their writing skills. Fourteen percent of all freshmen entering degree-granting postsecondary institutions take remedial writing courses (NCES, 2003b). And at public two-year institutions, 23 percent of entering freshmen take remedial writing. Even the best readers in high school do not necessarily write well enough to succeed in college or the business world—or perform well on the SAT, which will include a writing component as of 2005. Nearly 350 degree-granting postsecondary institutions have already decided to require students applying in 2005 to take the SAT writing component (College Board, 2004). Research supports the idea that writing instruction also improves reading comprehension. Many of the skills involved in writing, such as grammar and spelling, reinforce reading skills, and effective interventions will help middle and high school students read like writers and write like readers. Students need instruction in the writing process, but they especially need that instruction to be connected to the kinds of writing tasks they will have to perform well in high school and beyond. Attention therefore should be given not only to increasing the amount of writing instruction students receive and the amount of writing they do, but also to increasing the quality of writing instruction and assignments.

A Technology Component

Professionals and lay people are increasingly voicing support for inclusion of this element in a literacy program, because technology plays an increasingly central role in our society. Technology is both a facilitator of literacy and a medium of literacy. Effective adolescent literacy programs therefore should use technology as both an instructional tool and an instructional topic.

As a tool, technology can help teachers provide needed supports for struggling readers, including instructional reinforcement and opportunities for guided practice. For example, there are computer programs that help students improve decoding, spelling, fluency, and vocabulary, and more programs are quickly being developed to address comprehension and writing.

As a topic, technology is changing the reading and writing demands of modern society. Reading and writing in the fast-paced, networked world require new skills unimaginable a decade ago.

Ongoing Formative Assessment of Students

This element is included under instructional improvements because the best instructional improvements are informed by ongoing assessment of student strengths and needs. Such assessments are often, but not exclusively, informal and frequently occur on a daily basis, and therefore are not necessarily suited to the summative task of accountability reporting systems. Data should be cataloged on a computer system that would allow teachers, administrators, and evaluators to inspect students' progress individually and by class. These formative assessments are specifically designed to inform instruction on a very frequent basis so that adjustments in instruction can be made to ensure that students are on pace to reach mastery targets.

Infrastructural Elements

Extended Time for Literacy

None of the above-mentioned elements are likely to effect much change if instruction is limited to thirty or forty-five minutes per day. The panel strongly argued the need for two to four hours of literacy-connected learning daily. This time is to be spent with texts and a focus on reading and writing effectively. Although some of this time should be spent with a language arts teacher, instruction in science, history, and other subject areas qualifies as fulfilling the requirements of this element if the instruction is text centered and informed by instructional principles designed to convey content and also to practice and improve literacy skills.

To leverage time for increased interaction with texts across subject areas, teachers will need to reconceptualize their understanding of what it means to teach in a subject area. In other words, teachers need to realize they are not just teaching content knowledge but also ways of reading and writing specific to a subject area. This reconceptualization, in turn, will require rearticulation of standards and revision of preservice training.

Professional Development

Professional development does not refer to the typical onetime workshop, or even a short-term series of workshops, but to ongoing, long-term professional development, which is more likely to promote lasting, positive changes in teacher knowledge and practice. The development effort should also be systemic, including not only classroom teachers but also literacy coaches, resource room personnel, librarians, and administrators. Effective professional development will use data from research studies of adult learning and the conditions needed to effect sustained change. Professional development opportunities should be built into the regular school schedule, with consistent opportunities to learn about new research and practices as well as opportunities to implement and reflect upon new ideas. Effective professional development will help school personnel create and maintain indefinitely a team-oriented approach to improving the instruction and institutional structures that promote better adolescent literacy.

Ongoing Summative Assessment of Students and Programs

This element is listed under infrastructural improvements because of the substantial coordination that such assessment requires and because of its intended audience, which is the local school district administration, the state and federal departments of education, and others who fund and/or support the school, such as private foundations, the local community, parents, and students. In contrast to formative assessments, these assessments are designed specifically for implementation with continuous progress-monitoring systems. These systems would allow teachers to track students throughout a school year and, ideally, over an entire academic career, from kindergarten through high school. In addition, these systems would allow for ongoing internal and external evaluation of the implemented program. These data and more formative assessment data could be catalogued on a computer system that would allow teachers, administrators, and evaluators to inspect students' progress individually, by class, by cohort, and by school. These assessments are more formal than the formative assessments, but should go beyond state assessments and be designed to demonstrate progress specific to school and program goals, and, if possible, to also inform instruction. Ideally, the assessment results would be generated and shared in a timely fashion so that they might also be of use to teachers in planning instruction and to students in monitoring their success and progress in school.

Teacher Teams

This element ensures that the school structure supports coordinated instruction and planning in an interdisciplinary teacher team. This vision centers on teachers meeting regularly to discuss students they have in common and to align instruction. In the primary grades students see one teacher; in middle and high school grades, their daily routine changes, and they see many teachers during discrete blocks of time devoted to discrete subjects. This shift often causes a loss in consistency in literacy instruction. Teacher teams are viewed as helpful for reestablishing coordinated instruction in higher grades and as a way to promote teacher collegiality and heighten the likelihood that no child will slip through the cracks. Teacher teams that meet regularly allow teachers to plan for consistency in instruction across subject areas, which is an important step toward a comprehensive and coordinated literacy program.

Leadership

Without a principal's clear commitment and enthusiasm, a curricular and instructional reform has no more chance of succeeding than any other schoolwide reform. It is critical that a principal assumes the role of an instructional leader, who demonstrates commitment and participates in the school community. This leadership role includes a principal building his or her own personal knowledge of how young people learn and struggle with reading and writing and how they differ in their needs. In addition, a principal who takes on the role of instructional leader will attend professional development sessions organized primarily for teachers. This knowledge and experience will give a principal the necessary understanding to organize and coordinate changes in a school's literacy program. It will further give a principal the proper foundation for making the necessary decisions to alter structural elements, such as class schedules, to ensure optimal programming for student learning.

This element also applies to teachers, who should assume leadership roles and spearhead curricular improvements. Teachers play a role in ensuring the success of curricular reform, and their involvement is all the more crucial when a principal has not assumed the instructional leadership role. Without someone with an informed vision of what good literacy instruction entails leading the charge, instructional change is likely to be beset with problems.

A Comprehensive and Coordinated Literacy Program

In many ways, this component of a program is not obtainable without the other infrastructural improvements and is especially closely aligned to leadership and the establishment of teacher teams. Included in these teams would be additional school personnel, such as librarians, reading specialists, literacy coaches, and resource room teachers. Often in today's schools one teacher has no idea what another is teaching; this is particularly true in high schools. The vision for an effective literacy program recognizes that creating fluent and proficient readers and writers is a very complex task and requires that teachers coordinate their instruction to reinforce important strategies and concepts. It is important in a comprehensive and coordinated literacy program that teachers work in teams and are responsible for a cohort of students. This is not to advocate that math, science, and history teachers should become teachers of reading and writing, but rather that interdisciplinary teams that meet on a regular basis will provide opportunities for reading and writing teachers to better support content-area teachers. These teams can also create more consistent instruction by reinforcing reading and writing skills, such as note-taking and comprehension strategies. An effective literacy program should implement many of the instructional elements in a consistent and coordinated way.

Because the literacy needs of adolescents are so diverse, the intensity and nature of instruction in a comprehensive and coordinated literacy program—as well as which teachers are involved—will vary considerably. Some students need their content teachers to make only modest accommodations or adjustments; other students need learning strategies embedded in content material, explicit strategy instruction, or instruction in basic skills or even the basic language elements that are the foundation of literacy competence. Secondary schools must recognize adolescents' varying needs and develop a comprehensive program that will successfully address the needs of all their students.

A comprehensive and coordinated literacy program will also initiate or augment collaborations with out-of-school organizations and the local community to provide more broad-based interactions and greater support for students. These collaborations would further secure student motivation by providing students with a sense of consistency between what they experience in and out of school.

A Call to Action: What We Know About Adolescent Literacy and Ways to Support Teachers in Meeting Students' Needs
(http://www.ncte.org/about/over/positions/category/read/118622.htm)

NCTE Guideline

A guideline approved by the NCTE Executive Committee and found to be consistent with NCTE positions on education issues

A Call to Action: What We Know About Adolescent Literacy and Ways to Support Teachers in Meeting Students' Needs

A Position/Action Statement from NCTE's Commission on Reading
May 2004

Purpose: The purpose of this document is to provide a research-based resource for media, policymakers, and teachers that acknowledges the complexities of reading as a developmental process and addresses the needs of secondary readers and their teachers.

What is Reading?: The NCTE Commission on Reading has produced a statement, "On Reading, Learning to Read, and Effective Reading Instruction," that synthesizes current research on reading. Reading is defined as a complex, purposeful, social and cognitive process in which readers simultaneously use their knowledge of spoken and written language, their knowledge of the topic of the text, and their knowledge of their culture to construct meaning. Reading is not a technical skill acquired once and for all in the primary grades, but rather a developmental process. A reader's competence continues to grow through engagement with various types of texts and wide reading for various purposes over a lifetime.

What is Unique about Adolescent Literacy?:

In middle and high school, students encounter academic discourses and disciplinary concepts in such fields as science, mathematics, and the social sciences that require different reading approaches from those used with more familiar forms such as literary and personal narratives (Kucer, 2005). These new forms, purposes, and processing demands require that teachers show, demonstrate, and make visible to students how literacy operates within the academic disciplines (Keene & Zimmermann, 1997; Tovani, 2000).

Adolescents are already reading in multiple ways, using literacy as a social and political endeavor in which they engage to make meaning and act upon their worlds. Their texts range from clothing logos to music to specialty magazines to Web sites to popular and classical literature. In the classroom it is important for teachers to recognize and value the multiple literacy resources students bring to the acquisition of school literacy.

In effective schools, classroom conversations about how, why, and what we read are important parts of the literacy curriculum (Applebee, 1996: Schoenbach, Greenleaf, Cziko & Hurwitz, 1999). In fact, discussion-based approaches to academic literacy content are strongly linked to student achievement (Applebee, Langer, Nystrand, and Gamoran, 2003). However, high stakes testing, such as high school exit exams, is not only narrowing the content of the literacy curriculum, but also constraining instructional approaches to reading (Amrein & Berliner, 2002; Madaus, 1998) Limited, "one right answer" or "main idea" models of reading run counter to recent research findings, which call for a richer, more engaged approach to literacy instruction (Campbell, Donahue, Reese & Phillips, 1996; Taylor et al., 1999).

What Current Research Is Showing Teachers:

(1) That literacy is a dynamic interaction of the social and cognitive realms, with textual understandings growing from students' knowledge of their worlds to knowledge of the external world (Langer, 2002). All students need to go beyond the study of discrete skills and strategies to understand how those skills and strategies are integrated with life experiences. Langer, et al. found that literacy programs that successfully teach at-risk students emphasize connections between students' lives, prior knowledge, and texts, and emphasize student conversations to make those connections.

(2) That the majority of inexperienced adolescent readers need opportunities and instructional support to read many and diverse types of texts in order to gain experience, build fluency, and develop a range as readers (Greenleaf, Schoenbach, Cziko, & Mueller, 2001;Kuhn & Stahl, 2000). Through extensive reading of a range of texts, supported by strategy lessons and discussions, readers become familiar with written language structures and text features, develop their vocabularies, and read for meaning more efficiently and effectively. Conversations about their reading that focus on the strategies they use and their language knowledge help adolescents build confidence in their reading and become better readers (Goodman and Marek, 1996).

(3) That most adolescents do not need further instruction in phonics or decoding skills (Ivey and Baker, 2004). Research summarized in the National Reading Panel report noted that the benefits of phonics instruction are strongest in first grade, with diminished results for students in subsequent grades. Phonics instruction has not been seen to improve reading comprehension for older students (National Reading Panel, 2000). In cases where older students need help to construct meaning with text, instruction should be targeted and embedded in authentic reading experiences.

(4) That utilizing a model of reading instruction focused on basic skills can lead to the mislabeling of some secondary readers as "struggling readers" and "non-readers" because they lack extensive reading experience, depend on different prior knowledge, and/or comprehend differently or in more complex ways. A large percentage of secondary readers who are so mislabeled are students of color and/or students from lower socio-economic backgrounds. Abundant research suggests that the isolated skill instruction they receive may perpetuate low literacy achievement rather than improve their competence and engagement in complex reading tasks. (Allington, 2001; Alvermann & Moore, 1991; Brown, 1991; Hiebert, 1991; Hull & Rose, 1989; Knapp &Turnbull, 1991; Sizer, 1992). In addition, prescriptive, skills-based reading instruction mislocates the problem as the students' failure to learn, rather than the institution's failure to teach reading as the complex mental and social activity it is. (Greenleaf, Schoenbach, Cziko, and Mueller, 2001)

(5) That effective literacy programs move students to deeper understandings of texts and increase their ability to generate ideas and knowledge for their own uses (Newmann, King & Rigdon, 1997).

(6) That assessment should focus on underlying knowledge in the larger curriculum and on strategies for thinking during literacy acts (Darling-Hammond and Falk, 1997; Langer, 2000; Smith, 1991). Likewise, preparation for assessment (from ongoing classroom measures to high stakes tests) should focus on the critical components above.

What Adolescent Readers Need:

- Sustained experiences with diverse texts in a variety of genres and

offering multiple perspectives on real life experiences. Although many of these texts will be required by the curriculum, others should be self-selected and of high interest to the reader. Wide independent reading develops fluency, builds vocabulary and knowledge of text structures and offers readers the experiences they need to read and construct meaning with more challenging texts. Text should be broadly viewed to include print, electronic, and visual media.
- Conversations/discussions regarding texts that are authentic, student initiated, and teacher facilitated. Such discussion should lead to diverse interpretations of a text that deepen the conversation.

- Experience in thinking critically about how they engage with texts:
  - When do I comprehend?
  - What do I do to understand a text?
  - When do I not understand a text?
  - What can I do when meaning breaks down?

- Experience in critical examination of texts that helps them to:
  - Recognize how texts are organized in various disciplines and genre
  - Question and investigate various social, political, and historical content and purposes within texts
  - Make connections between texts, and between texts and personal experiences to act on and react to the world.
  - Understand multiple meanings and richness of texts and layers of complexity

What Teachers of Adolescents Need:

- Adequate and appropriate reading materials that tap students' diverse interests and represent a range of difficulty
- Continued support and professional development that assist them to:
  - Bridge between adolescents' rich literate backgrounds and school literacy
  - Teach literacy in their disciplines as an essential way of learning in their disciplines
  - Recognize when students are not making meaning with text and provide appropriate, strategic assistance to read course content effectively
  - Facilitate student-initiated conversations regarding texts that are authentic and relevant to real life experiences.
  - Create environments that allow students to engage in critical examinations of texts as they dissect, deconstruct, and re-construct in an effort to engage in meaning making and comprehension processes.

References

Applebee, A. (1996). *Curriculum as conversation: Transforming traditions of teaching and learning.* Chicago, University of Chicago Press.

Applebee, A., Langer, J., Nystrand, M., and Gamoran, A. (2003). Discussion-based approaches to developing understanding: Classroom instruction and student performance in middle and high school English. *American Educational Research Journal* 40: 3, pp. 685-730.

Allington, R.L. (2001). *What really matters for struggling readers: Designing research-based programs.* New York: Addison Wesley Longman.

Alvermann, D. & Moore, D. (1991). Secondary school reading. In R. Barr, M.L. Kamil, P. Mosenthal, & P.D. Person (Eds.), *Handbook of Reading*

Research (vol. 2, pp. 951-983). New York: Longman.

Amrein, A.L. & Berliner, D.C. (2002). *High-stakes testing, uncertainty, and student learning.* Educational Policy Analysis Archives, 10 (18). [Online]. Available: http://epaa.asu.edu/epaa/v10n18

Brown, R. G.(1991). *Schools of thought: How the polictics of literacy shape thinking in the classroom.* San Francisco: Jossey-Bass.

Campbell, J., Donahue, P., Reese, C. & Phillips, G. (1996) *National Assessment of Educational Progress 1994 reading report card for the nation and the states.* Washington, DC: National Center for Education Statistics, U.S. Department of Education.

Darling-Hammond, L. & Falk, B.(1997). Using standards and assessments to support student learning. *Phi Delta Kappan*, 79, 190-199.

Fehring, H., & Green, P. (Eds.) (2001). *Critical literacy: A collection of articles from the Australian literacy educator's association.* Melbourne, AU: Intrados Group.

Gee, J.P. *Social linguistics and literacies: Ideology in discourses.* (2nd ed.). London: Falmer.

Goodman, Y. and Marek, A. (1996). Retrospective *miscue analysis: Revaluing readers and reading.* Katonah, NY: R.C. Owens Publishers.

Greenleaf, C., Schoenbach, R., Cziko, C., and Mueller, F. (2001). Apprenticing adolescent readers to academic literacy. *Harvard Educational Review* 71: 1, 79-129.

Hiebert, E. (1991). *Literacy for a diverse society: Perspectives, policies, and practices.* New York: Teachers College Press.

Hull, G.A. & Rose, M. (1989). Rethinking remediation: toward a social-cognitive understanding of problematic reading and writing. *Written Communication*, 8, 139-154.

Ivey, G. & Baker, M. (2004). Phonics instruction for older students? Just say no. *Educational Leadership*, 61: 6, pp. 35-39.

Keene, E.O., and Zimmerman, S. (1997). *Mosaic of thought: Teaching comprehension in a reader's workshop.* Portsmouth, NH: Heinemann.

Knapp, M.S. & Turnbull, B. (1991). *Better schools for the children in poverty: Alternatives to conventional wisdom.* Berkeley, CA: McCutchan.

Kucer, S. (2005). *Dimensions of literacy: A conceptual base for teaching reading and writing in school settings.* Second edition. Mahwah, NJ, Lawrence Erlbaum.

Kuhn, M.R. & Stahl, S.A. (2000). *Fluency: A review of developmental and remedial practices* (Report No. 2-008). Ann Arbor, MI: Center for the Improvement of Early Reading Achievement.

Langer, J. (2002). *Effective literacy instruction: Building successful reading and writing programs.* Urbana, Illinois: National Council of Teachers of English.

Langer, J. (2000). *Teaching middle and high school students to read and write well: Six features of effective instruction.* Albany, NY: National Research Center on English Learning and Achievement.

Luke, A. (1995-1996). Text and discourse in education: An introduction to critical discourse analysis.

In M.W. Apple (Ed.), *Review of Research in Education* (Vol. 21, pp. 3-48). Washington, DC: American Educational Research Association.

Madaus, G. (1998). The distortion of teaching and testing: High-stakes testing and instruction, *Peabody Journal of Education*, 65, 29-46.

Moje, E., Young, J., Readence, J., and Moore, D. (20000). Reinventing adolescent literacy for new times: Perennial and millennial issues. *Journal of Adolescent and Adult Literacy,* 43: 5, 400-410.

Moore, D., Bean, T., Birdyshaw, D., and Rycik, J. (1999). *Adolescent literacy: A position statement.* Newark, DE: International Reading Association.

Morgan, W. (1997). *Critical literacy in the classroom: The art of the possible.* New York: Routledge.

National Reading Panel (2000). *Teaching Children to Read.* Washington, DC: National Institute of Child Health and Human Development.

Newmann, F., King, B. & Rigdon, M. (1997). Accountability and school performance: Implications from restructuring schools. *Harvard Educational Review,* 67, 41-74.

Sizer, T. (1992). Horace's compromise: *The dilemma of the American high school.* Boston: Houghton Mifflin.

Smith, M.I. (1991). Put to the test: The effects of external testing on teachers. *Educational Researcher* 20: 5, 8-11.

Street, Brian. (1995). *Social literacies: Critical approaches to literacy in development, ethnography, and education.* London: Longman.

Taylor, B.M., Anderson, R.C., Au, K.H., & Raphael, T.E. (1999). *Discretion in the translation of reading research to policy* (Report No. 3-006). Ann Arbor, MI: Center for the Improvement of Early Reading Achievement.

Selected Resources for Teachers

Allen, J. (2000). Yellow *Brick Roads: Shared and Guided Paths to Independent Reading.* York, ME: Stenhouse.

Atwell, N. (1998). *In the Middle*, 2d edition. Portsmouth, NH: Heinemann.

Beers, K. (2003). *When Kids Can't Read: What Teachers Can Do.* Portsmouth, NH: Heinemann.

Lenski, S., Wham, M.A., Johns, J. (2003). *Reading and Learning Strategies Middle Grades through High School.* Dubuque, IA: Kendall/Hunt.

Robb., L. (2000). *Teaching Reading in Middle School.* New York: Scholastic.

Schoenbach, R., Greenleaf, C., Cziko, C., & Hurwitz, L. (1999). *Reading for Understanding: A Guide to Improving Reading in Middle and High School Classrooms.* San Francisco: Jossey-Bass.

Smith, M. and Wilhelm, J. (2002). *"Reading Don't Fix No Chevy's": Literacy in the Lives of Young Men.* Portsmouth, NH: Heinemann.

Tovani, C. (2000). I *Read It but I Don't Get It.* York, ME: Stenhouse.

Wilhelm, J., Baker, T., and Dube, J. (2001). *Strategic Reading: Guiding Students to Lifelong Literacy.* Portsmouth, NH: Heineman.

Related Information:

- On Reading, Learning to Read, and Effective Reading Instruction: An Overview of What We Know and How We Know It (http://www.ncte.org/about/policy/guidelines)
- Features of Literacy Programs: A Decision-Making Matrix (http://www.ncte.org/about/over/positions/level/elem)

NCTE — A Professional Association of Educators in English Studies, Literacy, and Language Arts

The National Council of Teachers of English
1111 W. Kenyon Road, IL 61801-1096
Phone: 800-369-6283 Fax: 217-328-9645, Email: public_info@ncte.org

STEPS Middle & High School Literacy
Professional Development Courses

STEPS Middle & High School Literacy materials form a critical part of the STEPS professional development courses that promote a long-term commitment to educational change. Together, the professional development and the materials provide a strategic whole-school approach to improving students' literacy outcomes.

STEPS offers a full range of professional development courses that are conducted at the invitation of a school or district. Each participant who attends a two-day course receives

- *Reading to Learn: A Content Teacher's Guide*
- A reading course book to guide professional development
- Practical activities for classroom use

A selection of additional sessions, beyond the regular course, will also be available to meet the needs of teachers in different schools and contexts. These additional sessions can be selected in consultation with a STEPS Consultant.

For further information about STEPS Courses and Resources contact your nearest STEPS Professional Development office.

United States of America

STEPS Professional Development
The Cummings Center
Suite 421G
Beverly, MA 01915 USA
Phone 978 927 0095
Fax 978 744 0038
Toll Free 866 505 3001
www.stepspd.org

United Kingdom

STEPS Professional Development
Shrivenham Hundred Business Park
Majors Road
Watchfield SN8TZ
Phone 01793 787930
Fax 01793 787931
www.steps-pd.co.uk

Australasia

STEPS Professional Development
Edith Cowan University
Churchlands Campus
Pearson Street
Churchlands WA 6018 Australia
Phone 08 9273 8833
Fax 08 9273 8811
www.stepspd.com.au

Overview of the First Steps

Global Statement

Transitional Phase

In this phase, readers are beginning to integrate strategies to identify unknown words and to comprehend text. These strategies, combined with an increasing bank of sight words, enable readers to read texts such as novels, newspapers and websites with familiar content fluently and with expression. Transitional readers reflect on strategies used and are beginning to discuss their effectiveness.

Key Indicators

USE OF TEXTS
- Reads and demonstrates comprehension of texts by:
  - identifying the main idea(s), citing supporting detail
  - selecting events from a text to suit a specific purpose
  - linking ideas, both explicit and implicit, in a text, e.g. cause and effect.
- Locates and selects texts appropriate to purpose and audience, e.g. uses search engines, checks currency of information.

CONTEXTUAL UNDERSTANDING
- Recognises own interpretation may differ from that of other readers or the author/s.
- Recognises devices that authors and illustrators use to influence construction of meaning, e.g. visual clues, omissions.
- Recognises that authors and illustrators attempt to position readers.
- Recognises how characters or people, facts and events are represented, and can speculate about the author's choices.

CONVENTIONS
- Recognises an increasing bank of words in different contexts, e.g. subject-specific words, less common words.
- Explains how known text forms vary by using knowledge of:
  - purpose, e.g. to persuade
  - text structure, e.g. problem and solution
  - text organisation, e.g. headings, subheadings, an index, glossary
  - language features, e.g. conjunctions.

PROCESSES AND STRATEGIES
- Draws upon an increasing knowledge base to comprehend, e.g. text structure and organisation, grammar, vocabulary.
- Uses an increasing range of strategies to comprehend, e.g. creating images, determining importance.
- Determines unknown words by using word-identification strategies, e.g. reading on, re-reading.

Major Teaching Emphases

ENVIRONMENT AND ATTITUDE
- Create a supportive classroom environment that nurtures a community of readers.
- Jointly construct, and frequently refer to, meaningful environmental print.
- Foster students' enjoyment of reading.
- Encourage students to take risks with confidence.
- Encourage students to select their own reading material according to interest or purpose.

USE OF TEXTS
- Provide opportunities for students to read a wide range of texts.
- Continue to teach students to analyse texts, identifying explicit and implicit information.
- Continue to teach students to make connections within texts, using both explicit and implicit information.
- Model how concept knowledge and understandings can be shaped and reshaped using information from a variety of texts.

CONTEXTUAL UNDERSTANDING
- Discuss how readers may react to and interpret texts differently, depending on their knowledge, experience or perspective.
- Discuss how authors and illustrators have used devices to target specific audiences, e.g. quoting statistics.
- Provide opportunities for students to challenge the author's world view.

CONVENTIONS
- Continue to build students' sight vocabulary, e.g. less common words, subject-specific words.
- Continue to build students' graphophonic and word knowledge, such as:
  - recognising less common sound–symbol relationships
  - recognising letter combinations and the different sounds they represent
  - recognising how word parts and words work.
- Jointly analyse texts where combinations and adaptations of text structure and text organisation have been used.
- Teach students to identify the role of language features in a variety of texts.

PROCESSES AND STRATEGIES
- Continue to build students' knowledge within the cues, e.g. orthographic, world knowledge.
- Consolidate known comprehension strategies and teach additional strategies, e.g. synthesising, paraphrasing.
- Consolidate word-identification strategies.
- Continue to teach students how to locate, select and evaluate texts, e.g. conducting Internet searches, recognising bias.
- Model self-reflection of strategies used in reading, and encourage students to do the same.

© Western Australian Minister for Education: 2004

Reading Map of Development

ficient Phase	Accomplished Phase
strategy approach to identify unknown words and comprehend extbooks, novels and essays. They are able to select strategies y of the text. Readers have a greater ability to connect topic, ture knowledge with what is new in the text. Proficient readers y draw on evidence from their own experience to challenge or	Accomplished readers use a flexible repertoire of strategies and cues to comprehend texts and to solve problems with unfamiliar structure and vocabulary. They are able to fluently read complex and abstract texts such as journal articles, novels and research reports. Accomplished readers access the layers of information and meaning in a text according to their reading purpose. They interrogate, synthesise and evaluate multiple texts to revise and refine their understandings
of texts by: porting information relate to the author's purpose and the pecific audience t, in a text, e.g. thesis and supporting arguments. f texts and information in texts in terms of purpose and nd beliefs impact on the interpretation of text. ific text, and how the author has tailored the language, ideas and e and text organisation, e.g. historical account written as a tures such as: and bias, e.g. I think, It has been reported s, e.g. similarly — to compare, on the other hand — to contrast g. thief, bandit, pickpocket. comprehend, e.g. text structure and organisation, cultural/world de range to comprehend. g appropriate word-identification strategies.	**USE OF TEXTS** ♦ Reads and demonstrates comprehension of texts using both explicit and implicit information to achieve a given purpose. ♦ Synthesises information from texts, with varying perspectives, to draw conclusions. ♦ Locates and evaluates appropriateness of texts and the information in texts in terms of purpose and audience. **CONTEXTUAL UNDERSTANDING** ♦ Discusses reasons why a text may be interpreted differently by different readers, e.g. personal background of reader, author bias, sociocultural background. ♦ Discusses how the context (time, place, situation) of an author influences the construction of a text. ♦ Analyses the use of devices such as rhetoric, wit, cynicism and irony designed to position readers to take particular views. **CONVENTIONS** ♦ Uses knowledge of one text form to help interpret another, e.g. literary features in informational texts. ♦ Recognises the effectiveness of language features selected by authors. **PROCESSES AND STRATEGIES** ♦ Consciously adds to a broad knowledge base, as required, to comprehend. ♦ Selects appropriate strategies from a wide range to comprehend. ♦ Determines unknown words by selecting appropriate word-identification strategies.
ent that nurtures a community of readers. , meaningful environmental print. nfidence. reading material according to interest or purpose. d a wide range of texts. exts utilising information to suit different purposes and audiences. cuss how the ideologies of the reader and the author combine to entify devices used to influence readers to take a particular view. ulary, e.g. technical terms, figurative language. combine language features to achieve a purpose. manipulate texts to achieve a purpose, e.g. structure, organisation. within the cues. es. valuate texts. n reading, and encourage students to do the same.	**Major Teaching Emphases** and **Teaching and Learning Experiences** are not provided for this phase, as Accomplished readers are able to take responsibility for their own ongoing reading development.

MAY BE COPIED FOR CLASSROOM USE ONLY.